SEWING
TECHNIQUES

THE COMPLETE STEP-BY-STEP HANDBOOK

A PRACTICAL GUIDE TO SEWING, PATCHWORK AND EMBROIDERY, WITH
HOW-TO INSTRUCTION, CREATIVE PROJECTS AND A DIRECTORY OF STITCHES

DOROTHY WOOD

southwater

This edition is published by Southwater,
an imprint of Anness Publishing Ltd, Blaby Road,
Wigston, Leicestershire LE18 4SE; info@anness.com

www.southwaterbooks.com;
www.annesspublishing.com

If you like the images in this book and would like
to investigate using them for publishing, promotions
or advertising, please visit www.practicalpictures.com
for more information.

Publisher: Joanna Lorenz
Project editor: Simona Hill
Step-by-step photography: Rodney Forte
Special photography: Nicki Dowey
Illustrator: Penny Brown
Designer: Margaret Sadler
Editorial reader: Diane Ashmore
Production controller: Wendy Lawson

ETHICAL TRADING POLICY

At Anness Publishing we believe that business
should be conducted in an ethical and ecologically
sustainable way, with respect for the environment and
a proper regard to the replacement of the natural
resources we employ.

As a publisher, we use a lot of wood pulp in high-
quality paper for printing, and that wood commonly
comes from spruce trees. We are therefore currently
growing more than 750,000 trees in three Scottish
forest plantations: Berrymoss (130 hectares/320 acres),
West Touxhill (125 hectares/305 acres) and Deveron
Forest (75 hectares/185 acres). The forests we
manage contain more than 3.5 times the number
of trees employed each year in making paper for the
books we manufacture.

Because of this ongoing ecological investment
programme, you, as our customer, can have the
pleasure and reassurance of knowing that a tree
is being cultivated on your behalf to naturally
replace the materials used to make the book
you are holding.

Our forestry programme is run in accordance with
the UK Woodland Assurance Scheme (UKWAS) and
will be certified by the internationally recognized
Forest Stewardship Council (FSC). The FSC is a
non-government organization dedicated to
promoting responsible management of the world's
forests. Certification ensures forests are managed
in an environmentally sustainable and socially
responsible way.

For further information about this scheme, go to
www.annesspublishing.com/trees

Previously published as *The Practical Encyclopedia
of Sewing Techniques*

PUBLISHER'S NOTE

Although the advice and information in this book
are believed to be accurate and true at the time of
going to press, neither the authors nor the publisher
can accept any legal responsibility or liability for any
errors or omissions that may have been made nor for
any inaccuracies nor for any loss, harm or injury that
comes about from following instructions or advice
in this book.

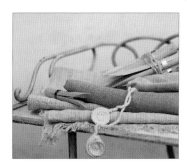

SEWING
TECHNIQUES

THE COMPLETE STEP-BY-STEP HANDBOOK

CONTENTS

INTRODUCTION 6

SEWING 8

PATCHWORK 94

EMBROIDERY 168

TEMPLATES 248

INDEX 252

INTRODUCTION

Today, you can buy a wide range of beautiful fabrics to suit virtually any requirement in every colour imaginable, from easycare fabrics for casual and holiday wear to the most exquisite materials for evening and special occasions. And with so many wonderful fabrics now available, it is hardly surprising that people are being tempted to rediscover sewing skills that were once taken for granted.

In addition to the purely practical skills of dressmaking, more decorative needlecraft skills such as embroidery, patchwork, quilting, and appliqué can be used to create beautiful pieces of work. These are all surprisingly easy to learn and add the finishing touches to any hand-crafted item. Simple garments and soft furnishings can be transformed, once a few basic skills have been mastered.

The Practical Encyclopedia of Sewing encompasses all aspects of sewing and needlecraft. This comprehensive reference manual includes everything you need to know to create practical and beautiful garments and items for the home, and exclusive gifts for friends and family. It is divided into three sections: dressmaking and soft furnishings; patchwork, appliqué

and quilting; and hand and machine embroidery. Each chapter covers all the basic and more advanced techniques for that particular discipline, including step-by-step instructions and photographs for working by hand as well as with a sewing machine.

Beginners will gain knowledge and confidence as they try out stitches at their own pace, while more experienced sewers who wish to try new techniques and learn different skills will find plenty of fascinating information.

Alongside the many different techniques shown, there are many photographs of beautifully worked pieces by talented contemporary designers. These have been chosen to show how the techniques can be applied and to provide inspiration for you to try out your own ideas. As you move from beginner to experienced stitcher, you will be surprised how quickly you produce results of which you can be quite proud.

As soon as you have mastered some of the techniques shown, you will have gained sufficient knowledge and confidence to start creating lovely pieces of your own. Whether you are making simple clothes, creating soft furnishings, making an heirloom patchwork quilt or adding the finishing touches to a hand-crafted item, this book will help you at every stage.

SEWING

Learning to sew opens up a whole new world of creative opportunities — choosing to make your own garments and soft furnishing items is not just cheaper than shop bought, it provides you with the opportunity to produce individualized items, with your choice of fabric, trims and finish. With the selection of fabrics available today, home-made need not be second best. Mastering sewing takes practice, but many items such as curtains require only basic sewing skills using simple seams.

Sewing equipment

Are your needles the right size, your pins rust-free and your scissors still sharp enough for fabric? Although most households have basic sewing equipment, it is worth checking that what you have is still in good condition before beginning to sew, and replace things that are past their best.

1 Bodkin
A bodkin is used to thread elastic, cord or ribbon through casings.

2 Dressmaker's carbon and tracing wheel
These are used together to transfer construction markings to the wrong side of fabrics. Select a colour of carbon paper close to the fabric colour that is still visible and always use white on white fabric (it shows as a dull line).

3 Fabric markers
Pencils are suitable for most hard-surfaced fabrics and can be brushed off with a stiff brush. Vanishing-ink pens wash out in water or fade over a few days. Tracing pens are used to draw a design on waxed paper that is transferred to fabric by ironing.

4 Fusible bonding web
This is a glue mesh that comes in various widths for sticking two layers of fabric together. The narrow bands (shown here) are useful for heavy-weight hems and facings and the wider widths are used for appliqué.

5 Needles
Sharps (medium length, all-purpose needles) are used for general hand sewing. For fine hand sewing, use the shorter, round-eyed betweens. Hand-sewing needles are numbered according to thickness and range from 1–10, with 10 being the finest.

6 Pin cushion
A pin cushion is useful for holding the pins and needles you are using. A wrist pin cushion is convenient when you are fitting a garment.

7 Pins
Pins come in a surprising number of shapes and sizes. Use household pins for normal sewing and wedding or lace pins for fine and delicate fabrics. Use ball-point pins for fine synthetic knit fabrics. Glass-headed pins are easy to see against fabrics.

8 Quilter's tape
Use this to mark accurate 5mm/^{1}/$_4$in seam allowances.

9 Rouleau turner
Use this metal tool to turn through rouleau loops.

10 Safety pins
Use to hold thick layers of fabric together safely.

11 Scissors
You will need a large pair of drop-handle (bent-handle) scissors for cutting out, a medium pair for trimming seams or cutting small pieces of fabric and a small pair of sharp, pointed embroidery scissors for cutting threads and snipping into curves. Never cut paper with your dressmaking scissors – it dulls the blade. Pinking shears are used to finish raw edges on fabrics that do not unravel easily.

12 Seam ripper
This is a small cutting tool for undoing machine stitching mistakes or cutting buttonholes.

13 Tape measure
Tape measures should be marked with centimetres and inches on the same side for quick reference. Buy a 150cm/60in tape with metal tips in a material such as fibreglass that will not stretch. A small metal ruler with adjustable guide is useful for pinning hems, tucks and buttonholes.

14 Tailor's chalk
Tailor's chalk is used to make temporary marks on the fabrics. Keep the edge sharp by shaving with medium scissors and test before using on the right side of fabrics to ensure it will brush off.

15 Thimble
A thimble is worn on the middle finger of your sewing hand. Although awkward at first, persevere because it will prevent accidental needle pricks.

16 Thread
Use a shade of thread that matches your fabric, or go one shade darker. For best results choose a thread that matches the fibre content of your fabric. Tacking (basting) thread is cheap, and poorer-quality. Use button-hole twist or linen thread for tailored buttonholes and strong thread for furnishing fabrics and hand quilting.

17 Tissue paper
When working with fine or delicate fabrics by machine, baste strips of tissue paper to each side of the seam before sewing. Tear off after use. Tissue paper is useful for lengthening or altering pattern pieces and transferring designs for embroidery.

The sewing machine

A sewing machine is one of the most expensive pieces of sewing equipment you will buy and you should take as much care choosing one as you would a washing machine or a car. Think about how much sewing you expect to do, not only next year but also ten or twenty years ahead.

Types of machine

All sewing machines sew a line of simple straight stitches, but new technology means there are many different types on the market.

Basic straight stitch and zigzag
The only basic straight stitch machines around today are antiques – but they still form beautiful stitches. Zigzag machines move the needle from side to side. The stitch width and spacing can be altered.

Automatic
Automatic machines can move the fabric backwards and forwards while stitching to produce stretch stitches, saddle stitch and overlocking. They have special discs inside called pattern cams that produce a variety of elaborate embroidery stitches.

Electronic
Electronic machines (above) are smoother and more sophisticated than ordinary automatic machines. The motor is controlled electronically and stops as soon as you lift your foot from the pedal. The machine can also sew very slowly if required with the same power. Electronic machines can be automatic or computerized, having either cams or a computer to create the stitches.

Computerized
Computerized machines (above) are advanced models with silicon chips, instead of pattern cams and are capable of a huge range of ornamental stitches. The stitches can be more complicated because the fabric can move in all directions. Touch-button panels or screens make them simple to use and some can stitch small motifs or your own embroidery designs when linked to a personal computer.

CHOOSING A SEWING MACHINE

Most people only ever use the straight stitch and zigzag on a sewing machine so think carefully before spending a lot of money on technology you don't really need. If you intend to make soft furnishings and curtains, a sturdy, second-hand flatbed machine may be best. Free-arm machines have a narrow arm that extends above the base to allow fabric to be moved around. They are more suitable for dressmaking.

Take samples of different fabrics such as jersey, silk and denim with you and try them out folded double on the machines. Check that threading up is easy and the bobbin case is not difficult to handle. Check that the electric fittings and attachments are well made.

Find out what accessories are included and if parts are easily replaced. Finally check that the machine packs away easily and isn't too heavy. After all, they're supposed to be portable.

Spend some time reading the manual and becoming familiar with the different parts. If you haven't used a sewing machine before, practise sewing on paper without thread first. For this, set all the dials at zero except for the stitch length, which should be between 2 and 3. Using lined paper, go up and down the lines, then try stopping and reversing, and very slowly, following curves and circles. Once you are comfortable, practise the same techniques on a double layer of gingham.

Know your machine

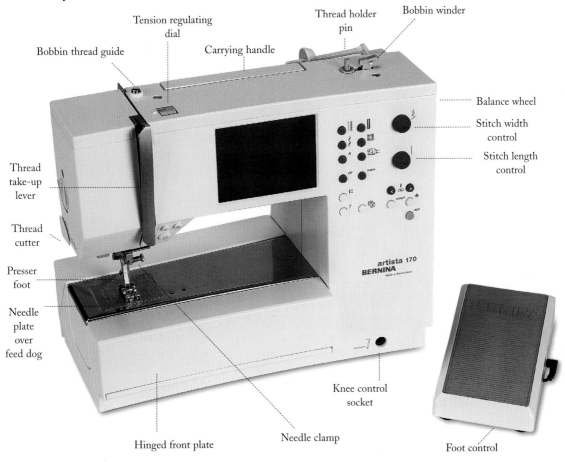

Tension regulating dial

Thread holder pin

Bobbin winder

Bobbin thread guide

Carrying handle

Balance wheel

Stitch width control

Stitch length control

Thread take-up lever

Thread cutter

Presser foot

Needle plate over feed dog

artista 170
BERNINA

Knee control socket

Hinged front plate

Needle clamp

Foot control

Balance wheel
This controls the sewing machine. On manual machines turn the wheel to lower the needle.

Bobbin winder
This allows you to fill the bobbin quickly and evenly.

Foot control/knee contol
This starts, stops and controls the speed that the machine stitches.

Needle clamp
This secures the shaft of the needle into the machine.

Needle plate
The needle plate surrounds the feed teeth and has a hole for the needle.

Presser foot
This holds the fabric flat on the needle plate so that a stitch can form.

Stitch length control
Use this to alter the length of straight stitch and the density of zigzag stitch.

Stitch width control
This controls the amount the needle moves sideways. Use a suitable presser foot so that the needle doesn't break.

Thread take-up lever
This feeds the correct amount of thread from the spool down through to the needle.

Tension regulating dial
The tension dial alters the tension on the top thread.

Thread cutter
This is situated at the back of the machine for cutting threads.

Thread holder pin
This holds the reel of thread when filling the bobbin and stitching.

Threading the upper machine

Unless a machine is threaded in exactly the right sequence it won't work properly. Every machine has a slightly different sequence, but in all of them the thread goes between the tension discs and back up through the take-up lever before it is threaded through the needle.

Always have the take-up lever at its highest point before threading. This brings the needle up to its highest point and lines up all the mechanical parts inside the sewing machine ready for inserting the filled bobbin case. The manual accompanying your sewing machine should have a diagram showing the correct threading sequence for your particular model.

Horizontal thread holders on the upper machine have a clip to hold the reel in position. The thread unwinds off one end of the stationary reel. Vertical thread holders have a disc of felt to help the reel to spin around as the machine is working.

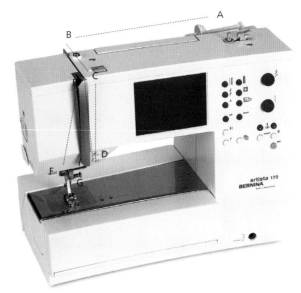

1 Fit the reel on to the thread holder (A), making sure that the thread can come off freely. Take the thread round B, between the tension disks (C) and down under the first thread guide (D).

2 Put the thread into the top of the take-up lever (E) and then through the thread guides (F) leading down the needle (G). Thread the needle from the grooved side (front to back).

Filling the bobbin

1 Fill the bobbin using the bobbin-winding mechanism on the machine. To begin, pass the end of the thread through one of the small holes in the side and fit it on to the spindle.

2 Click the bobbin-winding mechanism into place. This should automatically stop the machine from stitching – if not you will have to loosen the stop motion knob on the hand wheel. The bobbin will fill automatically to the correct level.

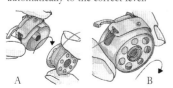

3 Insert the bobbin into the bobbin case (A) so that the thread is pulled back on itself through the spring (B).

4 Fit the bobbin case into the machine holding the case by the lever on the back. The open lever locks the bobbin into the case.

5 Push the case into the socket until it clicks and release the lever. Close the cover. If it does not click, the mechanism inside is not aligned.

The bobbin thread

1 To raise the bobbin thread, thread the needle and hold the upper thread out to one side. Some machines have an automatic thread-lifting mechanism but otherwise turn the hand wheel forwards until the needle has gone down and up again. Pull the upper thread to bring the bobbin thread right out. Take both threads through the slot in the presser foot and out of the back.

Choosing a needle

Always select a machine needle to suit the thread and fabric that you are using; this will reduce the likelihood of the needle breaking.

1 Universal needles
Universal sewing machine needles range in size from 70/9, used for fine fabrics to 110/18, used for heavy-weight fabrics. Size 80/12 is ideal for medium-weight fabric. Keep a selection to hand and change your needle when using different weights of fabric. A fine needle will break if the fabric is too thick and a large needle will damage a fine fabric.

2 Ballpoint needles
Ballpoint needles are used for synthetic fabrics, jersey and elastic. They have a round end which pushes between the threads instead of piercing them. This type of needle can also be used with fine silks and delicate fabrics which may snag.

3 Twin needles
Twin needles consist of two needles fitted to the one shank. They are used to sew narrow, parallel lines or, when the machine tension is altered, to sew pin tucks. You can also buy special stretch twin needles for working on jersey fabrics. When threading the machine with these needles you will need two reels of thread. For best results, take one thread down each side of the central tension disc.

4 Wing needles
Wing needles have a wide blade on each side of the shaft which cuts a decorative groove in the fabric as you stitch.

5 Spring needles
A spring needle allows you to embroider without a darning foot or embroidery hoop because it stops the fabric from moving about.

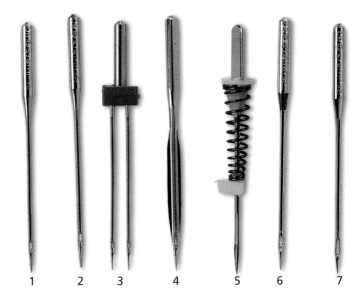

1   2   3   4   5   6   7

6 Embroidery needles
Embroidery needles have larger eyes than normal to allow sewing with a wide range of decorative threads. Some special embroidery needles have extremely large eyes for the thicker threads.

7 Top-stitch needles
Top-stitch needles have a very large eye to accommodate a thick, decorative thread. Jean-point needles have a specially elongated sharp point to stitch through heavy-weight denim and canvas fabrics.

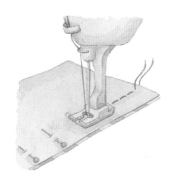

FITTING THE NEEDLE

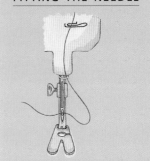

Machine needles can only be fitted one way because they have a flat surface down one side (the shank) and a long groove down the other side (the shaft). When the needle is inserted, this groove should line up directly with the last thread guide. When the machine is in use, the thread runs down the groove and scores a unique channel into the metal. So when you change thread, you should change your needle, too.

Machine feet

All machines have a number of interchangeable feet for different types of sewing. The most common ones are illustrated here but you can buy other specialist feet. These are designed for particular functions such as getting close to a zipper or guiding thread, cord or fabric while sewing.

Clear-view foot

Similar to the general-purpose foot, this foot allows you to see where you are stitching. It can be cut away or made from clear plastic. It can also be used for satin stitch because the underside of the foot is cut away to prevent the stitching from being flattened. Use it when working with bulky fabrics.

Hemming foot

A hemming foot has a curled piece of metal that turns a rolled hem on fine fabrics and feeds it under the needle. The hem can then be stitched with straight or fancy stitches.

Cording foot

This foot has a groove underneath which guides cord, round elastic or narrow ribbon under the needle for stitching.

Blind-hemming (blindstitching) foot

This foot has a metal guide for a turned-back hem. It is possible to adjust the needle position so that just a few threads are caught when stitching.

General-purpose foot

The basic metal general-purpose foot shown is used for all general straight stitching and zigzag on ordinary fabrics.

Darning foot

A darning foot is used for machine darning and free-style machine embroidery. The feed teeth on the machine are always lowered and the fabric is held flat against the needle plate using an embroidery hoop upside down. Set the stitch length at zero and sew straight stitch or zigzag with this foot.

Zipper foot

This allows you to stitch close to zipper teeth or piping. The needle can be adjusted to sew on either side. A special zipper foot is available to guide the teeth of invisible zippers.

Buttonhole foot

This foot has two grooves underneath to guide rows of satin stitch forwards and backwards leaving a tiny gap between for cutting.

Spacing guide (seam guide)

This attachment can be used with a variety of different feet as long as the rod and clip fits. By sliding the rod along, a particular distance can be stitched accurately. This guide is useful for stitching curves and for machine quilting.

Stitch tension

A new machine will have the tension correctly set, with the dial at the marked centre point. Try out any stitches you intend to use on a sample of your fabric.

To check the tension bring all the pattern and zigzag dials back to zero and set the stitch length between 2 and 3 for normal stitching. Place a folded strip of fabric on the needle plate, lower the needle into the fabric and sew a row of straight stitches. These should look exactly the same on both sides.

Above: The top and bottom threads lock together correctly in the middle of the fabric when the machine tension is correct.

Above: The top tension is loose and it is pulled to the wrong side of the fabric.

Above: The top thread tension is too tight.

Altering tension

To tighten the tension, turn the dial towards the lower numbers, to loosen it, turn towards the higher numbers. This will automatically affect the tension of the thread coming through the bobbin case. If the top tension dial is far from the centre the spring on the bobbin case is probably wrong.

Only alter the lower tension as a last resort. You should be able to dangle the bobbin case without the thread slipping through. Shake the thread and the bobbin case should drop a little. Turn the screw on the side of the bobbin case slightly to alter the tension. Try out the stitching again on a sample of fabric and alter the top tension this time until the stitch is perfect.

Maintenance and trouble shooting

Like a car, a sewing machine will only run well if it is used regularly and looked after. It needs to be oiled on a regular basis and cleaned out – this may be several times during the making of curtains or a garment. General maintenance only takes a few minutes but will ensure that your machine works well and lasts longer between services. Cleaning is essential when you change fabrics, especially if it is from a dark to a light-coloured one. Remove the sewing machine needle. Use a stiff brush to clean out the fluff (lint) along the route the top thread takes through the machine. Unscrew the needle plate and brush out any fluff from around the feed teeth. Remove the bobbin case to check that no thread is trapped in the mechanism.

Oil the machine from time to time using your handbook as a guide. Only use a couple of drops – too much oil can be damaging. Leave the machine overnight with a fabric pad beneath the presser foot and then wipe the needle before use. Some new machines are self-lubricating.

Even if you take care of your machine, problems can occur. Some of the more common problems are listed below.

The machine works too slowly

The machine may have two speeds and may be set on slow. More likely, it hasn't been used for a while and oil could be clogging the working parts. Run the machine without a needle for a minute to loosen all the joints. Check that the foot control is not obstructed. As a last resort, ask a dealer to check the tension belt.

No stitches form

Ensure the bobbin is full and inserted correctly. Check that the needle is facing in the right direction and threaded from the grooved side.

Above: Lace and velvet require extreme care when sewing. Always test a sample first to establish the correct tension.

The needle doesn't move

Check that the balance wheel is tight and that the bobbin winder is switched off. If the needle still doesn't move there may be thread trapped in the sewing hook behind the bobbin case. Remove the bobbin case and take hold of the thread end. Rock the balance wheel backwards and forwards until it comes out.

The machine jams

Rock the balance wheel gently to loosen the threads and take the fabric out. Remove the needle, unscrew the needle plate and brush out any fluff. Alternatively check that the machine is correctly threaded and the fabric is far enough under the presser foot when beginning.

The needle bends or breaks

A needle will break if it hits the foot, bobbin case or needle plate on a machine. Check that you are using the correct foot. When using a zipper foot, a common mistake is forgetting to move the needle to the left or right for straight stitching or to zigzag. Check the bobbin case is inserted properly. Make sure the take-up lever is at its highest point before fitting.

A needle that has been bent will break if it hits the needle plate. To avoid bent needles, sew slowly over pins and thick seams. A needle will also bend if there is a knot in the thread or if the fabric is pulled through the machine faster than the machine is sewing.

Fabric does not feed through

This can happen when the feed teeth are lowered in the darning position. Close zigzag or embroidery stitches will bunch up in the general-purpose foot, so change the foot to one that is cut away underneath to allow the stitches to feed through.

Stitches are different lengths

Check whether the needle is blunt or unsuitable for the fabric and that it is inserted correctly. Try stitching with the needle in the left or right position. On fine fabrics, put tissue paper under the presser foot.

The top thread keeps breaking

Manufacturers recommend that you change needles every time you change the type of thread. This is because each thread type scores a unique channel through the needle groove which will cause a different type of thread to snag and break. Label your needle packet to indicate what type of thread to use with each needle. This is particularly important when doing machine embroidery. Check also that you are using the correct thread and type of needle for the fabric. A knot or slub in the thread may also cause the thread to break.

The bobbin thread breaks

Check that the bobbin case is inserted correctly, has not been overfilled and the thread has no knots in it. Also check the bobbin case mechanism for trapped fluff. Occasionally, the spring on the bobbin case is too tight for the thread and the tension screw has to be loosened – refer to your user manual for instructions.

Understanding fabric

*The most exciting part of sewing, whether you are dressmaking or
sewing soft furnishings, is choosing the fabric. Making the right choice is
essential for the success of the finished project. The type of fabric chosen
will affect the drape and handling of the item as well as its lifespan.*

At one time it was quite easy to
choose fabrics as wool blanketing,
cotton lawn, viscose rayon prints and
silk dupion were instantly
recognizable. Even polyester and
nylon fabrics were distinct. Recent
advances in technology have made it
almost impossible to tell what a fabric
is made from just by looking at it.

Fibres form the basis of any fabric.
They are either fused together to
make a fabric like felt and fleece or
twisted together to form a yarn that is
then knitted or woven. There are a
huge number of different fabrics for
sale today and the majority are a mix
of several fibres. To make things easier
for the consumer, it is now law for
each fabric to carry a label listing the
type and proportions of all the

different fibres it contains where these
make up more than 5 per cent. If a
smaller quantity affects the behaviour
of the main fibre, it must be listed
too: for example 1 per cent Lycra or
Spandex will add a fair degree of
stretch to a fabric and will be included
on the label.

Natural fibres

These develop naturally in a fibrous
form either from a plant or animal
source. Cotton, linen, wool and silk
are the most well known but the
group also includes hemp used for
sacking or hessian (burlap) and luxury
animal hair fibres such as mohair,
alpaca, cashmere, angora, vicuna and
camel. Each natural fibre has an
unmistakable inherent character that

is reflected in the fabric: for example,
wool is soft and warm, cotton cool
and crisp, silk has a dry, papery
texture and linen a wonderful sheen.

Man-made and synthetic

Until the mid-nineteenth century,
natural fibres were the only materials
available for fabric production. As silk
was expensive, scientists experimented
with the aim of producing a cost-
effective "artificial silk". The first
rayon – made in 1892 – heralded a
new era for the textile industry.

Man-made and synthetic fabrics
are not the same – each type has
distinct properties. Man-made fibres
are produced from natural products,
primarily cellulose, but some rare
fabrics use regenerated milk protein.
Synthetic fabrics are made entirely
from chemical sources.

Recent developments have refined
the quality of both man-made and
synthetic fibres, making them
indispensable to today's fashion and
sportswear designers. Cosy, polar
fleece jackets are made from a
crimped 100 per cent polyester fibre.
Lycra and Spandex, two highly elastic
synthetic fibres, have transformed the
leisure-wear market. The range of
luxury fabrics has increased, too, as
man-made fibres, such as Cupro, have
been improved to produce exquisite
fabrics with a soft, silky texture. Not
only are these fabrics more accessible,
many are machine washable.

Left: Brightly coloured rayon machine
embroidery threads show how well this
man-made fibre takes dyes.

Cotton

Cotton fibres are harvested from the seed pods of the *Gossypium* plant. The fibres vary in quality and length depending on where the plant is grown, resulting in a vast range of cotton fabrics from the finest Swiss organdie to the coarsest Indian cottons. Cotton fabrics are highly absorbent with wet strength making them suitable for frequent laundering at high temperatures.

Batiste

A soft, finely woven fabric originally made from linen. It is usually only made in white or pastel colours and is used for handkerchiefs, lingerie or christening robes.

Calico

This name is a generic term for plain woven fabrics that are heavier than muslin. It is generally a neutral colour but can be bleached white. Calico is a cheap fabric, used for backing, linings and some home furnishings.

Canvas

This rather stiff, warp-faced cloth is made in different weights for interlinings, tents or deck chairs. Needlepoint canvas is an open-weave fabric used for embroidery.

Chambray

This is a medium-weight, plain-weave fabric woven from coloured warps and white wefts. It has the appearance of soft, stone-washed denim and can be striped or checked.

Cheesecloth (Butter muslin)

This is a sheer, plain-weave, white fabric that is used as a light-weight interfacing, as a pressing cloth or as a net curtain. It was originally used to line tins and baskets for draining the whey from soft cheese. Care must be taken when cutting out as the fabric is very loosely woven.

Chintz

This is a plain-woven fabric with one glazed surface. It is often printed with floral or natural motifs and used for soft furnishings.

Corduroy

This is a pile fabric that has cut weft threads which form cords running the length of the fabric. The cords can be fine or heavy creating different weight fabrics, such as needlecord and jumbo cord. Corduroy can be made on plain or twill weave and can be printed.

Damask

This is a reversible, jacquard-weave fabric. The fabric is woven on complex jacquard looms that create the intricate, embossed surface. It is flatter than brocade, which is woven in the same way.

Denim

Originating in Nimes in France, this strong twill weave is woven with indigo-dyed warps and white weft threads. It was traditionally used for jeans, but is now used for furnishings and kitchenware. The distinctive washed-out look of denim occurs because the dye fades with each wash.

Drill

This strong twill weave has a similar weight and feel to denim. It is known as khaki when dyed that shade.

Flannelette (Cotton flannel)

This is an imitation of wool flannel. Softly woven weft threads are brushed to produce a fluffy surface with a warm feel. It is flame-proofed when used for children's nightwear.

Right: 1 voile; 2 knitted cotton; 3 chambray; 4 ticking; 5 denim; 6 muslin; 7 cotton print; 8 flannelette (cotton flannel); 9 stone-washed denim; 10 moleskin; 11 winceyette; 12 gingham; 13 zephyr (shirtings).

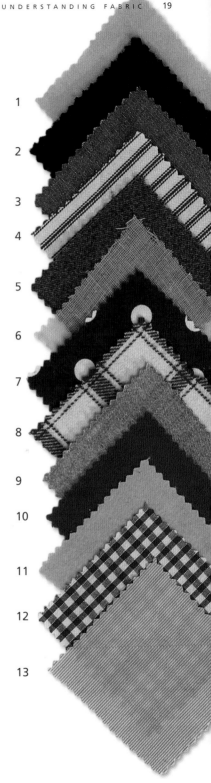

Left: Printed cotton fabrics are ideal for dresses, shirts and skirts.

Gingham

A firm, light-weight, plain-weave fabric that is woven with dyed yarns to produce the distinctive light, medium and dark checks. This is a hardwearing fabric, commonly used for smocked garments and home furnishing items.

Hessian (Burlap)

This is a coarse, heavy, plain-weave fabric made from jute, cotton or linen. It is used for sacking or as a backing for upholstery and rugs, since it is hard wearing, although it used where it is not seen. Jute is a cellulose fibre from India.

Indian cotton

The heavy weft threads are a distinctive feature of Indian cotton fabrics. The soft, bulky fabric is often dyed, printed or woven in stripes and checks. It is used for soft furnishings.

Jersey

This is a knitted fabric that originated on the island of Jersey. It is constructed in a tube shape in stockinette stitch. Natural-coloured cotton jersey is used for making rag dolls and a loose woven version is sold as a dish cloth (kitchen cloth).

Knitted cotton

Machine-knitted cotton is commonly used for summer sweaters and leisure wear. The fabric doesn't have the same "give" as knitted wool but is often blended with Lycra for sportswear.

Lace

Cotton lace is a heavy open-work fabric used for table linen, bridal wear and home furnishings. The threads are twisted, looped or knotted into complicated patterns on a complex loom that reads punched card patterns just like a musical organ.

Moleskin

This is a fairly hard-wearing, warm fabric used originally for workmen's trousers but now a fashion fabric available in a range of rich colours. It has the appearance of smooth suede or close-cut velvet.

Muslin

This is a term used for a wide range of soft, plain-weave fabrics that can be decorated with spots or embroidery. In the United Kingdom muslin is generally thought of as a sheer, roughly woven fabric whereas in the United States it is a closer woven fabric used for patchwork.

Organdie

This very fine, transparent fabric is treated with sulphuric acid to produce the characteristic crisp finish. It is used as a luxury dress fabric or as stiffening interfacing, for exquisite, fine household linen goods.

Piqué

Piqué refers to the raised cord weave that runs lengthways down a fabric. It can be embroidered to produce the characteristic holes and surface embroidery of broderie anglaise.

Printed cottons

Printed fabrics are not reversible as the dye colour does not penetrate completely through to the other side. Cotton is absorbent and accepts the colour well. There is a vast range of different printed patterned cottons in several weights used for dress fabrics, patchwork and home furnishings.

Scrim

This is a light-weight, open-weave fabric used as an interfacing, for pulled thread embroidery or for curtains. It can be made in cotton or linen and is often used for theatre backdrops.

Stone-washed denim

This is normal denim that has a faded, well-worn look. It has a soft feel achieved either by tumbling the denim with pumice stones or treating it with chemicals.

Ticking

A strong, durable twill-weave fabric with a distinctive lengthways coloured stripe. It was until recently purely a utilitarian fabric. Nowadays it is a fashionable fabric frequently used for kitchenware and soft furnishings.

Towelling (Terrycloth)

This distinctive, absorbent, loop-pile fabric is generally made from cotton. It can be woven or knitted with the pile on one or both sides.

Below: Gingham is a traditional woven cotton fabric that has recently become more fashionable. It is available in various widths as ribbon or as a fabric.

Voile

This is a sheer, light-weight fabric with a crisp feel. It has a plain, open weave with tightly twisted fibres. This fabric is usually starched to retain its crisp feel.

Winceyette

This medium-weight fabric is woven with a plain or twill weave and is brushed on each side for warmth. It has a similar appearance to flannelette. It is flame-proofed if it is to be used as a fabric for children's nightwear.

Zephyr (Shirtings)

This is a lightweight, finely woven fabric made primarily for shirting. It is either plain or twill weave and often has woven stripes or checks.

Right: 1 damask; 2 muslin; 3 lace; 4 batiste; 5 jersey; 6 organdie; 7 Indian cotton; 8 calico; 9 velvet; 10 piqué/broderie anglaise; 11 scrim; 12 hessian (burlap).

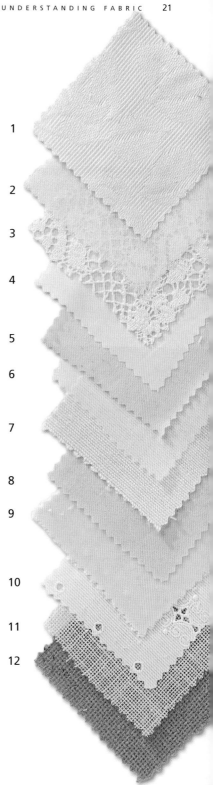

1

2

3

4

5

6

7

8

9

10

11

12

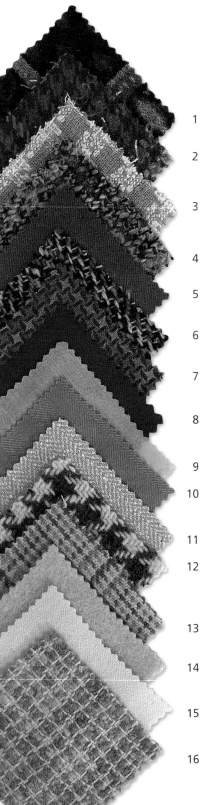

Wool

Wool fibres come from the fleece of a sheep. The quality is determined by the breed of sheep and the length of the fibres used. Wool fibres have a natural crimp that helps the fabric to shed creases but also allows folds to be pressed in with heat and steam. There is a wide variety of wool fabrics divided into two distinct groups – woollens and worsteds.

Woollens are made from fibres that are simply carded then spun. The resulting yarn is bulky and made into fabrics such as blazer cloth, flannel and tweed. Worsteds are much finer, made from combed fibres spun into a tight, smooth yarn. Fabrics such as tweed, gabardine and the new "cool wool" are made from worsted.

Blanket/Flannel

Blanketing is woven in plain weave and then brushed to raise the fibres on both surfaces to produce a soft pile fabric. It is light-weight but warm and ideal for bedding or coats.

Challis

This is a light-weight, soft, worsted wool fabric woven with a plain weave. It is suitable for shirts and blouses.

Cool wool

This fabric is woven from worsted wool and is smooth and light-weight. It has an unusual diagonal basket weave on the right side and a plain weave on the wrong side.

Crêpe

Wool crêpe has a soft feel with a delicate, pebbly surface. This is achieved by weaving in a random manner to produce top threads floating in an irregular pattern.

Above: Wool is a versatile fabric that can be made into a wide variety of fabrics and yarns. The design and colour are normally introduced by weaving two or more differently coloured threads together.

Dog's tooth check

The unusual weave pattern in this fabric is a variation of a twill weave. Hound's tooth is a larger version of the dog's tooth check.

Double face knit

This reversible fabric is made by knitting two layers and holding them together with binding threads. The fabric is less likely to curl than normal knit fabrics.

Twill weave

Herringbone and shepherd's check are variations of the twill weave that have distinctive pattens.

Wool blends

Man-made fibres with a similar texture to wool are blended with it to produce a wide range of less expensive suiting or coat-weight fabric.

Left: 1 knitted; 2 wool and mohair; 3 wool and silk; 4 coat weight; 5 crêpe; 6 coat weight; 7 dog's tooth; 8 cool wool;

9 challis; 10 twill weave; 11 herringbone weave; 12 hound's tooth; 13 wool blend; 14 blanket; 15 flannel; 16 fancy weave.

Silk

Cultivated silk is produced by the silk worm (caterpillar) of the *Bombyx mori* moth. The silk filament is very smooth and strong, creating fine fabrics with excellent draping qualities. Its strength allows sheer fabrics such as chiffon and georgette to be produced. Wild Tussah silk is produced by the caterpillar of the *Antheraea* moth. The filament of wild silk is very irregular, producing the well-known slub appearance.

Crêpe-backed satin

This beautiful fabric combines two weaves to produce a lovely soft fabric that drapes well. The satin and crêpe weaves are combined to give a crêpe fabric on one side with floating satin threads on the right side.

Dupion

This has an irregular texture that is woven from silk produced by double cocoons, created when two silk worms nest together. This gives the fabric its characteristic large slubs. It is a popular bridal fabric.

Futi

Silk futi is a beautiful soft shirt-weight fabric woven in a twill weave. The silk has been treated to produce a slightly brushed surface that gives it a warm feel.

Georgette

This is a sheer, dull crinkly fabric that is heavier than chiffon. It has a plain weave that is textured by crêpe, twisted yarns. It has a soft handle and is used for evening wear.

Habotai

Habotai is a general term for fine, soft, plain-weave silk fabrics that have been degummed. The lightest weights are used for lining, but heavier weights are sold as dress fabric.

Ottoman

This plain-weave fabric has a heavy corded effect caused by thicker weft threads. Normally used for evening wear, heavier weight Ottoman cloths are suitable for tailoring.

Organza

A sheer, stiff plain-weave cloth made from continuous filament silk in the gum. The threads are highly twisted to produce a crisp finish. Silk and metallic threads can be woven together to produce metallic organza.

Satin

The satin weave leaves long floating threads on the right side of this smooth fabric. It is available in various weights and qualities, with the heaviest known as duchesse satin.

Shantung

Shantung is a rough plain-weave cloth originally hand woven in China from wild silk produced by the Tussah moth.

Right: 1 satin; 2 duchesse satin; 3 dupion; 4 satin; 5 organza; 6 Ottoman; 7 crêpe-backed satin; 8 georgette; 9 habotai; 10 futi; 11 shantung; 12 duchesse satin.

Left: This soft, luxury fabric takes dye easily and is widely available in a vibrant palette of intense colours.

1

2

3

4

5

6

7

8

9

10

11

12

13

Linen

Linen fibres are found in the stem of the flax plant *Linum usitatissimum*. Jute and hemp are also obtained from the stem of plants. Flax fibres are extremely long – about 1m/1yd – when they are extracted from the plant but lose some length during processing. The long fibres give the linen its characteristic sheen. Linen is more absorbent than cotton and makes good tea towels (dish cloths) or table linen but has a lower resistance to abrasion. Originally, linen was bleached after weaving but a process has been developed for bleaching the fibres, which allows it to be blended with other fibres. Linens range from the fine batiste for handkerchiefs to heavy-weight jacquard suiting.

Batiste

This fine, antique, white Irish linen woven in a plain weave is calendered, a process that smoothes the surface and imparts a crisp, lustrous finish. It is used for making handkerchiefs, lingerie and fine household linens.

Left: 1 Jacquard weave; 2 batiste;
3 raw even weave; 4 white even weave;
5 bleached raw; 6 hand woven; 7 twill
weave; 8 scrim; 9 linen and silk; 10 stripe;
11 raw; 12 antique white; 13 cork.

Even-weave linen

This raw linen fabric has been woven in a "square" weave with exactly 31 threads running in each direction. The care required for weaving to such exacting standards makes it more expensive than ordinary linen. It is available as a raw or bleached fabric in a wide range of colours. The fabric is used for counted-thread embroidery.

Hand woven

This rough textured fabric is woven from a variety of thicknesses of yarn producing a soft, hand-woven look. It has been treated to make it more crease resistant than normal linen.

Jacquard

This 60 per cent linen/40 per cent cotton blend is woven on a Jacquard loom to produce the complex weave.

Pointed twill

The bleached linen yarn has been woven in a broken twill pattern to produce this attractive pattern of zigzags and stripes. The lustre of the linen fibres makes the weave particularly effective.

Below: Linen has a wonderful slubby texture which is often copied in other fibres.

Hair

These are any animal fibre other than sheep's wool or silk. Two types of fibre are collected: the long outer coat and the soft downy undercoat.

Alpaca

The alpaca is closely related to the llama. It produces fairly fine and soft fibres which can grow to 60cm/24in long if the animal is not sheared. The longer fibres are sometimes used for pile fabrics. Because the fibres are difficult to bleach they are used in their natural colour range of white, fawn, brown and black.

Angora

Angora comes from the long-haired angora rabbit. The fibres can be up to 7.5cm/3in long and are brushed from the animal. They are very soft and have a silky texture.

Camel

Camel hair is the long downy undercoat produced by the Bactrian camel. It is a soft but strong fibre that grows to about 16cm/6¼in in length.

Like sheep's wool, the fibre has surface scales that allow the fabric to be felted. It is used for overcoats and dressing gowns in its original colour because it is difficult to bleach.

Cashmere

Fibres from the downy undercoat of the Tibetan goat are very fine and grow to about 9cm/3½in long. Cashmere is soft and warm and is used to make luxury knitwear and shawls.

Mohair

These soft, smooth fibres come from the angora goat. The lustrous fibres have relatively few surface scales and are generally blended with worsted wool. Mohair fibres can be up to 30cm/12in long and are made into long-pile knitted or woven fabrics.

Vicuna

The soft hair of the wild vicuna, a small type of llama, is the finest of all the animals fibres. The fibres are about 5cm/2in long and are generally used in their natural colour.

Below: Because hair fibres are the most expensive fibres, they are often blended with other types to produce more affordable luxury yarns and fabrics.

Right: 1 cashmere; 2 vicuna; 3 alpaca; 4 camel; 5 alpaca; 6 cashmere; 7 vicuna; 8 vicuna; 9 cashmere; 10 wool and cashmere.

1

2

3

4

5

6

7

8

9

10

Synthetic fabrics

Synthetic fibres are produced entirely from chemical sources. Different fibre types are produced from different chemicals: nylon is a derivative of coke and tar, while polyester is a by-product of the petroleum industry. The range of fabrics is increasing as new ways to texture and process the raw filaments are developed. Synthetic fibres can melt and must be ironed on a cool heat setting.

Felt
Made with acrylic fibres or with wool, this soft, bulky fibre is made into felt by the application of heat, moisture and pressure.

Fleece
As the fabric is knitted, coarse yarn is laid in, then raised or fluffed up between teasels. Elastomeric yarn such as Lycra is often added to improve the stretch.

Jersey
Fine jersey fabric can be knitted from crimped nylon to produce a crêpe effect. The addition of an elastomeric yarn gives it a high degree of stretch.

Lycra
Lycra is a trade name for an elastomeric fibre made from polyurethane. This sheer fabric can stretch to double its length.

Microfibre
This beautiful, very fine polyester fibre looks like a luxury natural fabric, is easy to care for and has good crease resistance.

Mock peau-de-soie
This finely ribbed fabric has been made from Microfibre to emulate the exquisite peau-de-soie silk fabrics. It has superb draping and handling qualities with good crease resistance.

Mock suede
This smooth, soft fabric has a tight twill weave that has been raised on the right side by rubbing with carborundum. This process produces a napped surface. Spandex, an elasto-meric fibre, adds a degree of stretch.

Nylon net
Nylon is a hard fibre with poor draping qualities. These apparently negative aspects have been used to produce a stiff net that is ideal for making petticoats and costumes.

Polyester
Polyester is a generic term for a range of fabrics with good crease resistance and easy-care properties.

Taffeta
A crisp fabric with fine weft-way ribs, due to the weft and warp threads being of similar weight. The slub effect is used to emulate silk.

Below: Brightly coloured felts can be made from acrylic or polyester fibres.

Left: 1 acrylic felt; 2 polyester; 3 Lycra; 4 polyester fleece; 5 suedette and spandex; 6 taffeta; 7 Microfibre; 8 nylon net; 9 nylon velvet; 10 nylon jersey; 11 basket-weave polyester; 12 printed polyester; 13 polyester peachskin.

Man-made fabrics

The majority of man-made fibres are made from re-generated cellulose, which is the main component of cotton, linen, jute and hemp. The fibre is produced by extruding a solution of cellulose through a spinneret. The cellulose is then coagulated in filament form in an acid bath. The variety of man-made fibres are produced by modifying this basic procedure. Man-made fabrics are being improved and introduced all the time. They include rayon, viscose rayon, Cupro, cellulose acetate and Modal. Man-made fibres are often blended so that their combined properties make a fabric with improved handling and feel.

Acetate

This fabric is used as a lining. Made from cellulose acetate, it has a silky feel and excellent draping qualities.

Cupro

The soft draping qualities of Cupro have been given an added dimension by weaving to create the characteristic cord effect of a piqué fabric.

Jersey

This fine, jersey fabric has been blended with elastane to create a very stretchy fabric. It is much finer than cotton jersey and has a lovely soft feel.

Modal

This ribbed fabric has a watermarked effect known as moiré, produced by applying heat and steam while pressing the fabric between engraved rollers. The flattened areas reflect light in a different way producing the effect.

Printed viscose

Viscose rayon has a good affinity for dyes and so a wide variety of boldly coloured, printed, viscose dress fabrics are available. The viscose rayon creases readily unless specially treated.

Tencel gaberdine

Gaberdine is a firm, tightly woven twill fabric often made from fine worsted wool. Tencel is a strong man-made fibre with a similar feel to wool without the same shrinkage problems.

Velvet

This beautiful velvet fabric has a viscose rayon pile on a Cupro base fabric. Cupro has a soft lustre and good draping qualities. The viscose rayon makes a wonderful soft pile with a high sheen.

Viscose acetate

Viscose rayon and acetate blended together produce a fabric that is less likely to crease and takes a stronger colour of dye. The silk-like appearance of acetate is softened and the draping quality improved.

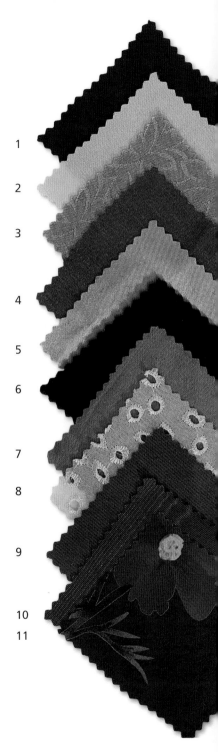

1
2
3
4
5
6
7
8
9
10
11

Right: 1 viscose acetate; 2 Tencel gaberdine; 3 polyester and viscose; 4 Tencel gaberdine; 5 cellulose acetate; 6 viscose and Cupro velvet; 7 viscose rayon jersey and elastane; 8 eyelet embroidery viscose rayon; 9 Cupro piqué; 10 Modal moiré; 11 printed viscose rayon.

Left: Manufacturing processes can produce a vast range of man-made fabrics, many of which handle similarly to natural fibres.

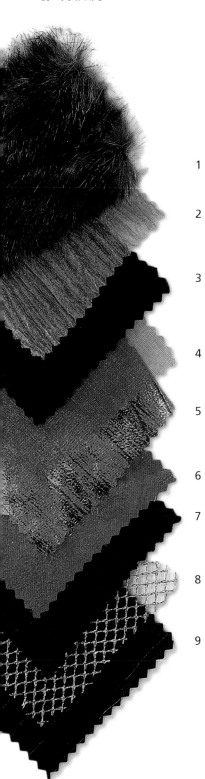

Decorative fabrics

In recent years fabric production has advanced with the constant introduction of new fibres and in the innovative way these fibres are being used. There is a huge range of decorative fabrics for evening wear, bridal wear and fun outfits. The majority of these fabrics require special handling, either in the way they are cut out, how they are stitched or the way they are cleaned.

Cotton lace

This is much heavier in weight than other lace fabrics. It is used for bridal wear and table linen. The edges are usually cut following the motifs of the lace rather than being hemmed. Lace can be fine and delicate or thick and heavy in appearance.

Cotton organdie

Organdie is a sheer, plain-weave fabric. The cotton yarn is tightly spun before weaving to give the fabric a very crisp feel.

Left: 1 imitation fur; 2 crushed organza; 3 PVC; 4 metallic organza; 5 paper lamé; 6 suede; 7 printed velvet; 8 nylon and lurex net; 9 vinyl crocodile skin.

Crushed organza

This fabric is made in the same way as metallic organza but has the creases set in to produce an unusual crimped fabric. It is used for scarves and evening wear.

Devoré velvet

This is a luxury fabric with a pile surface that has been "burnt out" in sections to create a velvet pattern on a sheer background.

Fun fur

The polypropylene base for this fabric softens at low temperatures and can be shaped easily to make hats. Fun fur is also used to make soft toys, soft furnishings and fashion garments.

Imitation fur

Advances in the production of imitation fur have shown how realistic it can be made to look. Imitation fur is light and is easy to stitch. The fur fabric shown has a knitted backing.

Below: Lace is made in different weights and fibres. The heavy, dress-weight lace shown here is used mainly for evening or bridal wear.

Above: Three different textures – velvet, net and satin – are combined here to produce an exquisitely simple bridesmaid's dress.

Lurex net

Nylon and Lurex yarns are knitted together to form a loose, open net. It is used for evening wear, hat veiling or for craft projects.

Metallic printed jersey

The silver appearance on this fabric is produced by printing small metallic dots over the jersey fabric. Despite being a stretch fabric, the metallic surface is distorted if pulled too much.

Metallic organza

The organza shown here has red silk threads in one direction and gold metallic threads in the other.

Nylon organza

The nylon shown here has been woven with Lurex threads to create an unusual checked organza. The nylon gives the fabric a rather harsh feel.

Panné velvet

Panné is a pressure finish for velvet that flattens the pile giving it a lustrous sheen. As this fabric is knitted, it has to be cut and stitched as a nap and stretch fabric.

Paper lamé

Lamé is a fabric made of metallic threads and another fibre. In this case the other fibre is nylon which gives the fabric a hard, crisp feel like paper.

Polythene (Plastic)

This plastic material is used primarily for shower curtains. It can be stitched, but care must be taken so that it doesn't rip along the stitch line.

Polyvinyl chloride (PVC)

This plastic is used as a coating on fabric to make it waterproof. It is used for rainwear, tablecloths and bags.

Sequin fabric

This polyester and nylon jersey fabric is knitted with a Lurex thread and then has small plastic sequins fused onto the surface. Stitch straight seams, between the sequins if possible.

Suede and leather

This is a natural fabric prepared from animal skin. Suede has a rough texture, whereas leather has a smooth surface. It is used for simply styled clothing, shoes, bags and furnishings. It is sold as part or whole skins.

Velour

This fabric can be knitted or woven and has a dense, short pile. The velour shown has a knitted, nylon backing and a multi-colour pile.

Vinyl

This is a thermoplastic material that can be moulded and heat set into shape, such as a crocodile skin surface. The plastic is quite stiff and is used for handbags or luggage.

Right: 1 panné velour; 2 cotton lace; 3 organdie; 4 nylon and Lurex organza; 5 imitation fur; 6 devoré velvet; 7 sequin fabrics; 8 polythene (plastic); 9 metallic printed jersey; 10 PVC.

1
2
3
4
5
6
7
8
9
10

Fabric structure

Fabrics made from natural fibres have been in existence from the earliest times and over the years a wide variety of different cloths have been produced, each with specific characteristics that make them instantly recognizable. Some construction methods, such as crochet and hand knitting, are labour intensive and only suitable for small-scale operations or for making luxury fabrics. Other methods, have been highly mechanized to produce vast quantities of fabric.

Weaving, knitting, lace-making, braiding and felting are the more traditional instantly recognizable methods of textile construction but stitch-bonding, laminating and needling are also used to create a wide range of fabrics.

Bonded fibre fabrics

These fabrics are generally used for interfacings, wadding (batting), disposable garments or cleaning cloths. They are not suitable for general use because of their poor recovery and draping qualities.

The fibres are made into a thick random layer called a batt and held together by several different methods. They can be fused with an adhesive, stitched together with rows of parallel stitching or needled. This last process uses rows of barbed needles to entangle the fibres together creating a lightweight felted fabric used for quilting.

Above, 1 laminated; 2 knitting; 3 net; 4 stitch binding; 5 weaving; 6 felting.

Below: This felt hat demonstrates how this sturdy fabric can be manipulated.

Braiding

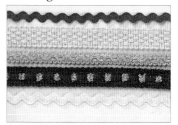

Braids are traditionally created by weaving a large number of warp threads together. The threads are woven in a bias direction to produce a narrow, interlaced band. Ric-rac braid (shown at the top of the samples above) is made in this way. Heavier furnishing braids are woven using warp and weft threads with the two groups of threads lying at right angles to each other.

Crocheting

Hand crocheting is produced using a single hook and a length of thread. Solid and lacy fabrics can be created by making the loops in different combinations. Filet crochet is a pictorial crochet technique that uses treble and chain stitches to create a design. The background has a square chain stitch mesh and the design is made from blocks of treble stitches. The yarn used for crocheting is generally smooth and tightly spun so that the hook catches it cleanly. Hand crochet was traditionally used to make mats, rugs and crochet lace borders but machines can now speed the process and crocheted garments are popular.

Felting

Felt is traditionally made by matting fibres together by applying heat, moisture, friction and pressure. Felting doesn't require any special equipment. Felted fabrics do not fray but they have no elasticity and will not return to their original shape once stretched. Modern craft felts are made from crimped synthetic fibres such as acrylic and polyester and created using bonded fibre techniques.

Knitting

Some knitted garments are still made by hand but are labour intensive and expensive to produce. Machine-knitted fabrics have become more widespread in recent years as technology has increased the variety of yarns that can be stitched by machine. Weft knitting is similar to hand knitting but is worked from one side only, either in a circular machine to produce a tube of fabric or on a flat-bed machine. Warp knitting is slightly different. A set of warp threads are worked parallel to each other and interconnected to produce knitted fabric. Knitted fabrics are very elastic and this can be increased by the introduction of an elastomeric yarn.

Laminating

This is a process where two layers are stuck together to improve stability or warmth, or to provide weather proofing. Laminating gives fabrics a different end use. A lining can be fused to a fabric before cutting to reduce construction costs and a thin layer of plastic can be fused to a fabric base to provide a waterproof barrier. Imitation leather, PVC and other vinyls are all made in this way.

Netting

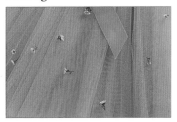

Netting is a versatile construction method that produces fabrics as diverse as fishing nets and delicate lace. There are two hand methods of lace-making – bobbin lace or needle-lace. Machine-made lace uses the same basic method as bobbin lace, where threads are twisted together to form a mesh of holes. The hexagonal mesh of stiff net is produced on a Leavers lace machine. Plain net and tulle is made on a bobbinet machine. Narrow and fabric width lace fabrics are made by a similar method on Leavers lace machines.

Weaving

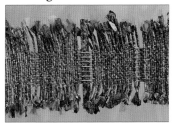

Woven fabrics are produced by interlacing two sets of threads together at right angles to each other. The warp threads are stronger and run lengthways down the fabric. The weft threads run across the fabric. The way these threads interlace produces the weave, which influences the appearance of the fabric and the way it handles.

There are a number of fabrics known by their weave, such as gaberdine, satin, twill and poplin. Other woven fabrics look and handle quite differently even though they use the same weave. Decorative weaves such as Leno, Dobby and Jacquard are produced on more complex looms. Leno weaving produces a lacy, open weave, whereas finely textured fabrics such as piqué are created on a Dobby loom, and brocades and damasks on a Jacquard loom.

Above: This evening jacket is trimmed with braid to give a crisp, decorative finish.

Lining, interfacing and thread

In sewing the design depends primarily on the quality and cut of the fabric to drape or lie in a certain way, but sometimes it is necessary to support the fabric with an interfacing or lining. The thread should always be chosen to suit the type of fabric being stitched.

Lining

Although linings are normally hidden from view, it is important to choose these undercover fabrics carefully. You need to pick one that will complement the outer fabric in weight and colour. Lining fabrics are now made to suit every eventuality. They can be woven or knitted and stretch or non-stretch.

With linings the fibre content is important, too. Pick a lining with a complementary fibre to the outer fabric. Man-made linings such as

Bremsilk or an acetate taffeta will work better with a natural fibre than a polyester taffeta. If the outer fabric can be washed, make sure the lining is washable too. Finally, select a lining that will move in the same way as the main fabric and one that will be as durable as the outer fabric. Seams in an ordinary lining will split during wear if the outer fabric is stretchy. A less durable lining fabric will wear out before the outer fabric.

Dressmaking patterns usually have separate pattern pieces for the lining.

Below: 1 stretch lining; 2 Bremsilk; 3 acetate taffeta; 4 Eton taffeta.

Right: A contrast lining has been used to effect inside the wide sleeves of this gown.

1
2
3
4

LINING FABRICS

Acetate taffeta
A basic general purpose lining that can be hand washed or dry cleaned. It has a medium weight and crisp handle.

Nylon jersey lining
A stretchy, light-weight translucent fabric, suitable for see-through fabrics. It has an anti-static finish and can be hand washed.

Stretch lining
An acetate fabric with 4 per cent Lycra added to give it stretch. It is an ideal lining for suiting fabrics, especially those with a percentage of Lycra added. Dry cleaning is recommended.

Bremsilk
A light-weight artificial silk lining made from Cupro. It is a wonderfully soft, lining fabric that handles well with natural fibres. It can be hand washed or dry cleaned.

Eton taffeta
A lighter weight, anti-static lining that can be washed to 50°C/122°F or dry cleaned. It is made from 100 per cent polyester.

Shot twill
This is an attractive suit lining fabric made from a mixture of viscose and acetate fibres. It is a heavier-weight lining with a soft feel. It must be dry cleaned.

Interfacing

Areas such as collars, cuffs and lapels are interfaced to hold their shape. Larger areas are interfaced to give support and add body to the outer fabric. Commercial patterns have separate pieces for interfacing, which is normally cut without seams and sewn or ironed in.

Interfacing is available in black or white and in light, medium or heavy weights – which one you choose will depend on the outer fabric colour and the amount of support required.

Iron or sew?

Interfacing is either woven or non-woven. Non-woven interfacing has no grain and can be cut in any direction. Where possible, iron-on interfacing should be attached to the facing rather than the outer fabric.

Standard interfacings are really only suitable for plain, cotton synthetic blends. Soft stretch and reinforced non-woven interfacings are also available for use with other fabrics.

1
2
3
4
5
6

Above: 1 fusible stitch reinforced;
2 medium weight; 3 light-weight stretch;
4 woven; 5 fusible stitch reinforced;
6 fusible heavy weight.

Thread

A good quality thread is strong and elastic with a consistent thickness. It has a smooth surface that resists tangling. Poor quality threads, often sold in bulk packs, have a fluffy texture and tend to snap readily. Such thread is only suitable for basting.

To blend in, thread should be the same colour or slightly darker than the fabric you are working with. Lay a single thread across the fabric surface to get the best match. If the fabric has several colours in it, match the predominant colour. Try holding some lengths of thread across the fabric to see which colour blends the best. Threads are available in a variety of fibres and thicknesses. Use this guide to find the best thread for the job in hand.

Mercerized sewing cotton

This is a strong, smooth thread with a soft sheen for general sewing on all fabric types. It is suitable for natural or man-made fabrics.

Synthetic sewing thread

Normally made from spun polyester, this very strong, elastic thread is suitable for all general sewing. It is especially recommended for use with synthetic fabrics and any jersey or knitted fabric.

Basting thread

Basting thread is poor quality thread used only for temporary hand stitching. It breaks easily so that the stitches can be removed quickly. Normally available in black or white, any poor quality coloured thread can be used. Avoid using dark threads on light fabric or vice versa.

Linen thread

Linen thread is a very strong thread that is used in tailoring for sewing on buttons. Run the thread through a wax block before use.

Silk thread

Silk thread is a soft, glossy, luxury thread designed for sewing silk and wool fabrics. It has plenty of "give" and is extremely durable. Silk thread is ideal for fine hand sewing and is also used for embroidery.

Strong thread

Strong thread is used for heavy-weight fabrics where there will be strain on the seams, on items such as coats, suits and furnishings. It is also used for top-stitching and quilting. Buttonhole thread, a strong thread with a predominant twist, is used for working hand-made buttonholes.

Ensuring good results

If an outfit you have sewn doesn't quite match up to one you can buy, it could be the choice of fabric or the way you have handled it that lets it down. With such a range of exquisite fabrics on the market there is no need for "hand-made" to mean a cheaper alternative or second best. Staff in most dressmaking shops will be pleased to pass on their knowledge about choosing the best fabric for a particular pattern.

Preparing fabric

If you choose a fabric with a large design, you will need to position the pattern very carefully when cutting out. Checked and striped fabrics work better on simple, uncomplicated designs that allow the fabric to make a statement. Large checks and stripes can be overwhelming, so choose your pattern carefully.

In commercial pattern books some designs are actually marked "unsuitable for stripes or plaids" because they probably have complicated seams that would be virtually impossible to match. As a rule, look out for paper patterns that illustrate the made-up garment or other item in a fabric similar to the one you are considering using. This should guarantee success.

Once you have chosen the right fabric and pattern for your project, the temptation is to get cutting straight away. Curb your enthusiasm – a little time spent checking and preparing your fabric before you begin will help prevent costly mistakes later.

Before beginning any sewing project, it is essential to straighten the fabric. This is because when the fabric is wrapped around the bolt by the manufacturer, it can be pulled slightly out of shape, and this may not become obvious until you have already started sewing. Such annoying problems as patterns not matching, cushion covers that aren't square, curtains not hanging straight, or fabric draping incorrectly are all caused by fabric being slightly off-grain.

It is always a good idea, therefore, to check whether your fabric is off-grain before starting any sewing project. You can do this by folding the fabric in half lengthways with the selvages together to see if the two crossways ends meet squarely.

Often, you will have to straighten the ends before you can check the grain, by tearing the fabric or pulling a thread. Sometimes it may not be obvious that the fabric is not straight because the bolt or roll was used as a guide for cutting by the store assistant – this can make the end look straight. Always check it anyway, it takes little time and will ensure good results.

Straightening fabric ends

If the fabric has an obvious weave or woven pattern such as a check, it can be cut straight easily, but you will probably have to tear or cut along a thread to guarantee a straight line.

Tearing is the quickest way to straighten a fabric end but this is only suitable for plain-weave fabrics such as calico or poplin. Try a test piece first to ensure that tearing your fabric won't ruin it for several inches on each side of the tear or cause it to suddenly tear lengthways instead. The safest way to straighten the end is by pulling a thread. It is time consuming, but worth the effort.

1 Look carefully at the weave of the fabric and snip into the selvage next to where the first thread goes straight across. Pull one of the crossways threads until the fabric gathers up. ◀

2 Ease the gathers gently along the thread as far as possible and then cut carefully along this line. Continue this process until you have cut right across the fabric.

Straightening the grain

Once the end of the fabric is straight you will be able to check if the fabric is off-grain. There are two ways to do this. You can either arrange the fabric flat on a square table or fold it in half lengthways with the selvages together. In both cases the ends should be square. If the corners don't match, the fabric needs to be straightened before you can begin cutting and sewing. If it is only slightly off-grain the fabric can be steam-pressed into shape.

Mis-shapen fabric must be pulled back into shape. This can be quite hard work and for a large piece of fabric you may need to enlist the help of a friend to pull from the opposite end. This step is essential and will affect the final drape of the garment or item, so don't be tempted to miss this stage.

1 Fold the fabric in half lengthways, with right sides together. Pin the raw edges together. Place upright pins into the ironing board every 13cm/5in along the selvage. Press the fabric from the selvage into the fold until the weave is absolutely straight, but avoid pressing the fold. Leave the fabric to cool before removing the pins.

2 To pull fabric back into shape, hold it firmly on each side of the narrow corners and pull your hands apart. Keep moving your hands down each side pulling firmly until you reach the other corners. This is easier to do if two people work from opposite corners. Check to see if the corner is square and press as in step 1.

PRE-SHRINKING FABRIC

Man-made or natural fibres will shrink when washed or dry cleaned unless they have been pre-shrunk by the manufacturer. Although shrinkage of 3 per cent may appear small, bear in mind that this can result in floor-length curtains being 5–7.5cm/2–3in shorter after cleaning.

• Problems also arise in dressmaking when interfacings don't shrink to the same degree as the outer fabric, causing collars and cuffs to pucker. Quilt-makers use this puckered effect to create instant "antique" patchwork quilts by washing a quilt in hot water after it has been stitched to shrink the cotton wadding (batting).

• Shrink cotton and other washable fabrics in a washing machine using no soap or in a basin of hot water. Fold the fabric to fit and leave it immersed for up to an hour. Lift the fabric out and roll it up to remove the excess moisture before hanging it up by the selvage. Keep the fabric in shape with regularly spaced clothes pegs, then press it on the wrong side while still slightly damp.

• Wool fabrics need to be handled with the utmost care and should be shrunk by dry cleaning if possible. Otherwise, straighten the ends of the fabric and fold it in half crossways. Place the folded fabric in the centre of a damp sheet. Fold the edges of the sheet on to the wool fabric and then roll it up carefully, keeping the sheet on the outside all the time. Leave the fabric overnight and then press lightly with a steam iron.

CHECKING FOR FLAWS

Once the fabric is ready for cutting, open it out with the right side facing up and examine it carefully for flaws.

• Flaws usually occur during the manufacturing process and may not be obvious on the wrong side. Sometimes a thread snaps during the weaving or knitting process causing a weak point or knot. Alternately, the printing may not be perfect or there may be a dirty mark.

• If you have enough fabric avoid the flaw, otherwise you will have to return the length to the shop or buy extra fabric.

• Some fabrics especially pale colours and synthetics can become quite badly soiled along the foldline while on display and will require cleaning before use.

Washing and caring for fabrics

Scientists are constantly searching for ways to make fabrics repel dirt and stay cleaner longer but until they succeed, the laundry is an essential part of all our lives. An average family will spend about 12 hours a week washing, ironing and putting away the clothes that they wear. Laundering itself, while caring for the fabric by getting it clean, is liable to cause some deterioration eventually by shrinking fabrics and fading colours. To help keep these problems to a minimum all clothes are labelled with the fabric they are made from and care information for treating them.

The present care labelling system is based on five symbols: the wash tub, an iron, a circle in a square (tumble dryer), a circle (dry cleaning) and a triangle (bleaching). These five symbols are used in groups on a label to describe exactly how to clean, iron or tumble dry a garment.

Sort clothes initially according to their colour. Keep whites separate, as even pale and neutral shades will eventually cause them to look grey.

In the United States, care instructions are written on labels.

Understanding the washcare symbols

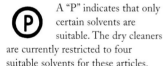 The number inside the wash tub symbol indicates the maximum recommended centigrade temperature you can use using a normal cycle.

 A single bar under the wash tub symbol indicates a gentler washing action. This symbol is used for synthetic fabrics.

 Two bars under the wash tub symbol indicates the wool wash or delicate cycle should be used.

 This symbol is used for hand wash garments only. The label will give other details such as temperature, drying and ironing.

 A crossed out wash tub indicates dry cleaning only. It is followed by another symbol giving information of the dry cleaning process to be used.

 The letter inside the circle indicates which solvents are suitable for dry cleaning the article. An "A" means that all solvents normally used for dry cleaning are suitable.

 A "P" indicates that only certain solvents are suitable. The dry cleaners are currently restricted to four suitable solvents for these articles.

 A bar under a circle indicates that the garment is sensitive to some dry cleaning processes and must be cleaned under strict conditions.

 A crossed out circle indicates that a garment is not suitable for dry cleaning.

 This symbol indicates that the garment may be tumble dried.

 A single dot inside the tumble drying symbol means that the garment should be dried on the low heat setting.

 Two dots indicate that the garment can be dried on the high heat setting.

 A crossed out tumble dry symbol means that the garment is not suitable for tumble drying. This symbol is usually followed by further instructions such as "dry flat".

 This tee-shirt in a square indicates that the garment should be dried flat away from direct heat. It is used for garments that can easily be pulled out of shape.

 The iron with one dot is used for synthetic fabrics that melt at low temperatures. Set the iron at its coolest setting.

Fabric terminology

The success of a project depends on the correct folding and accurate placement of pattern pieces, so it is important to learn the terms commonly used in commercial patterns. Some fabrics handle very differently if cut on the crossways grain rather than on the lengthways grain and designs or motifs can end up facing in the wrong direction. Most fabrics are cut with the right sides of the fabric together and can be folded on the lengthways or crossways fold. Nap designs have a design or surface texture that means the fabric must be folded lengthways or not at all.

Above: Wool fibres mat together to make felt if they are roughly handled or washed with hot or boiling water.

Two dots on an iron indicate a medium heat setting. It is used for wool, silk and some synthetic fibre mixtures.

Three dots indicate the hottest setting on an iron. This symbol appears on cotton, linen and man-made fibres such as viscose.

A crossed out iron means do not iron. This usually indicates that the fabric has a special finish or embellishments which will be damaged with an iron.

A crossed out triangle means do not use chlorine bleach.

The triangular symbol is found on garments that have been imported. It refers to chlorine bleach only and not to the bleaching agents found in most heavy-duty washing powders.

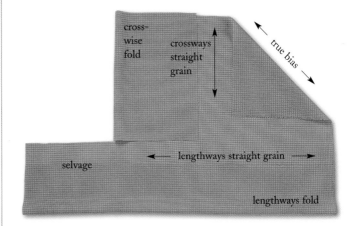

Bias

Bias is any diagonal line across woven fabric. Fabric cut on the bias has more stretch than fabric cut on the straight grain and the most stretch is achieved on the true bias. This occurs when the selvage edge on one side is folded over to run parallel to the crossways grain. Patterns cut on the bias drape beautifully. Bias strips are used for binding or piping curved edges.

Folds

Fabric is usually sold off a roll or from a bolt (a flat cardboard base). On narrow widths the fabric is flat with a selvage at each edge, but more often the fabric is folded in half lengthways so that the selvages lie together. This fold is used for centre front seams and should be in the centre of a large pattern. Crossways folds are used when cutting wide pattern pieces.

Grain

Woven fabrics are made up of two sets of threads. The crossways, or weft, threads go over and under the stronger warp threads that run the length of the fabric. The grain is the direction in which these threads are woven. Warp threads running parallel to the selvage are on the lengthways grain. When the weft threads run perpendicular to the selvage they are on the crossways grain.

Selvage

This is the narrow flat band running lengthways down each side of the fabric. The threads are strong and closely woven and provide a straight, ready-finished edge for centre back seams or cushion cover zipper openings. On some fabrics, such as jersey, the selvage is rather ragged and it is better to trim it off.

Cutting paper patterns

Commercial patterns usually come with a cutting guide. This tells you how to fold the fabric and arrange the pattern pieces and is carefully worked out. You may make a mistake if you change things around. If there is no cutting plan, the following information will be useful.

Fabrics are usually folded lengthways with right sides together. This makes it easy to mark the fabric on the wrong side and allows you to sew pieces together quickly.

The straight grain line is the most important line on the pattern piece. This line is placed to follow the lengthways grain on the fabric and runs parallel to the selvages. If the grain line is inaccurately placed the item or garment will not hang straight. Check carefully even after the pattern is pinned to the fabric.

1 Place the pattern lengthways on the fabric. Measure an equal distance to the selvage from each end of the pattern and insert a pin at the top and the bottom.

2 Pin around the sides every 7.5–10cm/3–4in to firmly secure the pattern to the fabric. Refer to the tips before cutting out.

Seam allowances

Check whether seam allowances are included in the pattern pieces or if they have to be added. If required, use tailor's chalk and a ruler to add 15mm/⁵⁄₈in extra for the seam allowance on all sides except for the foldlines.

1 Arrange this type of pattern piece so that the foldline lies exactly along the fold of the fabric. Pin along the fold every 7.5–10cm/3–4in, then all around the edges.

TIPS FOR SUCCESSFUL PATTERN CUTTING

• Select the cutting guide to match the width and type of fabric and size of pattern. Draw a circle around the cutting guide you intend to use.

• Pin all the pattern pieces on to the fabric before cutting out.

• Check the straight grain lines are parallel to the selvages and foldlines are on the fold.

• Make sure that any alterations to the main pattern pieces have been applied to corresponding pieces such as facings.

• Cut out pattern pieces with the printed side facing up unless stated otherwise. This is shown as shaded in the cutting guide.

• When a pattern piece has to be repeated, draw around the pattern with tailor's chalk, marking the notches then move it to another location.

• Sometimes a "cut 1" pattern piece overhangs the fabric in a cutting guide. Cut all other pieces first and then open out the fabric with right side up. Pin in place using the foldline as a guide for the straight grain.

• Hold your hand flat on the pattern piece and cut the fabric with large shears using long even cuts. Move around the table rather than moving the fabric, keeping your hand resting on the fabric at all times so that you do not accidentally move it.

Dealing with directional fabrics

Many plain, or small, patterned fabrics can be cut out quite easily without much thought as to how the pattern pieces are laid out. Directional fabrics, on the other hand, have a textured surface or pattern that requires greater care when folding, positioning and cutting out.

Fabrics such as velvet, devoré, moleskin and corduroy have a pile and can only be cut in one direction. Hold the fabric lengthways against your body and move your hand across the surface to determine the direction of the pile. It should feel smooth when you stroke your hand up the fabric. Dress patterns and curtains are normally cut with the pile facing upwards so that the colour looks richer, but they can also be used in the other direction for a paler effect. Whatever you decide, ensure it matches throughout.

Follow the same approach for one-way prints and dyed fabrics such as ombré, which shade from top to bottom by making all pattern pieces face the same way. All these fabrics are known as directional or "with nap" and also include satin and brocade. They have to be treated as directional because of the way the light reflects from the surface.

The cutting guide will have a pattern layout for using "with nap"

Below: Everyday clothing and mundane checks and stripes have been pieced into an unusual patchwork quilt.

Above: Velvet has a directional nap that requires careful handling.

fabrics if the design is suitable. Fold the fabric lengthways with right sides together to give you a smooth surface on which to pin the pattern. Don't fold directional fabric crossways before cutting because the pattern or pile on the lower layer will be facing in the opposite direction to that on the top layer. If your pattern is too wide for the lengthways fold, cut the fabric in half crossways and rotate the top piece until both layers face in the same direction.

Patterned fabrics

Most of us will probably use patterned fabric for a sewing project at least once. Small random prints can be cut out in the same way as plain fabric, but large designs, checks and stripes need to be studied closely and the patterns arranged carefully before cutting. The position of a large bold design on the finished item can be crucial to its success.

Border designs that are positioned along the hem of garments and curtains can be difficult because the exact finished length needs to be determined before cutting. Mark the hem line on the pattern allowing for turnings and position the border design just above the line.

On dress patterns or cushions, any large bold designs are usually positioned centrally. You will find this easier if you make complete pattern pieces from tracing paper before you begin. Work with the fabric in a single layer with the right side facing up, and position, for example, the front bodice pattern piece centrally on the design. Cut other corresponding pattern pieces so that the design will be at the same level on the garment.

Soft furnishings such as loose covers and curtains will also look wrong if a large design is badly positioned. Plan the cutting layout allowing extra fabric for matching seams and positioning the design.

Checks and stripes

These are made up of stripes arranged horizontally and vertically across the fabric to form a repeating pattern. This pattern can be even or uneven, depending on the arrangement of the stripes. Because the bold lines of a checked design should match horizontally and vertically on a finished garment or soft furnishing item, it is essential to test these fabrics before cutting as some fabrics that appear to be even are actually uneven.

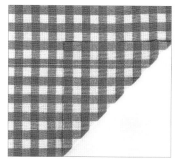

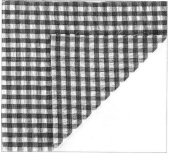

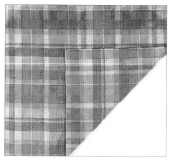

1 Turn over a corner of the fabric so that the fold lies centrally through the squares of the check design. In an even check the line widths and colours match in both directions.

2 This check appears to be even, but when folded on the diagonal it is obvious that the horizontal lines are stronger than the vertical lines.

3 In an uneven check the line widths and colours may match if folded vertically or horizontally but don't match on the diagonal fold.

Left: Striped fabrics work well with simple designs and are particularly associated with country style furnishings.

Cutting checked fabrics

Fabrics with even checks can usually be cut on the normal "without nap" pattern layout. Open the fabric out and refold it down the centre of the main check line.

1 Insert pins along the foldline. Work out from the centre pinning along each main check line, making sure that both layers match exactly.

2 Place the pattern pieces so that the centre front line and back seam lines are exactly on the dominant check line. Move the pattern pieces up or down this line until the side seam notches match across the garment.

3 When making garments with front facings, make sure the notches match the corresponding pattern piece. Sleeves are placed with the dominant check line running down the centre of the pattern piece and matched by placing the notch on the front sleeve head at the same level as the armhole notch on the bodice.

Cutting uneven checks

Cutting fabrics with uneven checks is not suitable for a beginner and it is advisable to choose simple patterns to reduce the amount of matching required. Seam lines cut on an angle should have the check lines coming together as shown, but this can look very fussy if there are a lot of seams. The principle for pattern cutting is the same as for even checks, but, since the check can only be matched in one direction, use a "with nap" layout. It may also be easier to open the fabric out and cut it on a single thickness, making sure you turn the pattern pieces over to cut the left-hand side. Pin the seams carefully and baste if necessary, before sewing to ensure neat, accurate matching.

Cutting striped fabrics

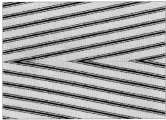

Striped fabrics are easier to match than checked ones because the lines run in one direction only, but the same preparation and cutting principles apply. Horizontal striped fabrics can be cut more accurately if the stripes are pinned at regular intervals. First determine the garment length and position the hem line along the dominant stripe. The pattern can then be matched across the way by placing corresponding notches on the same stripe. Facings should match the main pattern piece, too. Position sleeves so that the front sleeve head notch is on the same stripe as the front armhole notch. Unbalanced horizontal stripes must be cut on a "with nap" layout.

Above: Striped silk has a formal appearance, particularly if it is used on a grand scale to furnish the home.

Right: Large and small-scale gingham checks in natural fabrics will soften with age.

Fabrics requiring special handling

Although it is much easier to stitch a plain cotton fabric than a knitted velour, your dressmaking will be rather dull if you don't try using some of the more unusual fabrics, such as lace, leather, fake fur or any of the sheer fabrics. There are some wonderful fabrics available today that can make a simple design exceptional and quite unique.

Lace

Lace or lacy fabrics are unique because of their loose, open construction. They can be used for the whole garment or just a part such as the bodice, sleeves or skirt. Lace is normally lined on the bodice and skirt but cut on its own for sleeves. When used in this way, lace garments are usually luxury items, since they require special laundering and care.

Lace works well with a variety of fabrics such as velvet, crêpe, satin or taffeta. Choose a pattern to suit the main fabric with simple lines to show off the lace. When using lace with another fabric, check that both fabrics require similar laundering.

Lace is constructed differently from woven or knitted fabrics and is backed with a fine mesh. It can be cut in any direction. Look at the motifs and the pattern they create and decide if the lace motifs can be used as a border or the hem of the garment. Lace is non-fray and can be cut around the motifs to produce an attractive scallop edge.

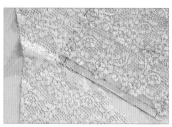

1 Position the stitching line of the pattern piece along the bottom of the lace motifs. The lace can be trimmed neatly along this line and then cut in the normal way for the other seams.

Sheer and satin fabrics

Voile, muslin, georgette, organza and batiste are all sheer fabrics with quite different handling. Crisp sheers such as organza are quite easy to cut and stitch, but the softer sheers such as georgette tend to slip requiring greater care when dressmaking. Sheer fabrics can be stitched in multiple layers to produce a moiré effect but need to be lined in certain parts to make them less transparent. Satin fabrics handle in a similar way to soft sheers when stitching. Use narrow, rolled hems and choose methods of fastening that will keep machine stitching on the right side to a minimum. Rouleaux loops and invisible or prick-stitched zippers are suitable methods to use.

Soft sheer fabrics and satin are quite difficult to sew. The fabric tends to shift and slide and can snag as it is stitched. Use a new needle – a ballpoint needle is often recommended because it slips between the threads without splitting them.

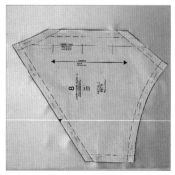

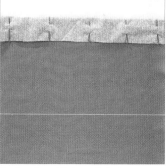

Above: Satin has a smooth, glossy appearance and is soft to the touch making it ideal for lingerie.

1 Satin and sheer fabrics can be permanently marked by pins. Place the pins in the seam allowance.

2 On sheer fabrics, stitch the seams between two layers of tissue paper. The paper can be torn away later.

Fur fabrics

Imitation fur fabrics should be treated as a pile fabric. The pattern pieces are pinned with the pile going in the same direction. When cutting long hair fabrics, use a small pair of pointed scissors to snip the fabric leaving the pile intact on the surface.

1 Stitch a seam and then ease the long hairs out of the seam using a large, blunt needle from the right side to make it almost invisible. Excess fur can be trimmed from the seam allowance on the inside to reduce bulk.

Leather and plastic

Leather, suede and plastic fabrics such as vinyl, PVC, imitation leather and polythene shower curtain fabric can all be stitched on a domestic sewing machine. Choose simple styles with few seam lines and avoid seams that need to be eased. It is important to make sure there are no pins used outside the seam allowance. Tape and paper clips are suitable alternatives. Use the tape to fix the pattern pieces and both methods for seams.

Below: Seams on leather can be pressed on the wrong side using a dry, medium iron.

1 Masking tape and paper clips can be used to hold leather or plastic materials instead of pins.

2 Use a long stitch as small stitches tear more easily and plastic especially will split along the seam line like perforated paper. Ensure that the seams are stitched correctly first time.

3 If seams are stitched in the wrong place on plastic or leather they can be taken in but not let out. The previous stitches leave an unsightly row of holes on the right side.

4 To make it easier to stitch leather or plastic, use a roller foot or place strips of tissue paper on each side of the seams to help it slip under the presser foot.

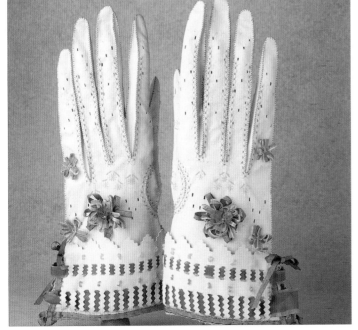

Marking up fabric

Printed pattern pieces contain information that must be transferred on to the fabric before sewing. The position of darts, centre front and centre back lines, buttonholes and seam openings are the most common, but every symbol and line you transfer will make sewing much easier.

Tailor's tacks

Tailor's tacks are threads used to mark points such as the top of darts. The symbol for a tailor tack is a dot on the pattern. They are suitable for many fabrics. Use a different colour for large and small dots on the pattern and work with a long double strand of thread without a knot.

1 Take a small stitch through the pattern and fabric. Leave a long tail. Make a second stitch on top of the first, pulling the thread through until a loop is formed.

2 To save time, work groups of tailor's tacks, leaving a long strand between each one. Snip the middle of the loops and the strands between each one.

3 Pull the layers apart gently and snip the threads between the layers leaving short tufts on each piece. Handle the pattern pieces carefully to prevent the tufts from coming loose.

Carbon and tracing wheel

Use these to mark the wrong side of closely woven, hard-wearing fabrics such as PVC, plastic and leather. Use a smooth wheel for a solid line.

Dressmaker's carbon paper is available in a variety of colours. Choose a colour that will show up on the fabric without being a contrast. Try out the carbon paper on a scrap of fabric and steam press or hand wash to ensure the marks will disappear.

1 With the pattern in place, inset a carbon sheet on each side of the folded fabric with the coloured side facing the wrong side of the fabric.

2 ◄ Using the wheel, trace along the lines to be transferred, pressing hard enough to produce a light line on both pieces of fabric. If necessary, use a ruler to keep the wheel straight. Mark dots and other symbols with a short line or cross.

Tailor's chalk and pins

Tailor's chalk is generally used for drawing around pattern pieces before cutting out or for last-minute marking on soft-surfaced fabrics. It can be rubbed off easily, so you should baste along the chalked lines to make a more permanent mark.

1 Push a pin through the pattern and both layers of fabric at each point to be marked.

2 ◄ Peel back the tissue paper leaving the pins in the fabric and chalk the fabric where the pins are, joining them up if necessary.

Pinning and basting

These techniques are quick, temporary methods of joining or marking pieces of fabric. Any thread that contrasts with the fabric can be used, but avoid using dark colours on white fabric, or vice versa, since fibres will remain in the holes and leave a coloured mark. Use a long needle. Cut a length of thread long enough to sew the whole length and secure with a knot or a loose back stitch that can be easily pulled out.

Pinning for hand sewing

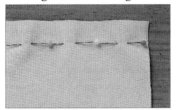

Insert pins along the seam line before basting. Arrange them in the same direction as you sew to avoid pricking your finger and only remove pins as you reach them. Use as many pins as required to hold the fabrics together. You will need more on a curved or gathered edge.

Uneven basting

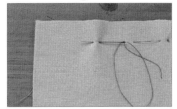

Basting is used on seam lines to hold two layers of fabric together, or for marking guidelines such as the centre front of a garment. You can also use basting to attach lining or interfacing to the main fabric or to baste a hem before sewing it in place.

Strong basting

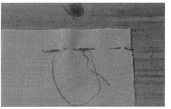

Use this stitch where there will be a lot of strain on the seam during construction or fitting. Simply work a back stitch every few basting stitches. Strong basting is ideal for holding together two different textures such as satin lining and wool.

Pinning for machine sewing

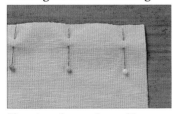

If you intend to sew by machine without basting, insert the pins across the seam line. Stitch slowly over the pins and the needle will slip over each without bending. Insert pins across the seam line when easing or gathering fabric before basting. Insert the pins up or down depending on whether you are left- or right-handed so that you can remove them easily as you stitch over them.

Slip basting

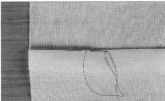

Work from the right side of the fabric for final fitting adjustments or to ensure perfect matching of checks, stripes and patterns. Fold under the seam on one side and crease. Place the folded edge on the seam line of the other piece, matching the pattern carefully and pin. Take small stitches alternately through the fold, then through the other piece. Slip basting looks like even basting if the seam is opened out for sewing.

Diagonal basting

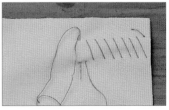

Diagonal basting is a large stitch used to insert interfacing and hold linings and facings in place. Work the stitch on a flat surface unless you are using it to hold the roll line on collars and lapels. Take small straight stitches through the fabric at right angles to the edge, forming long diagonal stitches on the top side and short parallel stitches on the underside. Don't pull the thread tight or ridges will form.

Sewing by hand

In the days before sewing machines, every garment, curtain or furnishing item was sewn by hand. It seems miraculous now that so much was achieved often in poor light. Sewing machines have, without doubt, taken the drudgery out of sewing, but they cannot entirely replace hand sewing. Hand sewing should not be hurried as the quality of your stitches will affect the finished appearance of the project.

Beginning a hand stitch

Hand-sewn stitches are normally worked in thread that closely matches the fabric colour and fibre content. Work in good light either close to a window or with an angled lamp. Use a short length of thread and a short fine needle to suit the fabric you are using.

1 Pull a length of thread from the reel no longer than the distance

between your elbow and wrist. Cut the thread at an angle to make it easier to feed through the eye of the needle. Pull the cut end through the eye to about three-quarters of its length.

2 Wind the end of the thread once around your forefinger about 12mm/½in from the tip and hold it in place with your thumb. Rub your finger down your thumb until the threads form a twisted loop. Slide your finger and thumb down the thread to tighten the loop and form a small knot. On fine or see-through fabric where a knot would show, use a small double back stitch.

3 Take the first stitch on the wrong side preferably hidden in a seam or fold.

Finishing off

Finish hand sewing with a knot or several back stitches, one on top of the other, on the wrong side, ideally

hidden in a seam or a fold. If using back stitches, weave the thread in and out before cutting off. The finishing knot is flatter than a beginning knot.

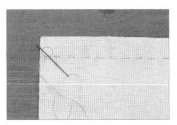

1 Make a loop by taking a tiny back stitch on the wrong side. Take the needle through the loop and pull through until a second loop forms.

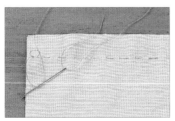

2 Finally take the needle back through the second loop and pull tight. Snip off the long end.

Hand stitches

Hand stitches are used where machine sewing is awkward or undesirable. There are many types for particular uses.

Running stitch

This basic stitch is used for gathering, smocking and quilting. Make several small even stitches at a time, weaving the needle in and out of the fabric at regular intervals. Use longer stitches for gathering and leave the thread end loose for pulling up.

Back stitch

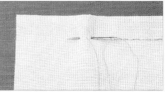

Use this strong stitch for repairing or sewing lengths of seam that are difficult to reach by machine. Bring the needle up through the fabric on the seam line. Take a small stitch back along the seam and bring the needle out an equal distance in front of where the thread last emerged.

Half back stitch

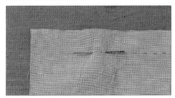

Half back stitch is suitable for stitching seams or inserting sleeves by hand. The small stitches are more attractive and stronger than ordinary back stitch. The stitch is also used on facings to prevent the edge from showing on the right side of the garment. Work this stitch in the same way as back stitch but take only a half stitch back and a whole stitch forward. This forms small even stitches on the top side and long overlapping stitches on the underside.

Slip stitch

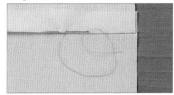

Slip stitch is used to close gaps, attach pockets and insert linings. A variation of it known as slip hemming is used to sew hems. When worked neatly, it is an almost invisible stitch. Take a small stitch through the fold and then another through the fabric underneath. Make the stitches the same length and keep the threads straight. Pull the thread taut without causing the fabric to pucker. Slip hemming is worked in the same way but only a tiny stitch is taken through the underneath fabric.

Oversewing

Oversewing is used to hold two folded edges together. It is more visible, but also much stronger, than slip stitching. Work with the two folds held together in your hand. Take a tiny stitch straight through both folds, if possible catching only one thread. Continue along the folds making a row of very small slanting stitches on the right side. In traditional patchwork the oversewing which holds patches together is worked from the wrong side.

Prick stitch

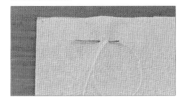

Prick stitch is an almost invisible stitch. It is used to insert zippers in fine or sheer fabrics and to sew layers of fabrics together from the right side where a row of machine stitching would be too stiff or unsightly. Work in the same way as half back stitch but take the needle back over only one or two threads each time to form a row of tiny surface stitches with longer reinforcing stitches on the wrong side.

Hem stitch

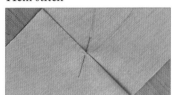

This is a diagonal stitch worked to hold down a fold of fabric such as a binding. Despite its name, it is not suitable for hemming a garment or curtains because it shows on the right side. Hem stitch can be worked into a row of machine stitching to finish cuffs or waistbands on the inside. Take a tiny stitch through the fabric and diagonally up through the edge of the fold at the same time. Continue in this way keeping the stitches 3–5mm/$^1/_8$–$^1/_4$in apart depending on the fabric thickness.

Blanket stitch

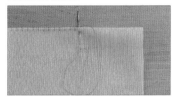

Traditionally used to neaten the raw edges of wool blankets, this stitch is quick to work and ideal for preventing fabric from fraying while working embroidery. It can be used as a decorative stitch and also for appliqué. Secure your first stitch at the edge of the fabric and then work from left to right with the edge towards you. Insert the needle through the right side about 5mm/$^1/_4$in from the edge. Bring the needle back out over the thread loop and pull taut. Continue working evenly spaced stitches in this way adding an edge to the fabric.

Sewing by machine

Few people would even think of beginning a sewing project without a sewing machine. Sewing by machine is quick and if the tension has been set correctly, extremely neat. Machine stitching is indispensable when sewing long straight seams in soft furnishings and also produces strong seams in dressmaking. Use machine stitching in conjunction with hand sewing for the most professional result.

Sewing a seam

One of the first tasks in any sewing project is stitching a seam. Most soft furnishing and dressmaking patterns use a 15mm/⁵⁄₈in seam allowance – any alteration will affect the final fit.

1 Baste or pin the seam across the seam line with the right sides of the fabric together. This will hold the fabric together while you sew.

2 Place the fabric under the presser foot so that the edge of the seam is next to the 15mm/⁵⁄₈in line on the needle plate and the fabric is 5mm/¹⁄₄in behind the needle. Use the hand wheel to take the needle down into the fabric, then begin to sew.

3 Sew at a speed that is comfortable for you, guiding the fabric along the 15mm/⁵⁄₈in line on the needle plate.

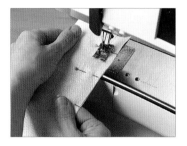

Turning corners and sewing curves

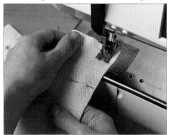

1 Stitch down the first length leaving a 15mm/⁵⁄₈in seam allowance. Slow down as you approach the corner and work the last few stitches by turning the hand wheel. Stop 15mm/⁵⁄₈in from the edge with the needle in the fabric. Lift the presser foot and swing the fabric around until the next seam is lined up with the guideline on the needle plate. Lower the foot and continue sewing. You may have to turn the fabric back and take another stitch or two until the edge is exactly on the 15mm/⁵⁄₈in line on the needle plate.

2 Sew slowly around soft curves, keeping the edge of the fabric opposite the presser foot on the guideline of the needle plate. On tighter curves stop and turn the fabric slightly into the curve before beginning. Keep stopping every few stitches to adjust the line of the fabric until the curve is complete. To ensure that two curves are exactly the same, for example on a collar, make a template of the shape along the sewing line and cut out. Mark the second curve along the seam line before sewing.

Removing stitches

1 Unless the fabric is fine or delicate, the easiest way to remove stitches is with an unpicker. Slip the point underneath a stitch and cut it against the sharp curved edge of the tool. Cut every two or three stitches and then turn the fabric over and pull the reverse side thread out. Brush the loose threads from the right side and steam press to close the holes. You can run the unpicker up the seam to rip stitches, but you risk cutting the fabric. On fine or delicate fabrics, lift and cut the stitches one at a time.

Machine stitches

The type of machine you have will determine the range of stitches at your disposal. The stitches listed here are the ones most commonly used in general sewing. Check your handbook for the range of stitches possible on your machine. Try out a stitch on a double scrap of fabric before you start.

Overlocking

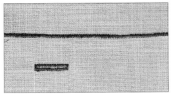

Overlocking is worked directly over the edge of the fabric, stitching and finishing the seam in one. Alternatively, stitch along the seam line and trim, as shown above.

Satin stitch

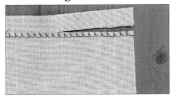

Satin stitch is a zigzag with the stitch length set almost at zero. It is used for buttonholes and machine appliqué. Use a clear-view foot to allow enough room for the bulky stitch underneath. Satin stitch can make the fabric gather if the stitches are too wide, so check that the stitch width is right for the fabric before you start. Buttonholes consist of two parallel rows of narrow satin stitches with a few double-width stitches at each end to finish.

Straight stitch

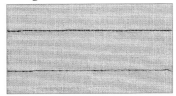

This is the stitch most widely used to join two pieces of fabric together. For ordinary fabric set the stitch length dial between 2 and 3. If the fabric is very fine or heavy, alter the stitch length to suit: use a shorter stitch for fine fabrics and a longer one for heavy fabrics. If you have an automatic sewing machine you can work a stretch straight stitch, which is useful for sewing fabrics such as jersey. Quick basting stitches can be worked by machine. Use the longest straight stitch possible to make it easy to pull out the thread at a later stage.

Blind-hemming (blindstitching)

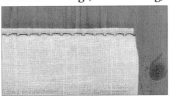

To work this stitch, a blind-hemming (blindstitching) foot must be attached first. This stitch is suitable for heavy or bulky fabrics where the stitch won't show on the right side. The hem is basted and then fed under the foot and is sewn with a series of straight stitches followed by a zigzag stitch which picks up the main fabric. Adjust the zigzag to make the stitch into the fold as small as possible.

Zigzag

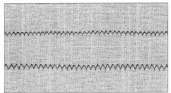

Zigzag stitches are used for finishing edges, for machine appliqué and as decoration. Try different lengths and widths of stitch to find which one suits the fabric best. In general, the stitch should be as small and narrow as possible. Wider versions of zigzag such as triple zigzag and herringbone stitch are useful for sewing elastic onto fabric. Triple zigzag can be used for finishing seams on soft or fine fabrics. Both stitches can be used to prevent the edges of towelling (terrycloth) or knitted fabrics from curling before sewing.

Machine embroidery stitches

The most advanced machines have a silicone chip to create a huge range of decorative stitches which can be selected at the touch of a button. These stitches take time to stitch as the fabric moves in a circular motion to create the pattern, but the results are very effective. Automatic machines have a smaller range of stitches based on satin stitch.

Sewing seams

Seams are a crucial part in any sewing project. The perfect seam joins two pieces of fabric without puckering or stretching and lies or hangs exactly as expected. If the seam isn't right, it is better to unpick and restitch it than continue, because a poor seam will spoil the end result.

Before deciding what sort of seam to sew, think about the type of fabric used and the amount of strain and wear the seam will take. The main types of seams and their special uses are listed here.

Seams can be neatened in a number of different ways to prevent them from fraying and becoming weakened, although this is not necessary if they are enclosed by fabric or a lining.

Sew angled fabric pieces in the direction of the grain rather than against it. Generally, this is from the wide end of the pattern piece to the narrow end. If you run your finger along the edge of the fabric with the grain the threads will smooth down, but will fray if against the grain.

Plain seam

This functional seam is the basis of nearly all other seams. Use a 15mm/⅝in seam allowance. Press along the stitch line to "set" the stitches into the fabric before pressing the seam open. This seam can be worked in a narrow zigzag stitch or with the stretch stitch on automatic machines to prevent the seam from splitting on knitted or stretch fabrics.

Understitching

Understitching is used to prevent an armhole or neck facing rolling out on to the right side of the garment. Grade and notch the curve. Press the seam allowances towards the facing. Work a row of small back stitches along the right side of the facing, catching the seam in at the back. Understitching can also be worked by machine.

Taping

Taping strengthens a seam and prevents it from stretching out of shape. It is often used on shoulder seams and waistlines. Use a woven seam tape and baste it in place along the seam line so that it overlaps slightly into the seam allowance before stitching the seam as normal.

Plain turned-under

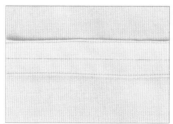

Finish off seams on light-weight, closely-woven fabrics by turning under 5mm/¼in down each edge of the seam and pressing. Machine straight stitch close to the folded edge through the seam allowance only.

Plain bound

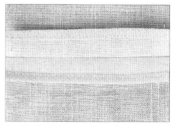

On bulky fabrics that tend to fray, for example, in unlined jackets or coats, enclose the edges of the seam allowance with seam binding for a neat finish. Seam binding is slightly wider on one side and this should be underneath. Baste the seam binding in place and machine stitch as shown.

Self-bound seam

A self-bound seam is used to enclose the raw edges of light-weight fabric and looks a little like a French seam once complete. It is the ideal way to finish the inside bottom edge of a yoke (shoulder) and useful when one side of the seam is gathered.

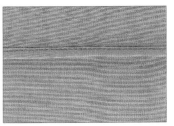

1 Trim one side of the seam allowance to 3–5mm/¹/₈–¹/₄in. Press the edge of the seam allowance over.

2 Fold the pressed edge over to the machine stitching and baste. Machine stitch close to the fold or hem into the machine stitching.

French seam

A French seam is used on fine, sheer fabrics and gives a beautiful straight finish. It is ideal for silk blouses, christening robes or lingerie. Unlike other seams, begin a French seam by pinning the wrong sides of the fabric together.

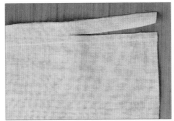

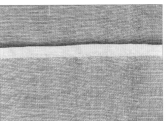

1 Stitch the wrong sides of the fabric together, using 9mm/³/₈in from the seam allowance. Trim this seam to 4mm/³/₁₆in. Press the seam open.

2 Fold the fabric over with right sides together, enclosing the raw edges. Press the edge flat and stitch along the seam line, 5mm/¹/₄in from the edge. Press the seam to one side.

Mock French seam

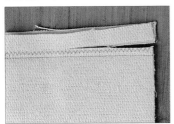

This seam looks like a French seam from the right side. It is suitable for heavy-weight fabrics or curved seams in sheer and light-weight fabrics. With right sides together, stitch a plain seam 15mm/⁵/₈in from the edge. Then machine zigzag both layers of the seam allowance together close to the seam and trim.

Plain zigzag seam

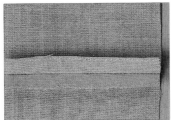

A zigzag stitch provides a quick method of finishing the raw edges of a plain seam. It can be used successfully on quite bulky fabrics. It is not a particularly neat finish and is generally used where it will not be seen. Stitch zigzag part way into the seam allowance and trim close to the stitching.

Stretch seam

A stretch seam is worked either with a very narrow zigzag or using the stretch stitch on an automatic machine. It is used to stitch jersey fabrics or other fabrics that have a high degree of stretch. The stitching "gives" with the fabric and prevents the seam from bursting open.

Trimming a plain seam

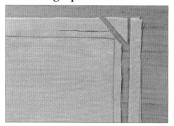

Only trim a plain seam when you are enclosing it with fabric and you need to reduce its bulk, for example, before turning a collar through. Trim the seam to 5mm/¹/₄in and cut the corners diagonally close to the stitching.

Grading a seam

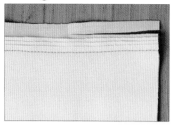

When more than two layers of fabric are joined together, the seams must be graded to reduce bulk. Trim each layer closer to the stitching as shown, making the deepest layer next to the right side of the garment. The trimmed seam allowances can be narrower on enclosed pattern pieces.

Plain pinked

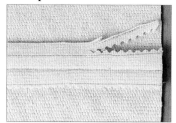

For a quick method of finishing seams on fabric that doesn't unravel, cut the edge of the seam allowance with pinking shears. This is not a very secure seam finish but can be strengthened with a row of machine stitching 5mm/¹/₄in inside the pinked edge.

Clipping curves

A curved seam needs to be snipped at regular intervals to allow it to lie flat when it is turned through. If the fabric is bulky, the seams should be graded first.

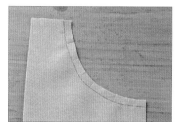

1 On inward-facing seams, snip into the fabric to within a few threads of the stitching at 1–2.5cm/¹/₂–1in intervals, depending on the curve.

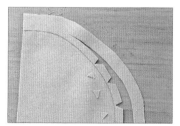

2 On outward-facing curves cut small notches out of the seam at 1–2.5cm/¹/₂–1in intervals. Cut more notches when the curve is sharp.

Decorative seams

Most seams are meant to be barely noticeable on the right side of the fabric, but sometimes a more decorative seam finish is required, for example in sports and casual wear.

Lapped seam

Use this seam on fabric that can be pressed into a neat fold. Turn under and press the overlapping piece of fabric along the seam line. Working from the right side, pin the folded edge along the seam line of the other fabric piece. Stitch close to the fold.

Tucked seam

The tucked seam has a flap on the right side. Baste a 15mm/⁵/₈in plain seam. Press the seam allowances to one side. On the right side, stitch 5mm/¹/₄in away from the seam through all layers, using contrasting thread if desired. Remove the basting.

Welt seam

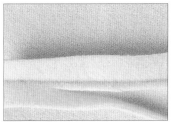

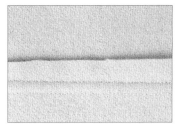

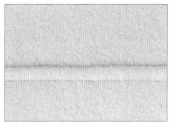

A welt seam is similar to a top-stitched seam. It is worked on straight seams in non-fray fabrics. It is a fairly flat seam even on bulky fabrics because one seam allowance layer is trimmed. Stitch a plain seam and open out. Trim one side of the seam allowance to 5mm/¹⁄₄in.

1 Press the seam allowances to one side to hide the trimmed edge. Machine stitch through the top fabric and seam allowance enclosing the trimmed edge inside.

2 From the right side, the seam looks like a top-stitched seam. If the fabric has a lot of give, use a stretch stitch throughout.

Flat fell seam

The flat fell seam is the classic seam used on denim jeans and casual trousers to give the distinctive double row of stitches on the right side. On reversible garments, slip stitch the inside seam allowance in place.

1 With wrong sides together, stitch a plain seam and open out the seam allowance. Trim one side of the seam allowance to 3mm/¹⁄₈in.

2 Turn under the other seam allowance and fold over the trimmed side. Baste in place and stitch through all layers close to the fold.

Slot seam

A slot seam has two tucks facing with a piece of fabric showing behind. The seam looks particularly effective when two contrasting fabrics are used.

You can make the slot very narrow or quite wide to create a contrast panel on the garment, in which case use a wider strip in step 2.

1 With right sides together, baste a plain seam. Press open.

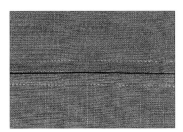

2 Cut a strip of fabric slightly wider than the seam allowances. Baste in place over the seam on the wrong side.

3 On the right side, top stitch the same distance away from the seam line down both sides. Remove the basting thread.

Making and using bias binding

Bias binding is used to enclose raw edges along seams on the wrong side or around the edge of a neckline or armhole in place of a facing. It consists of a strip of fabric cut across the diagonal to give it stretch. You can buy pre-folded bias binding in various widths or make your own.

Making bias binding

Use a fabric of similar or lighter weight than the main fabric such as a closely woven cotton fabric with a crisp finish. For standard 12mm/¹⁄₂in binding, cut strips 4cm/1¹⁄₂in wide.

Binding an edge

Before using bias binding, steam press the strip to remove some of the slack. If the binding is going around a curved edge, turn under 5mm/¹⁄₄in down each long side. Press, then fold

the strip in half lengthways. Steam press into a soft curve and open out before use and stitch along the pressed line.

You can buy a small tool that turns under the edges ready for use.

1 Fold the fabric over in one corner to form a diagonal at 45° to the selvage and cut along the fold. Mark strips of fabric four times the width of the finished binding plus a 5–9mm/ ¹⁄₄–³⁄₈in allowance depending on the fabric thickness. Cut along the lines.

1 Pin the bias binding so that the seam line on the bias binding follows the seam line on the main fabric. Baste 5mm/¹⁄₄in away from the raw edge of the bias strip.

2 Machine stitch next to the basting line and then trim the main fabric so that it is slightly narrower than the binding seam. Press the binding away from the main fabric.

2 With right sides together, overlap two ends at right angles. Stitch across the diagonal corner and press open. Trim the seam allowance flush with the bias binding. Join extra pieces as required.

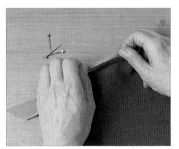

3 Turn under 5mm/¹⁄₄in and fold over to the wrong side. Pin and baste the binding in place.

4 Secure the binding with tiny hem stitches. For extra strength, work the stitches into the machine stitching.

Working with decorative piping

As well as providing a decorative feature on clothes and soft furnishings, piping also strengthens a seam and can protect the edge from wear. It is made by wrapping a bias strip of fabric around piping cord and enclosing it within a seam. You can use either a matching or a contrasting fabric, but it must be the same or a lighter weight than the main fabric.

Using piping cord

Piping cord is available in several widths to suit a range of different fabrics. Wrap fabric around several sizes of piping cord to check which one looks best. A lighter-weight fabric usually ooks better with thin piping cord.

Piped seams are often used as a decorative feature in soft furnishings or on suits and jackets. A softer piped seam can be made without any cord.

Below and below right: Piping provides an ideal opportunity to introduce accent colours to your design. The design on the right uses a contrasting fabric type.

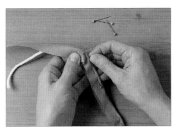

1 Wrap a piece of bias fabric around the cord and add a 3cm/1¼in seam allowance to each side. Cut as many bias strips as you need to that width and steam press them to remove the excess stretch. Wrap the bias strip around the cord and pin. Stitch close to the cord using a zipper foot.

2 Pin the piping to one piece of the main fabric, matching the raw edges, and stitch close to the previous stitching. Pin the second piece of fabric on top, matching the raw edges, and stitch through all layers as close to the piping cord as possible.

Making perfect hems

A hem adds weight to a garment and helps it to hang correctly. It is usually the last thing to be sewn and the fabric and style of garment influences the choice of hem and its depth. A perfect hem looks absolutely level and, if hand stitched, is almost invisible from the right side.

Measuring up

A normal hem allowance is 7.5cm/3in but for narrow hems on a full circle, bias or stretchy garments it can be as little as 3mm–2.5cm/¹⁄₈–1in. These should be hung for 24 hours before marking the hem line. Reduce excess fullness evenly and keep the stitches loose to prevent ridges forming.

Mark the hem at the final fitting when all other adjustments have been made. Put on any clothes that will be worn with the garment for the fitting.

1 Use a floor-standing hem rule and insert pins horizontally at the same height all the way around the garment to mark the bottom line. Some garments such as full skirts and trousers may look better if the hem slopes slightly to the back. Make this adjustment gradually so that it is not noticeable. Turn the hem up to the inside of the garment along the pin line.

2 Baste along the foldline, removing the pins as you go.

3 Measure and mark the depth of hem required and then trim off the excess fabric.

Zigzag or overcast hem

This hem lies flat because there are no turnings. It creates a very smooth finish on the right side and is suitable for most weights of fabric. The raw edge can be zigzagged or overcast. Baste along the hem just below the zigzag, easing in any fullness as you go. Turn over the top edge and hold down with your thumb to slip stitch the hem to the main garment. Work two small running stitches in the hem and take a tiny stitch into the main garment. Continue around the hem keeping the stitches loose. Press the hem from the wrong side.

Plain turned under

This hem is suitable for light- and medium-weight washable fabrics. It must be pressed from the wrong side otherwise a ridge will form on the right side. Turn under 5mm/¹⁄₄in along the raw edge and machine stitch close to the fold. Slip hem, sliding the needle along the fold and taking a tiny stitch into the main fabric.

Seam binding

Seam binding is added to fabrics that fray easily before turning up the hem. The binding is much thinner than the main fabric and makes a neat hem finish. Seam binding is often used on trousers to protect the hem from being caught on a shoe. On the right side, machine stitch the seam binding about 5mm/¼in from the raw edge of the main fabric. Turn the hem up to the required length and baste. Hem the seam binding to the main fabric.

Machine-stitched hem

A machine-stitched hem is visible from the right side of the garment. It is suitable for knitted fabrics and on garments where top stitching is a feature, such as a shirt or unlined jacket. To create a design, machine stitch along the bottom fold as well. Baste the hem in position and ease any fullness evenly as you work. It may help to press the hem from the wrong side before machine stitching.

Hand-rolled hem

A hand-rolled hem is a delicate, soft finish for lingerie and other dressmaking using silk or sheer fabrics. It is often used to finish the edges of silk scarves. It is quite time consuming but well worth the effort. Machine stitch 5mm/¼in from the hem line. Trim the hem allowance close to the stitching. Roll the raw edge to enclose the machine stitching and slip stitch catching a single thread at each stitch.

Double hem

A double hem is similar to a narrow hem but is used when the fabric is transparent. The turning is the same width as the hem itself so that no raw edge is visible through the layers of fabric. It is used for the edges of sheer curtains or for sheer fabrics such as cotton organdie. Mark the hem length and then decide on the depth of the finished hem. Cut the hem allowance twice the depth of the finished hem. Fold the hem allowance in half so that the raw edge lies along the hem line. Fold the hem up and pin or baste in place. Machine stitch or slip stitch.

Narrow hem

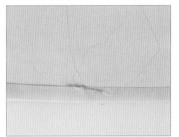

A narrow hem is suitable for light-weight fabrics on blouses, shirts and lingerie. The edge can be machine stitched or slip stitched. Turn under 5mm/¼in along the raw edge and turn up a narrow hem. Slip stitch along the fold. This type of hem can be worked along a gentle curve if it is eased carefully.

Machine-rolled hem

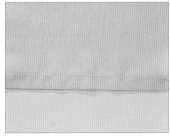

A machine-rolled hem is much stiffer than a hand-rolled hem because it has two rows of machine stitching. Use it on crisp, fine fabrics such as cotton lawn. Turn under 5mm/¼in and machine stitch along the fold. Turn under an additional 5mm/¼in and machine stitch through all the layers of the hem.

Tucks, pleats, darts and gathers

In dressmaking, flat fabric is stitched together to fit the curves of the body. To some extent pattern pieces are curved and shaped, but further shaping is usually needed to create a three-dimensional garment. The method chosen to control fullness and manipulate the fabric is very much part of the overall design. Darts, tucks and pleats control the fabric in a precise way, while gathers and shirring create a softer effect.

Tucks

These are narrow folds of fabric that are stitched to produce a decorative effect. The basic technique is the same for all tucks but the width, spacing and length can be varied to create different effects. Tucks are always worked on the straight grain. They can be narrow or wide, touching or spaced and stitched either all the way down or only part way down for fullness. When adding tucks to a garment, for example on a plain sleeve or yoke (shoulder), work the tucks in the fabric before cutting the pattern piece.

1 Decide on the width and spacing of the tucks. Cut a piece of paper to use as a guide to make the gauge. Mark the foldline of the tuck and the stitching lines down both edges of the fabric.

2 Draw a single thread from the fabric down the foldline of each tuck. Fold the fabric along the pulled thread lines and press. You can press the tucks without drawing a thread but it is more difficult to keep the tuck exactly on the straight grain.

Above: These tucks are worked in a circular motion, first stitching one way, then the other, to produce a wave-like effect.

3 Baste the tucks along each stitching line. Use the gauge as a guide if the weave of the fabric is too fine. Place the basted fold under the presser foot. Use the edge of the presser foot or needle plate guide to gauge the width of the tuck and stitch parallel to the foldline. Press along each stitch line and then press the tucks to one side. Press the entire tucked area from the wrong side.

Above: Using the Cathedral Windows' patchwork technique, one fabric is inset on another. The edges of the lower fabric are rolled over the inset fabric and hand-stitched in place.

Pin tucks

Pin tucks are very narrow tucks often used on baby clothes or blouses. The tucks can be stitched in the same way as spaced tucks but it is quite difficult to stitch neatly so close to the fold. For the best result insert a twin needle in the sewing machine and thread up with two reels of thread. The upper tension can be loosened slightly to make the tucks more pronounced. Use the side of the presser foot as a guide to space the tucks.

Spaced tucks

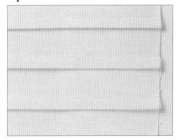

Spaced tucks have a fixed space between each tuck. The width and spacing of the tucks should be worked out carefully to produce a balanced appearance on the garment.

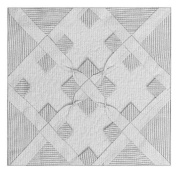

Top right and right: Calico has been folded, pleated, tucked and manipulated to create interesting surface textures.

Released tucks

Released tucks are blind or spaced tucks that are only stitched part way along the length allowing the fabric to open out at one or both ends. The fabric at the end of the tuck is never pressed and falls in soft folds to create fullness. Released tucks are often worked with the fold on the wrong side.

Blind tucks

On blind tucks the distance on the gauge between the fold, stitching line and space between are the same so that the fold of each tuck touches the machine stitching.

Scalloped tucks

Scalloped tucks are blind or spaced tucks that are stitched by hand to create a pretty shell effect. Soft delicate fabrics are most suitable for this type of tuck. The tucks can be stitched entirely by hand or stitched by machine and scalloped by hand. Baste the tuck and machine stitch then mark every 9mm/³/₈in along the stitched line. Slip a threaded needle through the tuck to the first mark. Sew two tight stitches over the tuck and slip the needle through the tuck to the next mark.

Crossed tucks

Crossed tucks are always worked before the pattern is cut out. Measure and stitch the spaced tucks in one direction first and press very carefully. Measure the tucks at right angles to the first set and baste. Machine stitch with the first tuck folds facing downwards so that the presser foot slips over each tuck. Place the pattern piece with the horizontal tucks facing towards the bottom and the straight grain running along one of the vertical tucks. Cut out and stay stitch the edges of the pattern piece to keep the tucks flat while making up.

Pleats

Pleats are folds in fabric that provide controlled fullness in a garment, for example on a skirt. They are usually stitched part way down the length and then pressed flat. Perfect pleats hang closed while the wearer is standing still but open to allow freedom of movement. Whether it is a small kick pleat at the back of a dress or a skirt pleated all the way around, it is necessary to be very precise during the making. Transfer all markings carefully and baste down the entire length of a pleat before stitching. Choose fabrics carefully for a pleated garment. They should be of light- to medium-weight and hold a crease when pressed. Suitable fabrics include wool and wool blends, linen mix fabric, heavier silks and some synthetic or man-made fabrics. Choose a pattern for a pleated skirt by the hip measurement rather than the waist measurement because it is easier to alter the waistline.

Marking pleats

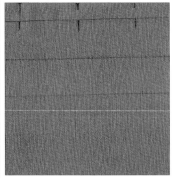

Successful pleats depend on accurate marking of the three pleat line indicators. Pleats that are left unpressed have a roll line and pleats that are pressed into a flat crease have a foldline. Both pleats also have a placement line; the roll- or foldline is brought up to this line and stitched.

Pleats can be stitched either from the wrong side or top stitched on the right side. Pressed and unpressed pleats are made in the same way, it is the final pressing that makes the difference. Leave the basting thread holding the pleats closed in place until the garment is complete.

Knife pleat

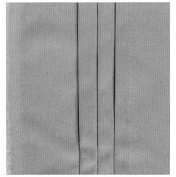

This basic pleat is a double fold of fabric pressed flat. Knife pleats all face in the same direction in a garment.

Box pleat

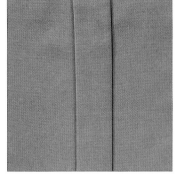

This pleat is created from two knife pleats. The underneath folds meet on the wrong side.

Inverted pleat

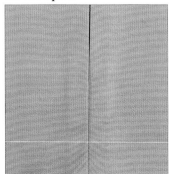

An inverted pleat is the opposite of a box pleat. The two knife pleats face each other and meet in the centre on the right side of the fabric.

Accordion pleat

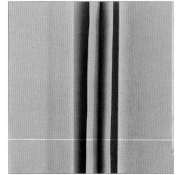

Accordion pleats lie partly open during wear. The pleats are normally permanently pressed in alternate valley and mountain folds.

Working from the wrong side

1 Mark pleat lines with basting thread or dressmaker's carbon on the wrong side of the fabric. Fold the fabric right sides together and baste along the full length of the pleat matching fold and placement lines.

2 Mark the length of the stitched pleat and stitch down to this line. Reverse back along the line for several stitches for strength. Take out the basting thread in the stitched area only and press the pleats flat.

Removing excess bulk

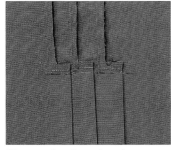

Pleats can be trimmed on the wrong side to remove excess bulk, especially around the waistline. Lift each pleat away from the main fabric on the wrong side and stitch crossways at the end of the pleat stitching. Baste along these stitch lines to hold the pleats in position. Trim the fabric above the line leaving a 15mm/⅝in seam.

Working from the right side

1 Mark pleat lines with basting thread on the right side of the fabric. Bring the foldline up to the placement line and pin, then baste along the whole length of the pleat.

2 Mark the length of the stitched pleat and stitch down to this line. Take the thread ends to the wrong side and sew in securely.

Fitting pleated garments

Minor adjustments to pleated items can be made at the side seams but for a larger alteration make small adjustments to the top of each pleat. Divide the number of pleats by the alteration required and add or take that measurement from each pleat. If your garment has four pleats, 2.5cm/1in can be added or removed by moving the foldline of each pleat just 5mm/¼in.

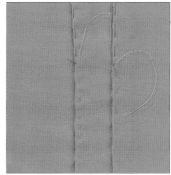

1 From the wrong side, enlarge a garment by moving the seam line into the seam allowance slightly. Reduce the garment by moving the seam allowance into the main fabrics.

2 From the right side, enlarge a garment by moving the foldline over the placement line. Reduce the garment by moving the foldline back from the placement line.

Pleats with separate underlay

Some pleats have a separate underlay. Form the pleat from an extra wide seam allowance. Working from the wrong side, baste the pleat foldlines with right sides together. Stitch, then press open. Stitch underlay in place. Tidy the raw edges. Baste the top of the underlay to hold it in position.

Darts

Darts are one of the basic dress-making techniques. It is essential to check the position of the darts on a garment before cutting out because the angle and length of each dart is crucial to the final fit and appearance.

Darts should point towards the fullest part of the body, for example the point of the bust or hip bone. If necessary, re-draw the dart, beginning about 2.5–4cm/1–1½in away from the new point. Keep the base of the dart the same size and join the lines in a similar shape to the original.

When fitting patterns or garments, always wear the correct underwear and the shoes that will be worn with the finished item.

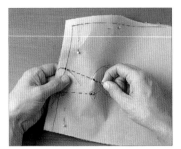

1 Mark darts by inserting a tailor's tack at each of the large dots on the pattern piece. If the outside lines of a dart are curved, it is advisable to mark along the lines as well. Darts can also be marked using dressmaker's carbon or tailor's chalk.

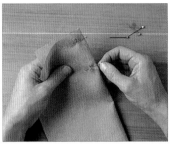

2 Pull the two layers of fabric slightly apart and snip the tailor's tacks. With right sides together, fold the dart along the centre and match the tailor's tacks. Insert pins across the dart and baste between the tailor's tacks.

3 Machine stitch the dart from the widest part tapering to a point. Stitch inside the basting thread and work the last few stitches along the fold. Tie the ends of the thread together rather than reversing as this can cause an unsightly bump.

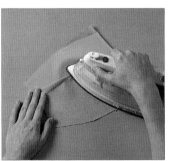

4 Press along the stitch line to set the stitches and then press vertical darts towards the centre of the garment and horizontal darts downwards. Press from the wrong side, using the tip of the iron to shape the point end of the dart. Slip a strip of brown paper under the dart before pressing to prevent an impression forming on the right side.

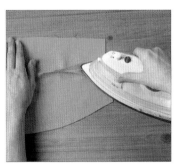

5 Deep darts or those worked in heavier fabrics can be slashed and pressed flat to reduce the bulk. Cut the dart along the foldline as far as possible and open out. This method is only suitable for lined garments where the raw edges won't fray.

6 Darts in sheer fabrics can be trimmed to make them less conspicuous from the right side. Press the dart flat and trim leaving 5mm/¼in outside the stitches. Overcast the raw edges and press the dart to one side.

Gathering

Work gathering by hand or machine. Use gathering to ease fabric into a waistline, yoke (shoulder) or cuff.

The width of fabric to use is determined by the weight of fabric and the amount of fullness required in the finished garment. If the fabric is very wide, work the gathering stitches in batches to prevent the thread snapping as it is pulled up. Insert pins between the batches of stitches for securing the thread ends.

Machine gathers pull up easily if the top tension is loosened slightly before stitching with a long stitch. Use a strong thread, such as nylon or quilting thread in the bobbin to prevent the thread from snapping.

1 Sew the gathering threads onto the fabric. If hand sewing, work two parallel rows of small running stitches across the fabric on each side of the seam line. Try to keep the stitches and spacing the same size on both rows.

2 Place the two pattern pieces together with right sides facing, pin at both ends and wrap the ends of the thread around the pin in a figure of eight to secure. Mark the centre on the edge to be gathered and the flat pattern piece.

3 Match the two pieces and pin in the centre and at the other end. Continue pinning between the inserted pins to distribute the fullness evenly along the length.

4 Pull up the gathering threads until the folds lie flat and wrap the ends around the other pin in a figure of eight.

5 Pin along the folds to hold the gathers in place. The gathers can be basted, or stitch carefully across the pins using the point of small scissors to straighten the gathers as you sew.

Above: Gathering has been made into a design feature on this velvet top.

Shirring (Gathering elastic)

This is a pretty, stretchy, gathered panel that hugs close to the body. It is used to gather sleeves into cuffs and for young children's clothes. For this technique, shirring elastic rather than thread is wound onto the bobbin in the usual way and fitted into the bobbin case. Set the machine for a long straight stitch and sew several lines of stitches from the right side. Use the side of the foot as a guide for subsequent rows. It may help to hold the fabric taut as you stitch and work slowly so that the stitch lines are even.

Smocking

Smocking is a traditional decorative technique that has been used all over the world. It is an ornamental way to control fullness in garments. The smocked panel has a degree of elasticity making it comfortable to wear. It was traditionally used to make practical smocks for agricultural workers, but nowadays it is more commonly used for baby wear.

There are several ways to gather fabric for smocking. The method you choose depends on the type of fabric to be smocked. Gingham fabric is particularly associated with smocking because the regular squares make it easy to work accurately and evenly. Other fabrics have regular dots or tiny motifs that can also be used as a spacing guide. If the fabric is plain or has an all-over pattern, you can use a smocking transfer sheet. There are different spacings of dots on these sheets to suit a variety of fabrics. The lighter weight the fabric,

the closer the dots should be. As a guide, light-weight fabrics generally require dots spaced between 5–12mm/ ¼–½in.

Gathering

The gathered section of a piece of fabric often looks completely different from the actual fabric. The way the fabric is gathered can change the surface pattern dramatically and it is advisable to try out different ways of gathering to see what happens.

Gingham fabrics can be stitched at the edge of each square to produce

tucks in alternate colours or stitched in the middle of the light squares to produce a dark panel or vice versa.

Fabrics with small motifs or dots may look plain when gathered. The dots or motifs can form lines across the tucks to give a striped effect. These lines also help to keep your stitching straight. Match the colour of the motif for a strong design.

Subtle all-over cotton prints look very much the same when gathered. This type of fabric looks very good with smocking worked in thread colours that tone in with the fabric.

Getting started

1 Cut a piece of smocking transfer to fit across the width of the fabric. Place the paper dot side down on the wrong side of the fabric and press with a hot iron to transfer the dots.

2 Some fabrics have dots or a regular pattern that you can use as a guide for the gathering stitches. If the dots are too far apart you can take an extra stitch in between each one.

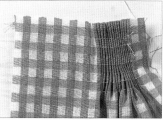

3 Gingham squares make ideal guidelines for smocking. You can take a stitch on the lines between the squares or stitch into the centre of alternate squares.

FINISHING THE SMOCKING

• Once the smocking is complete, pin it embroidered side down, on the ironing board.

• Hold a steam iron above the tucks and use the steam to set the folds and the stitches.

• Leave the piece to dry. Carefully untie the thread ends, then pull out each of the gathering threads.

Working a smocked sample

Try a small sample of gathering on your chosen fabric to find out the best spacing of the running stitches and to work out the width of fabric required. Generally allow three to four times the width of fabric. A 15–20cm/6–8in piece of fabric, for example, will produce approximately 5cm/2in of smocking. The amount of fabric also depends on the thickness of the fabric and the spacing of the dots. Measure the fabric before and after gathering and multiply the width to fit the yoke (shoulder) or garment section.

Different stitches give varying amounts of control in smocking. Stem or cable stitch hold the tucks quite firmly and are good outline stitches, usually worked along the top edge, whereas wave stitch produces a much looser effect. Whichever stitches you choose, remember that an even tension is as important in smocking as in knitting. A piece of smocking should give quite easily. If you stitch to a tight tension, allow extra width in the fabric to compensate.

Work a small sample first on your chosen fabric before smocking a garment or soft furnishing item to establish the correct tension.

1 Cut the required width of fabric. Mark dots on the wrong side with a transfer sheet if necessary. Cut a long length of strong thread and tie a knot in the end. Work across the fabric with running stitch, picking up a couple of threads at each mark. Complete all rows in the same way.

2 Hold all the gathering threads together and pull up until the folds are close together but still slightly loose. Tie pairs of thread ends together securely. Turn the gathered fabric over so that the tucks are facing upwards. Ease the tucks until they are evenly spaced and straight.

3 Work a row of stem stitch along the top of the tucks. It is easier to follow a guideline to keep the stitching straight. The pattern of this fabric has produced lines of dark blue dots to stitch along. Otherwise open the tucks slightly as you stitch to keep level with a gathering thread.

4 Continue stitching bands of smocking stitches across the tucks. Count the tucks and plan the placement of zigzag and diamond patterns carefully. Choose stem or cable stitch for the last row for stability or a zigzag stitch such as chevron stitch to release the gathers.

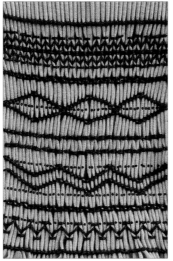

Above: A single colour thread makes a strong contrast on this background.

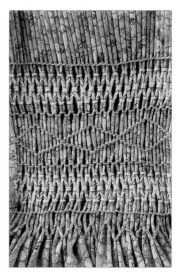

Above: Subtle all-over cotton prints look most effective when smocked in thread colours that tone in with the fabric.

The stitches

It is the delicate stitching on the surface of smocking which holds the rows of tucked fabric together.

Honeycomb stitch

This stitch can be worked directly on top of the dots or on gathered tucks.

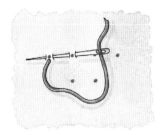

1 Take a small stitch at the top left to secure the thread, then pick up a few threads at the second and then the first dot.

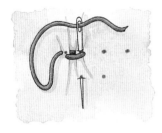

2 Take a second stitch over the first then slide the needle under the fabric to the dot below.

Above: Making a stitch sampler is a good method of learning which stitches you enjoy working, and which threads work well on your chosen fabric. Try working bands of stitches across the fabric and arrange them into a pleasing composition.

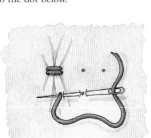

3 Work two stitches to pull the next two dots together.

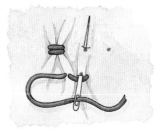

4 Take the needle back up to the dot in the row above.

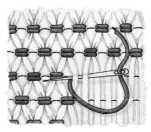

5 Continue working backwards and forwards across the rows in this way.

Cable stitch

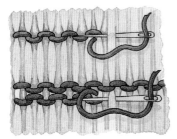

Pick up every tuck in turn, keeping the needle absolutely straight.

Stem stitch/Outline back stitch

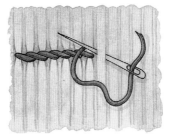

Take back stitches through each tuck keeping the thread below the needle.

Chevron stitch

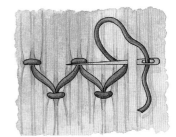

This is similar to surface honey-comb stitch, but the diagonal thread goes across two tucks rather than one.

Wave stitch

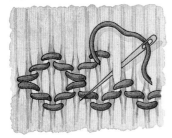

Start in the middle on the left. Take a stitch through two tucks and bring the needle out between them. Stitch over the next two tucks, continuing up in a diagonal. Bring the needle out below the stitches to work back down.

Surface honeycomb stitch

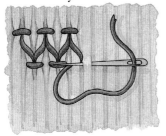

Start at the top left. Stitch through two tucks and bring the needle out between them. Take a stitch below, through the same tuck, then stitch over two tucks, bringing the needle out in the middle as before.

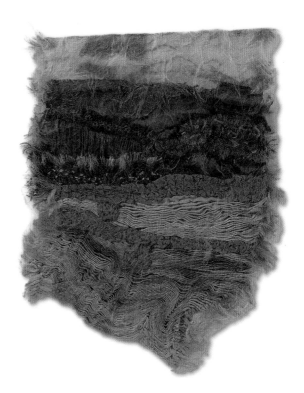

Above: This piece of textural embroidery uses a technique called gauging which is similar to smocking but without the stitches. The fabric is gathered with rows of running stitches and supported with a backing fabric.

Darning and patching

A garment will need some repair work when an area becomes worn or gives way due to constant wear or an accidental tear. Preventive strengthening measures can be taken in certain garments, such as decorative patches on elbows and knees and rivets on jeans or work-wear pockets. Garments can also be reinforced with interfacing on the wrong side before sewing on buttons and pockets.

Darning by hand

Choose a thread for darning that matches the fabric colour as closely as possible. Use one that is slightly thinner than fabric threads otherwise the darning will be too thick.

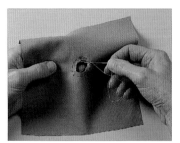 

1 Work with a long length. Begin by basting a circle or square of small running stitches around the outside edge of the worn area.

2 Work small running stitches back and forwards across the fabric within the marked area. Leave a slight loop at the end of each row so that the darn doesn't become too tight. At the worn area, leave the thread lying in parallel rows across the hole and work running stitches on each side.

3 Turn the work so that the laid threads are horizontal. Begin to weave over and under the stitches and threads until the entire area is covered with a woven patch. Avoid pulling the threads tight.

Darning by machine

Machine darning is suitable for strengthening worn areas such as the knees of trousers, but can be rather solid if used to fill a hole. Use a darning foot on the machine and stitch with finer thread in a colour to match the fabric. Set the machine for straight stitch and reduce the stitch length to zero.

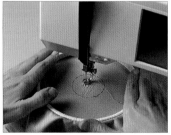 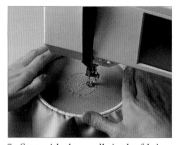

1 Baste a circle of running stitches around the outside of the worn area. If possible, fit the garment into an embroidery hoop so that the fabric lies flat against the needle plate. Lower the darning foot and work parallel rows of stitching fairly close together backwards and forwards across the marked area.

2 Stop with the needle in the fabric and turn the hoop until the stitches lie across the other way. Stitch more parallel rows slightly further apart to form a stitched grid over the marked area. If filling a hole, turn the hoop back around and work a third set of parallel rows across the hole.

Hand patch

This type of patch is normally used to repair garments. To make the patch less obvious, cut the fabric to match the colour and pattern of the worn area as closely as possible.

1 Cut a patch 3–4cm/1¼–1½in larger than the worn area. Baste it 5mm/¼in from the raw edge and notch any curves. Turn under and baste the raw edge. Work small hemming stitches to secure the patch.

2 On the wrong side, trim away the worn fabric leaving a 5mm/¼in allowance. Work overcasting or buttonhole stitch over the raw edges without stitching into the front side of the patch.

Machine patch

This quick and easy patch is a hardwearing way of repairing most utility items around the home. Use fabric from another similar item or pre-wash a new piece of fabric to soften it. Stitch the patch with a matching thread.

1 Cut a square or rectangular patch about 2–3cm/¾–1¼in larger than the worn area and baste it in position on the right side, matching the grain of the fabric. Machine zigzag over the raw edge to secure the patch.

2 Turn the garment over and trim the worn areas of the patch to 9mm/⅜in. Machine zigzag over the raw edge. The patch will have two rows of zigzag showing on the right side of the fabric.

Right-angled tear

1 Bring the edges of the tear together by loosely oversewing them. Beginning and ending 5mm/¼in beyond each end of the tear, work tiny stitches across the tear.

2 On a worn garment or pocket tear, iron a square of iron-on interfacing to the wrong side before working the stitches. Pin the pocket back in position and re-stitch over the repair.

3 A button can be replaced over a right-angled tear once this has been repaired with interfacing and machine stitching.

Buttonholes

Unlike buttons, buttonholes are solely functional rather than decorative and normally match the colour of the garment. Take into account the design of the garment and the fabric used before deciding what sort of buttonhole to sew. Hand-worked buttonholes are suitable for soft and delicate fabrics; bound or piped buttonholes give a more tailored look, and machine-sewn buttonholes can be used on more casual garments.

Buttonhole size

Dress patterns include the designer's choice of button size with the corresponding buttonhole position and length marked, but these need to be checked and altered if you are using your own choice of buttons and fabric.

1 The shape and size of the button will determine the size of the buttonhole. The minimum length required is the diameter of the button plus its thickness and an extra 3mm/ ¹⁄₈in for ease.

2 To measure a shaped or rounded button, wrap a thin strip of paper around the widest part and pin the ends together. Slip the strip off the button and fold in half. This is the buttonhole length plus 3mm/¹⁄₈in added for ease.

Above: Luxury fabrics need perfect stitching, especially on details such as buttonholes or imperfections will show.

BUTTONHOLE POSITION

The position of buttonholes should be marked, along with darts and centre lines, after the pattern pieces are cut out. Buttonholes are not usually made until quite late in the dressmaking process and should be marked once again with basting lines on the right side just before they are made.

• Baste along the straight grain of fabric, slightly longer than the proposed buttonhole and mark the buttonhole length with pins.

• Baste across the first line to show the finished length.

• Horizontal buttonholes are stronger than vertical ones and will close when under any strain.

• Horizontal buttonholes begin 3mm/⅛in to the seam side of the centre line. This allows room for the shank of the button and keeps the centre lines in place.

• On centre front or back openings, vertical buttonholes tend to gape and make the button pop out when put under strain. They are used on loose shirts or where there is a narrow front band. On women's clothing make sure that one of the buttonholes is positioned between the bust points. Space the other buttonholes accordingly.

• Vertical buttonholes begin on the centre line, 3mm/⅛in above the actual button position. This allows for the natural tendency of buttons to pull downwards.

Hand- or machine-stitched buttonholes?

Buttonholes are worked once the garment is complete. Baste the position of the buttonhole through all layers. For hand-sewn buttonholes, use a 45cm/18in length of strong thread or buttonhole twist in the needle. Hand-worked buttonholes have a round end where the button lies and a square end opposite.

Machine-stitched buttonholes are suitable for casual clothes and men's shirts. You will be able to machine stitch buttonholes if your machine has a zigzag stitch, but most automatic machines have an in-built mechanism that alters the width and direction at the touch of a button.

Use a clear-view buttonhole foot on the machine so that you can see your markings on the fabric. This foot has grooves on the underside to guide the fabric so that the slot between the rows of satin stitch is the right width.

By machine

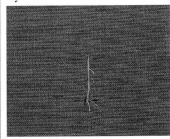

1 Mark the position of the buttonhole along the straight grain with basting thread. Work the first side, finishing with the needle on the right-hand side.

2 Work the bar across the bottom and continue up the second side, finishing with the needle on the outside edge.

3 Work a bar across the top and then use several very small straight stitches to anchor the thread. Trim the thread ends and cut carefully between the rows of satin stitch to open the buttonhole. Use small embroidery scissors or a seam unpicker for this.

By hand

1 Cut the buttonhole exactly along a straight thread. Use small embroidery scissors or special adjustable buttonhole scissors. On light-weight fabrics use a seam unpicker.

2 Take the needle through the facing about 2.5cm/1in from the buttonhole and bring it out at the opposite end to where the button will be. Take the needle through the slot and work 3mm/⅛in buttonhole stitches along the first side.

3 Oversew stitches in a fan shape around the button end of the buttonhole. Work buttonhole stitches down the second side making the stitches the same length as those on the other side.

4 Slip the needle between the two layers of fabric and work several bars of thread across the end of the buttonhole. Work blanket stitch over the bars keeping the loops facing into the buttonhole. Sew in the thread ends on the wrong side.

Bound buttonholes

Bound buttonholes can give a neat tailored appearance and are suitable for light-weight, closely-woven fabrics. They are begun before the facing has been attached and are completed at a later stage. It is essential to make and work each buttonhole exactly the same size, so careful, accurate marking is required.

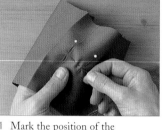

1 Mark the position of the buttonhole with tailor's tacks – through both layers if there is a self-facing and cut the layers apart.

3 Mark the buttonhole with basting thread. Beginning on one side, stitch a rectangle 3mm/⅛in away from the thread. Leave the needle in the fabric to turn the corner and carefully count the stitches to work the other side exactly the same distance away.

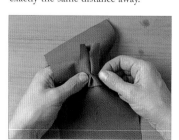

5 Pull the fabric rectangle through to the wrong side. Fold the fabric to form an inverted pleat at each end, with the folds of the binding meeting in the centre of the slot. Oversew each end securely.

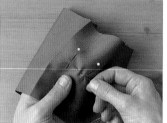

2 Cut a piece of fabric 5cm/2in wide and 3cm/1¼in longer than the buttonhole. Pin this centrally over the tailor's tacks with right sides together.

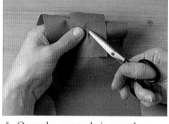

4 Once the rectangle is complete, trim the thread ends. Cut a slit down the centre of the rectangle and cut carefully into each corner.

6 When you are ready to complete the facing, slash along the tailor tacks and pin the facing over the back of the buttonhole. Turn under the edge and hem an oval shape on the wrong side.

ROULEAUX LOOPS

A rouleau is a self-filled fabric tube used to make single or continuous fabric loops that can be used as a button fastening. Rouleaux loops are sewn into a garment between the main fabric and the facing.

• Cut a bias strip four times the desired finished width. Steam press to remove the excess stretch and fold it in half with right sides together. Stitch down the centre of the folded strip. Slide a rouleaux turner into the tube and hook the end. Pull the tube through.

• On the right side of the fabric, baste parallel lines to mark the seam line and the depth of the loops. Plan and mark the loop position and width with thread. Pin the tubing in a curve to the fabric within the guidelines.

• Secure the tubing with diagonal basting and pin the facing in place. Baste along the seam lines and check the loops before stitching the seam.

Piped buttonhole

1 Work this buttonhole before the facing is complete. Mark the position with basting thread. For the piping, cut a 2.5cm/1in-wide fabric strip on the straight grain. Iron fusible web to the wrong side, remove the backing and fold the strip lengthways. Press to seal the layers. Trim to 5mm/¹⁄₄in.

2 Cut two lengths of piping longer than the buttonhole and pin along the marked buttonhole line with raw edges touching. Baste along the centre of each piece of piping without catching the facing as well. Work all the buttonholes to the same stage each time for accuracy.

3 Baste the folded edges of the piping together. Trim the piping to 9mm/³⁄₈in from the end of the buttonhole. Mark the buttonhole ends with tailor's chalk. Beginning in the middle of one piece of piping, stitch to the mark, along to the other end and back to the middle.

5 Push the piping through the slit from the right side and sew the edges together with diagonal basting. From the right side, tuck the tiny triangles at each end under. Stab stitch around the buttonhole edge.

Below: Choose threads to complement the colour scheme when stitching buttonholes.

4 Repeat for the second side, counting the stitches to ensure each side is the same length. On the wrong side, cut between the parallel rows of stitching and carefully into each corner.

6 When you are ready to complete the facing, pin the facing over the back of the buttonhole and slash along the buttonhole line. Turn under the edge and hem stitch an oval shape on the wrong side.

Adding buttons

Buttons are more than just functional fasteners; they also form a decorative feature. Changing the buttons can alter the look of a garment. When cheap buttons are replaced with better quality ones, a garment can be made to look more expensive than it actually is.

Buttons come in an amazing range of styles, colours, shapes and sizes, and need to be chosen carefully to suit the garment. Pin buttons in place to find which ones are most suitable before making any buttonholes. Buttons are sewn on the buttonhole line 3mm/ ⅛in from the end of the buttonhole.

Carefully pin the garment closed, matching the centre front line and insert a pin through the buttonhole to mark the button's position. Use a strong thread to match the colour of the button. The length of thread shank between the underside of the button and the fabric should equal the thickness of the garment at the buttonhole plus a little room for ease of movement.

Two-hole button

1 Make two tiny back stitches where you are going to sew the button. Thread the needle through one of the holes on the button and hold the button in position. With the holes either horizontal or vertical to match the direction of the buttonhole, make the first stitch. Insert a pin under the thread and sew on the button.

Four-hole button

This is sewn on in the same way as a two-hole button. Either sew through the holes to form two bars or work a cross stitch. Work the shank and blanket stitch bars as for a two-hole button.

Shank button

2 Remove the pin and bring the needle out underneath the button. Wrap the thread around several times between the button and the garment to create a shank, then take the needle through to the wrong side.

3 On the wrong side work blanket stitch over the thread bars. This step is often omitted but does reinforce the thread and helps prevent buttons from falling off at a later date.

A shank button has a plastic or metal loop or stem on the wrong side for fixing. Attach the button with tiny stitches worked through the hole in the shank. If the fabric of the garment is very bulky, a thread shank will be required as well. Align the narrowest part of the shank with the buttonhole.

Covered buttons

Buttons can be covered to match the garment fabric for a more subtle effect or when you can't find suitable buttons. Covered buttons can look very effective in a contrasting fabric to match piping or binding. Self-cover buttons can be decorated with a number of embroidery techniques to create unique designs. Personalize your garment with tiny cross-stitch initials or appliqué a different design on each button.

Self-cover buttons are either plastic or metal. They are covered with a circle of fabric that is stitched or fitted using a small tool that you can buy. Use plastic buttons if the garment is likely to be washed regularly and metal buttons if it is to be dry-cleaned, making sure the button type suits the garment fabric.

Covering buttons by hand

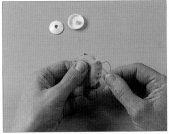 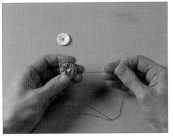

1 Cut a circle of fabric as indicated in the manufacturer's instructions. If the fabric frays, iron light-weight interfacing to the wrong side before cutting out. Work tiny running stitches around the edge of the circle.

2 Hold the button top in the middle of the fabric circle and pull the thread up tightly. Ease the gathers into position and sew the end in securely. Fit the back over the shank and press until it clicks into place.

Using a plastic tool

1 Cut a circle of fabric. Select the corresponding hole in the plastic tool and centre the fabric on top. Push the button top into the recess so that the fabric edges turn over. Fit the back over the shank and press into place.

Centring a motif

1 Cut the required circle from tracing paper and hold it over the fabric to find the best area to cover the button. Pin and cut out carefully centring any motif. Cover the button. The plastic tool has a hole in the base for you to check the position before fitting the button back.

Right: Buttons are made from many different materials such as plastic, metal, wood and leather or are covered in fabric.

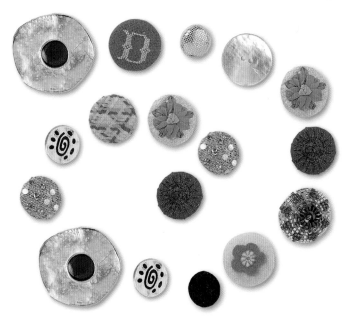

Fasteners for fabrics

Fasteners come in a variety of types and sizes to suit different fabrics. They are worked through two layers of fabric or a single fabric and interfacing. Hooks and eyes are sewn on the wrong side of garments and are invisible when in use. Add fastenings once the garment is complete. If the fabric edges touch, use a hook and eye, but if they overlap use a hook and bar. The hook is sewn in the same position in both cases.

Hooks and eyes

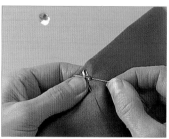

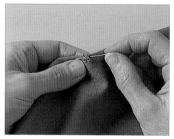

1 Hold the hook 3–5mm/¹⁄₈–¹⁄₄in back from the folded edge on the wrong side. Work several stitches over the hook end to hold it in place, making sure it does not show on the right side.

2 Bring the needle through the layers of fabric and out next to a loop on the hook. Work buttonhole stitch around both loops to secure this to the fabric. Fasten the eye into the hook.

3 Position the eye on the other side of the garment so that it extends over the edge by 3–5mm/¹⁄₈–¹⁄₄in. Take a back stitch across the eye to hold it in place and unfasten. Work buttonhole stitch around the two loops to secure.

Buttonhole bars (Thread eyes)

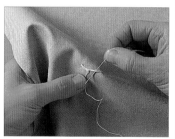

1 Use thread loops for securing single buttons at the neck edge where they are worked on the fold of fabric. Using strong thread or buttonhole twist, work several large stitches of the required length through the fabric. Allow extra length for ease depending on the button thickness.

2 Work buttonhole stitches over the thread loop, keeping the stitches straight and close together. Make sure that the loop doesn't twist as you cover it with stitches. Finish off with a couple of tiny back stitches on the wrong side.

Eyelets

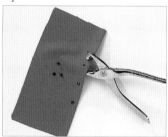

1 Mark the position of the eyelets with a pencil and punch a hole through the fabric at each mark. The hole should be just large enough for the eyelet to fit through.

2 Insert the eyelet from the right side of the fabric and use eyelet pliers to fit it into the hole.

Press studs (Snap fasteners)

These are quick-opening fasteners useful for cushion covers and on overlapping garment edges where there is little strain. They come in black, silver or plastic and in a range of sizes to suit different fabrics. Sew the thinner knob of the stud on the under side of the top layer of the opening. Use a strong thread as finer threads tend to fray against the sharp metal edge of the holes. The stitches should be worked through the facing and interfacing only.

Poppas (Rivets)

There are many different types of poppa (rivet) fasteners on the market suitable for a wide range of casual clothes. The sets of poppers come with a small tool that you use with a hammer to fix them in position. Always follow the manufacturer's guidelines.

It is advisable to try out the technique on a spare piece of fabric first. Always double check the position of the poppas as they can't be removed once they have been hammered into place.

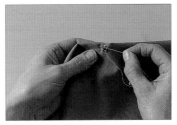

1 Work a few small back stitches where the base of the stud is to go. Hold the stud in position and work four or five buttonhole stitches into each hole to secure it in place.

1 Mark the position of the poppas (rivets) on the top layer of the garment and use a pin to transfer the position to the lower layer. Fit the appropriate sections into the tool and place on each side of the fabric.

2 Tap the hammer sharply against the tool to join the sections.

2 Feed a pin through the fabric and up through the stitched stud. Fit the other half of the stud on top and position the other side of the garment on top. Hold the stud in place and sew on with buttonhole stitches.

Velcro

This is an easy-to-use fastener that can be substituted for most other types of fastenings. It is useful for children's wear and where garment adjustments are required, such as in maternity wear and for those who have difficulty with other fasteners.

Velcro is available in strips and in small circles. One side has plastic hooks which attach to the soft loops on the other side. Self-adhesive Velcro is used on soft furnishings.

1 Select the hook piece of Velcro and attach it to the top fabric with small hem stitches.

2 Check the position of the lower layer and sew on the loop pieces of Velcro by hand or machine.

3 Fit the sections for the lower part of the poppa into the plastic tool and secure them into the fabric using the hammer. Make sure the lower sections align with the top part.

Choosing and inserting zippers

Zippers are one of the most common methods of fastening items and there is one to suit every fabric and sewing requirement. They fall into three categories – those with metal or plastic teeth (chain zippers), those with interlocking nylon or polyester coils (coil zippers), and invisible zippers.

Invisible zippers look like a seam on the right side of the fabric. Toothed zippers are stronger but fairly bulky, and coiled zippers are more flexible but can pull apart under any strain. Choose a zipper to suit the fabric weight and type of garment: for example, a jacket requires an open-ended zipper, whereas jeans and trousers need a heavy-duty zipper.

Skirt or neckline zipper
These are the most common weight of zipper and are available in different lengths. This zipper is designed to be

inserted in the seam of a garment, down the centre back or on one side.

Light-weight zipper
The tape on a lightweight zipper is much finer than that on ordinary zippers. This makes it more delicate, but also more flexible, than ordinary zippers and it is ideal for fine fabrics. It is available in lengths from 18–56cm/7–22in.

Jeans (brass) zipper
This is a heavy-weight zipper made with large brass teeth on a very strong

tape. It is quite bulky and only suitable for trousers made in heavy-weight fabrics such as denim or corduroy.

Open-ended zipper
There are several weights of open-ended zippers to suit different applications. Jacket zippers are available to match the heavy brass jeans zipper and there are lighter-weight chunky zippers for other garments. Dress-weight zippers are also available in an open-ended version. These are available in different lengths.

Hand-sewing a zipper

This method is used to insert zippers into sheer or delicate fabrics. It is fairly strong but shouldn't be used where there is a lot of strain.

1 Stitch the seam to the bottom of the zipper opening. Hand or machine baste the zipper opening and press open. Position the zipper along the seam line and pin in place.

2 From the right side, baste 5mm/^{1}⁄₄in to each side of the seam line. Prick stitch along the basting lines making the tiny stitches about 3–5mm/^{1}⁄₈–^{1}⁄₄in apart.

3 Pull the basting thread out from the seam line of the zipper opening.

Above from left to right: jacket zipper, open-ended zipper, jeans (brass) zipper, invisible zipper, skirt-weight zipper and light-weight zipper.

Inserting a semi-concealed zipper

This method is used for centre front or back positions in a garment or in a slot in a side or back seam.

1 Machine stitch the seam up to the bottom of the zipper opening. Turn under the seam allowance and baste down 5mm/¼in away from the fold.

2 Place the pull tab 5mm/¼in below the top seam line. Pin the fabric on each side of the zipper so that the folds run up the centre of the teeth.

3 Diagonal baste the folds together to prevent them opening while stitching. Baste along the guidelines and remove the pins. Using a zipper foot attachment, stitch just outside the basting lines down one side.

4 Leave the needle in the fabric and turn to stitch across the bottom and back up the other side.

Top: Zippers are a good choice for small children's outfits.

Inserting a concealed zipper

This is used for inserting a zipper into the side seam of a skirt. It is ideal for cushions and other items of soft furnishings and makes an unobtrusive and neat fastening, since a fold of fabric overlaps the zipper so that it cannot be seen. This doesn't affect the fit because the stitching line is brought forward 3mm/⅛in on the back section and set back 3mm/⅛in on the front section.

1 Machine stitch the seam up to the bottom of the zipper opening. Press the opening along the seam line on the back section of the garment. Fold the seam allowance 3mm/⅛in out from the pressed line and baste.

2 Baste a guideline on the front side 7.5mm/³⁄₈in from the fold. Position the pull tab 5mm/¼in below the top seam line. Pin and baste the back section next to the zipper teeth. Machine stitch close to the fold.

3 Pin and baste the front section in place matching the original seam lines. Machine stitch along the guideline. Leave the needle in the fabric then turn and stitch across the bottom of the zipper.

Making decorative tassels

Tassels are extremely versatile. They come in all shapes and sizes and are used to decorate garments and cushions and can make very effective tie backs. Although there is a tremendous choice, sometimes it is not possible to get exactly the right colour or type of thread. Simple tassels are easy to make. Embroidery thread, crochet cotton and tapestry or crewel wools (yarns) are all suitable depending on the effect you want.

Simple tassel

1   Cut a piece of card (card stock) slightly wider than the finished tassel length. Wrap thread around the card until you have enough wound on to make the required size of tassel.

2   Slip a double length of cord under the threads. Tie the double cord to hold the threads together. Hold the threads securely in your hand and then snip along the bottom edge.

3   Fold a single thread into a long loop and hold against the tassel with the loop at the top. Wrap the other end several times around the tassel to create a "neck".

4   Slip the working end through the loop and pull the other end to take the loop under the wrapping. Snip the thread ends and trim the tassel neatly.

Right: Tassels are quick to make and require the minimum of materials. Use toning shades of one colour for a subtle effect.

Corded tassel

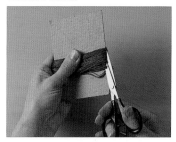

1 Cut a piece of card (card stock) slightly wider than the finished tassel length. Wrap thread around the card until you have enough to make the required size of tassel and cut along one edge.

2 Tie a large knot in a piece of cord to form a loop and place it on top of the bundle of threads so that the knot lies just below the mid-point. Tie a strong thread around the tassel above the knot.

Above and below: These elaborate tassels are ideal for soft furnishing items such as tie backs or to decorate the corners of throws.

3 Ease the threads evenly around the knot to cover it and then let the top threads drop down over the knot to form the tassel.

4 Wrap thread around the tassel to make a neck (see Simple tassel, steps 3 and 4). Carefully trim the end of the tassel level.

Making cushions

Cushions can add the finishing touch to any room and make it more comfortable and inviting. They can be simple and stylish to complement a classic chair or more adventurous in colour to jazz up a plain sofa. Use fabric that complements the other fabrics in the room.

Cushions can be filled with a variety of materials. The most luxurious is feather and down, but there are cheaper alternatives such as foam chips and polyester wadding (batting). If you choose to make your own cushion pad, use a heavyweight calico for the pad cover to prevent the filling from escaping and pack the cushion pad quite firmly as the contents will settle and flatten once it is in use. Make your cover slightly smaller than the cushion pad dimensions to ensure

the cushion is really plump when made up. By the time you've taken the seam allowances from a 45cm/18in panel it will fit snugly over a 45cm/18in cushion pad. When the fabric has a bold pattern such as stripes, it is a good idea to make a pattern to ensure that patterns match where necessary.

You can fit a zipper in any position on the wrong side of a cushion but the simplest place to insert it is 5–7.5cm/2–3in from the top edge.

Zipper fastening

1 Cut the shape of the cushion from tracing paper and mark the centre lines with a felt pen. Position the pattern on the fabric and pin in place. Add seam allowances and cut out.

Above: The motif on this fabric is the ideal size for this cushion.

2 Cut a back panel adding an extra 4cm/1½in seam allowance. Cut across the panel 7.5–10cm/3–4in from the top edge. Turn under 15mm/⅝in along the top edge of the larger piece and pin to the zipper tape. Baste and machine stitch close to the zipper using a zipper foot in the machine.

4 Baste and machine stitch along the basted guideline using the zipper foot. Remove all basting and open the zipper slightly before sewing the back and front panels together with right sides facing.

3 Turn under 2cm/¾in along the bottom edge of the narrow piece and baste a guideline 15mm/⅝in from the fold. Pin the folded edge over the zipper so that it just covers the machine stitching.

Envelope (Overlap) opening

1 The envelope opening is a discreet and easy-to-make cushion opening. Cut the front panel the required size plus seam allowances. Cut two pieces for the back each measuring half the depth of the front plus an extra 7.5cm/3in. Press under a small hem along one long edge of both pieces. Machine stitch in place.

2 On a flat surface, place the front panel right side up. Pin one back panel to the left-hand side and one to the right-hand side, matching raw edges. Overlap the two pieces so that the lower flap comes from the top of the cushion. Pin the side seams. If you prefer not to stitch over pins, baste around the edge.

3 Machine stitch around the edge of the cushion. Keep the stitching at the corners square by leaving the needle in the fabrics before swinging the cushion around to stitch the next side. Reverse stitch over the overlap for extra strength. Trim across the corners to reduce bulk and turn through.

Making a flange

Cut a front cushion panel and make a back panel with either an envelope or zipper opening. Baste with wrong sides together. When cutting the flange, if the fabric has an obvious pattern or weave, cut four pieces horizontally and four vertically.

Above: A flange makes a cushion appear much larger. It can be decorated with cord, ribbons or buttons.

1 Cut eight strips of fabric each 7.5cm/3in wide and 15cm/6in longer than each cushion edge. Fold back one corner of each strip until raw edges align. Trim each diagonal.

2 Pin the corners right sides together and stitch, stopping 15mm/ $^{5}/_{8}$in away from the inside edge. Make two square flange panels in this way and press the corner seams flat.

3 Pin the two flange panels right sides together. Machine stitch around the outside edge. Clip the corners and trim the seams to reduce bulk.

4 Turn the cover right side out. Ease out the corners and press flat. Tuck the basted cushion panels inside the flange then pin and machine stitch.

Flap opening

A flap opening is usually positioned on the front of the cushion. The flap can be shaped in various ways and fastened using buttons, ties, poppers or Velcro. These instructions are for a 45cm/18in cushion. It is a good idea to cut stripes for the front and back panels in the opposite direction to avoid matching problems.

Above: Stripes going in opposite directions avoids difficult matching at seams.

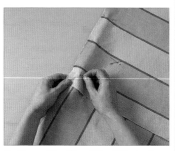

1 Cut a 45 x 60cm/18 x 24in back panel and a 30 x 45cm/12 x 18in flap panel. With right sides together, pin the flap to the top of the back panel. Cut a 45cm/18in square front panel with the top edge on a selvage or add an allowance for a small hem.

2 Machine stitch 15cm/6in down the sides and along the top edge. Trim the seams and clip the corner. Clip into the seam allowance where the stitching ends on both sides.

3 Turn the flap through, ease out the corners and press. Pin the front panel to the back with right sides together. Stitch around the remaining sides, trim the seam allowances as before, and turn through. Add the fastening of your choice.

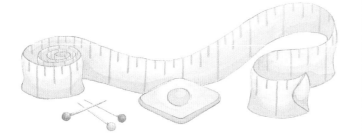

Adding a cord

Cushions can be decorated by sewing cord around the edges. This is done once the cushion has been made up.

Above: Choose a cord that has the same colour as the fabric or go for a complete contrast to add accent colours.

1 Unpick about 2.5cm/1in of the stitching along the bottom seam. Beginning at this point, sew the cord invisibly but securely to the seam line on the front of the cushion.

2 Trim the ends to 2.5cm/1in and tuck them into the gap. Stitch the gap closed securing the cord ends.

Adding a flanged cord or piping

Both these types of decorative edging have a projecting edge that can be stitched to the cushion panel: on flanged cord it is made from tape; on piping it will be a raw fabric edge.

1 Pin the piping along the seam line of the cushion front panel with the tape or raw edge facing outwards. Clip into the tape to help the cord go around the corners. Machine stitch the cord or piping in place using a zipper foot in the machine.

2 Pin the back panel on top and baste securely. Machine stitch as close as possible to the cord or piping. Trim across the corners and turn the cushion pad through.

Making a bolster cushion

Bolster cushions are quite different in shape from other cushions. Tubular cushion forms are available in different shapes and sizes.

The cover consists of a tube of fabric with two end panels. These can be flat circles or gathered panels. The opening for the cushion pad is usually along the tube seam. Either leave a gap for hand sewing or insert a zipper.

The end of the bolster cushion can be decorated with a flanged cord, fabric-covered piping cord or left plain. Finish the end with a matching tassel or a fabric-covered button to complement your colour scheme.

Right: Bolster cushions, once associated with formal furnishings and rigid fillings, can be dressed to suit almost any style of decor.

1 Measure the length and circumference of the bolster cushion pad and cut a panel that size. Measure the radius of the cushion pad and add a 2.5cm/1in seam allowance. Cut two strips that width to fit across the end of the tube panel. Pin the flanged cord across the short ends of the large panel on the right side. Machine stitch close to the cord using a zipper foot.

2 With right sides together, pin the end panels on top and machine stitch as close as possible to the cord using the zipper foot. Work two rows of machine gathering stitches along the outside edge of each end panel.

3 With right sides together, pin and stitch the long seam of the cushion panel. If the cord is very bulky you will have to hand sew that part of the seam. Gather the tube ends. Insert a tassel cord from the right side and wrap the gathered end as tightly as possible with a piece of strong thread.

Curtain equipment

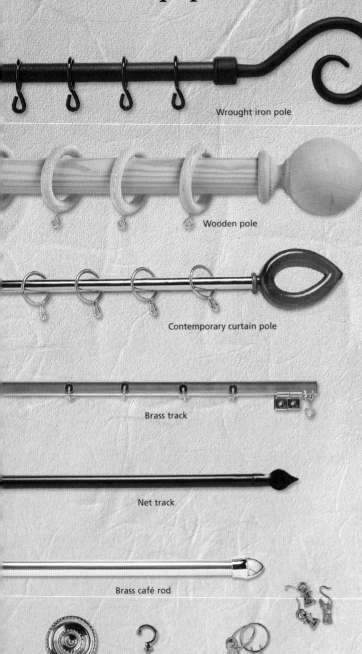

Wrought iron pole

Wooden pole

Contemporary curtain pole

Brass track

Net track

Brass café rod

Hold back

Hook for a tie back

Brass curtain clips

Brass track

This high quality traditional rail is ideal for conservatories because it can withstand high temperatures without distorting. It has a certain unique design appeal in ultra-modern houses and the metal rollers run very smoothly.

Brass café rod

This beautiful brass rod is too elegant to cover. It can be used with a self-heading curtain but looks particularly elegant when the curtain is hung from café rod clips.

Contemporary curtain pole

The finials on this retro-look curtain pole are available in a range of shapes and colours to suit your decor. You can choose from three different poles and fit matching tie backs to create a distinctive and individual look.

Wrought iron pole

Wrought iron poles make a distinct design statement in the home. These poles are less heavy than traditional wrought iron and are suitable for light- to medium-weight fabrics. Several different finials are available to suit your particular decor.

Wooden pole

Wooden poles are normally supplied with matching curtain rings. They are available in a variety of different wood and paint finishes and with a choice of carved finials.

Brass curtain clips

Curtain clips are an alternative to traditional hooks. They do away with curtain tapes and are ideal for simple curtains. Curtain clips are spaced evenly along the top of the curtain (in the same way as bulldog clips grip paper), and the hoop at the top of the grip slides on to the pole.

Hold backs

Hold backs are used to hold the curtain away from the window. With some, the curtain is simply draped over the pole and held in place by the decorative disc, and with others a tie back is used.

Net wire

This steel wire with a plastic coating can be cut to length and simply fitted using hooks and eyes. It is suitable for sheer or light-weight fabrics with a simple self-heading.

Net track

This light-weight, extendible track is suitable for sheer and light-weight fabrics. Some types can be fitted to the window with hooks or fittings. Others have adhesive pads for use with plastic frame windows.

Valance

This standard valance track is fitted behind the curtain rail fittings and can be bent to fit a bay window. It is strong enough to be used for all weights of valance.

Cord track

Cord tracks are pre-corded to allow easy access for opening and closing curtains without touching them. This type is suitable for straight runs with medium-weight curtains.

PVC curtain track

This is a basic general purpose curtain track which is easy to fit and to remove for decorating. It is suitable for medium-weight curtains and can be bent into shape.

Curtain hooks

Curtain hooks are made to fit particular curtain tracks. End hooks have a screw to keep them in position. The smaller hooks are used for attaching linings to curtain tape.

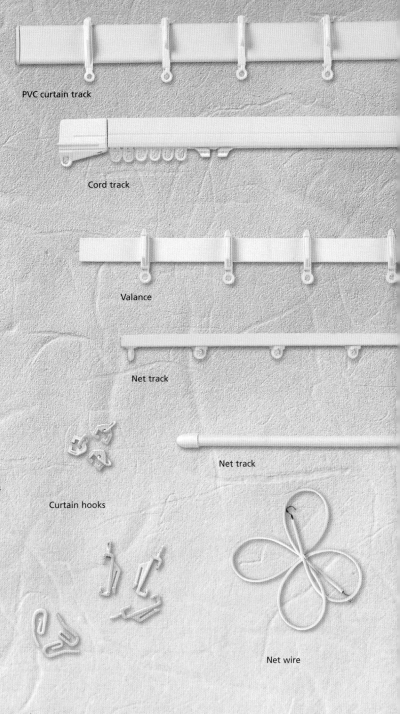

PVC curtain track

Cord track

Valance

Net track

Net track

Curtain hooks

Net wire

Making curtains

It is not difficult to make curtains that look professionally made. All you need is a sewing machine and the ability to sew straight. Curtains are made to cover a window and add a decorative touch to a room, but they also cut out light, provide privacy, dampen noise and add warmth. The type of curtain you choose depends on the shape and position of your window, the depth of the recess and the effect that you want to create.

Sheer curtains on net wires are usually fitted inside the recess while tracks or rods are fitted above the window and extend out on each side. How much they extend will depend on the position of the window and the thickness of the fabric used. You should be able to pull the curtains almost clear of the window to allow as much light in as possible.

Before you determine the amount of fabric required you must first decide on the type of rod or track and where it will be fitted. Most curtains are two to three times as wide as the curtain rod or pole depending on the type of heading used. Valances are generally fuller and require about four times the width.

Above: Plain cream or white fabric always looks elegant at the window. The matching pelmet adds a formal touch to the room.

In practice, the width of the fabric will determine the final fullness of the curtains because the number of "drops" or lengths of fabric sewn together to make the curtain are generally worked out in full or half widths. Most curtain fabrics are 120cm/48in wide and measurements are rounded up or down to the nearest 60cm/24in. So for example, on a 200cm/80in-wide window each curtain should be anything from 400–600cm/160–240in wide. Two drops on each side would be 480cm/196in, slightly more than twice the width; whereas two and a half drops on each side would be exactly three times the width. Half widths are stitched to the outside of each curtain.

Joining curtain drops

Curtains must match across each seam and between the two curtains, so extra fabric may have to be bought if a fabric has a large pattern. Join the fabric selvage to selvage, keeping any half widths on the outside.

Inside the recess

Curtains that hang inside the recess are normally fitted near the top unless they are café-style curtains. Measure inside the recess in both directions to get the width and the length. Multiply the width by both one-and-a-half and two-and-a-half, then work out the number of drops of fabric required so that it lies between the two measurements. Add about 20cm/8in to the length of each drop for hems.

Outside the recess

Curtain poles and tracks are fitted either just above the recess with the curtain hanging just below the window sill or to reach to the floor. This measurement will be the length of the drop. The width of the curtain depends on the length of the curtain pole or track rather than the width of the recess. Depending on the type of heading tape used (fancy tapes such as pinch pleats or goblets use more fabric), multiply the width by both two and three, then work out the number of drops of fabric required so that it lies between the measurements. Round up, rather than down for these curtains. Add about 20cm/8in to the length of each drop for hems.

Above: Unusual black and white striped curtains are finished off with a swag and decorative rose.

Unlined curtains

Unlined curtains are simple to make but can fade in the sunlight. If you are using satin or velvet, sew the hems by hand.

Cut the fabric according to the style of curtain you are making and join the drops as required.

1 Turn under a 12mm/½in hem down each edge and machine stitch.

2 ◄ Turn under 12mm/½in along the bottom edge and then turn up a 5–7.5cm/2–3in hem. Machine stitch, and then slip stitch the gaps at each side of the hem.

Lined curtains

Lined curtains hang better than unlined curtains and provide more insulation. Lining is sold in narrower widths than curtain fabric so the same number of drops may not require an adjustment of width.

1 Cut the fabric according to the curtain style and join the drops. Cut the lining 15cm/6in shorter and about 13cm/5in narrower than the curtain. Turn up 7.5cm/3in at the bottom of the curtain and a 5cm/2in hem at the bottom of the lining and stitch.

2 With right sides together, pin the lining so that its hem overlaps the top of the curtain hem by about 2.5cm/1in. Machine stitch the side seams and press the seams open.

3 Turn the curtain through and centre the lining. Pin along the top edge and baste down each side making sure the curtain and lining are lying flat. Slip stitch the corners of the hem.

TYPES OF HEADING TAPE

The type of heading tape you choose will determine the look of the curtains and the amount of fabric you need to buy.

• **Narrow tape** – for simple curtains that are fitted inside a recess or underneath a valance.

• **Pencil pleat** – a basic heading tape for curtains that requires about twice the width of fabric to look good. The folds are about 12mm/½in wide.

• **Pinch pleat** – one of several fancy headings that need a specific width of fabric to hang properly. They normally require about three times the width and are used in more formal settings.

• **Loose lining tape** – a narrow tape that fits along the top edge of the lining. It fits with standard hooks to the curtain tape.

• **Sheer curtain tape** – a lightweight transparent pencil tape specially made for sheer fabrics. This tape is used if the curtains are to open.

• **Velcro curtain tape** – a pencil tape with bands on the reverse side that stick to Velcro. It is used to fit curtains into window recesses and on to valance boards.

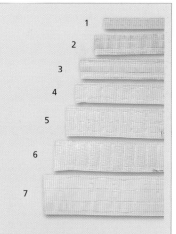

Above: 1 lining tape; 2 sheer Velcro tape; 3 sheer curtain tape; 4 narrow tape; 5 pencil pleat; 6 pencil pleat for Velcro; 7 pinch pleat.

Narrow tape

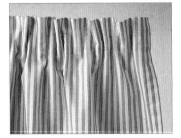

1 You will need between one-and-a-half times and twice the width for this heading tape. Tie the cords at one end of the curtain tape together.

2 Turn down a 3–5cm/1¼–2in single hem at the top of the curtain. Pin the curtain tape over the raw edge and baste in place. Trim the ends of the tape and turn under.

3 Machine stitch along each edge of the curtain tape. Draw up the cords to the correct width and tie off the other end.

Pencil pleats

Pinch pleats

1 You will need between two and three times the width for this heading tape. Turn down a 2cm/¾in hem along the top edge of the curtain. Draw out the cord at one end of the tape and knot together.

2 Pin the heading tape along the top edge of the curtain, turning the ends underneath the hem. Stitch along the guidelines at the top and bottom edges of the tape.

You will need about three times the width for this heading tape.

1 Attach the tape to the curtains in the same way as pencil pleats making sure that the tape is facing in the right direction so that when you pull the tape up, the pleats will fan out at the top.

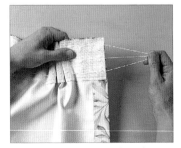

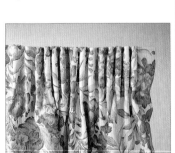

3 Pull the cords out singly at first and then hold the ends together and ease the curtain to the correct width. Tie the cords to secure and tuck the ends inside between the tape and the curtain.

TIP

On very wide curtains tie the cord ends to a door handle before pulling them up.

Detachable lining

This type of lining can be fitted to most curtain tapes and is a good choice where the curtain will be frequently washed or dry cleaned. The lining does not have to be as full as the curtain. Cut the lining so that it is between one-and-a-half times and twice the width of the window or track and the same length as the curtain. Turn under and sew a double hem down each side of the fabric.

Open the loose lining tape and fit it over the top raw edge of the lining. Pin and machine stitch the tape in place. Trim the end of the tape and turn it under. Pull out the cord and ease the lining to fit the width of the curtain. Turn up a double hem along the bottom edge so that the lining is about 2.5–5cm/1–2in shorter than the curtain and machine stitch. Attach the lining to the curtain tape with standard hooks.

Self heading

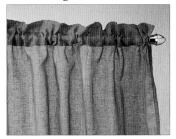

Sheer or net curtains that will stay closed can be hung from spring wires on a narrow window and from a narrow brass rod or slim pole on wider windows. In each case the top of the curtain is turned over to form a casing. It is not necessary to join the seams if there are several drops as the selvages are less visible than a seam.

1 Turn up the hem and make the curtain up as for an unlined curtain. Turn down a 3–5cm/1¼–2in hem along the top edge depending on the width of the spring wire or rod. Machine stitch the hem along the bottom edge and again, 1–2cm/½–¾in away to make a casing for a rod.

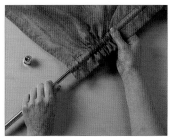

2 Sew in the thread ends and press the curtain. Remove the finial from one end of the curtain rod. Feed the curtain onto the rod or spring wire. Even out the gathers along the length of the curtain. Hang the rod from hooks fitted at each end.

Fitting curtain hooks

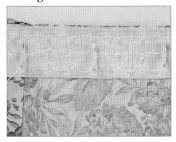

Curtain hooks are normally fitted in the middle row of loops on the curtain tape, unless the curtain has to fit on a rail very near the ceiling. Insert a hook every 10–15cm/4–6in along the tape, depending on the weight of fabric. A heavier fabric will need smaller gaps between the hooks. Fit a hook with a screw in the last

space at the left or right depending on which way the curtain will open. Measure the curtain rail and gather each hooked curtain up to fit on half the rail. The hooks can slide onto the rail or will "snap-on" if pushed gently. Close the curtains and rearrange the pleats so that they spread evenly along the track.

Tied curtains

These are made from a basic unlined curtain which has been machine stitched with a 2cm/³⁄₄in hem along the top edge. These curtains create an informal look.

Ties can be made from cord, ribbon or tape and fitted in the same way as the fabric tapes shown here.

1   Decide on the length of tie required by pinning the centre of a strip of fabric to the curtain and tying the raw edges in a bow over the pole. Work out how many strips are required spacing them every 10–15cm/4–6in. When calculating the quantity of fabric, remember to add seam allowances.

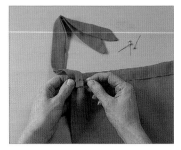

2   Cut each strip twice the finished width plus a 1cm/¹⁄₂in seam allowance. Fold the strips in half lengthways. Leaving a gap in the middle for turning, machine stitch along the length and across both ends 5mm/¹⁄₄in from the raw edge. Make the ends taper to a point.

3   Trim across the corners and turn through. Ease out the points of the tie with a blunt, narrow tool such as a bodkin or blunt needle. Roll the tie so that the seam lies exactly on the edge and press flat. Neatly slip stitch the gap closed.

4   Fold the tie in half crossways and pin the fold on the wrong side of the hem at the top of the curtain. Using good quality thread, stitch in a square to secure the tie. Sew in the ends of the threads. Stitch the other ties in place, evenly across the width of the curtain, in the same way.

Eyelet curtain

1   Make an unlined curtain and turn down and sew a 2.5cm/1in hem along the top edge. Make a mark at 7.5–10cm/3–4in intervals along the top hem of the curtain and an equal distance from the fold. Use the special tool supplied with the eyelets and a hammer to cut a hole in the centre of the hem at each mark.

2   Turn the curtain with the wrong side facing up. Fit the tube section of the eyelet through the hole and drop the ring on top. Cover with the tool and hammer into position.

3   Thread the cord through each hole leaving a loop to fit over the pole. Tie the ends of the cord in a knot and trim neatly. This type of curtain also looks good with nautical-theme fabric on a wooden curtain pole.

Café curtain

Café curtains are an attractive way to screen the lower half of a window and at the same time allow light through the top half. The curtains normally hang inside the recess across the window but can be hung across the window from a curtain pole. The width of the curtain will depend on whether it is to hang flat or have soft gathers. These scalloped-top curtains can be made in a single colour or in two contrasting fabrics as shown here.

Draw out a pattern for the curtain tops. Decide on the length, making sure the finished curtain will reach the window sill, and add a 5cm/2in hem allowance. The end of the tabs can be any shape – simply alter the pattern below before cutting out. Try out your paper pattern over the rod first before cutting fabric.

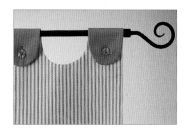

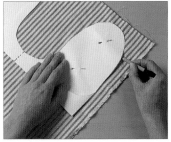

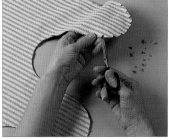

1 Fold the pattern over to make a straight edge and pin to the fabric. Draw around the pattern with tailor's chalk and move along to complete the shaping. Cut out along the lines and cut the contrasting fabric to match.

2 With right sides together, sew down the sides and around the curves. Trim the seams to 5mm/¹⁄₄in. Notch the outward curves as shown and clip the inward curves. Turn the curtain through and press.

3 Work a vertical buttonhole if required on each tab. Fold the tab over the pole and check the buttonhole position. (The button will sit at the top of the buttonhole). Sew the buttons in place. Fit the curtain over the pole and pin up the hem. Make the hem 1–2.5cm/¹⁄₂–1in shorter on the inside of the curtain.

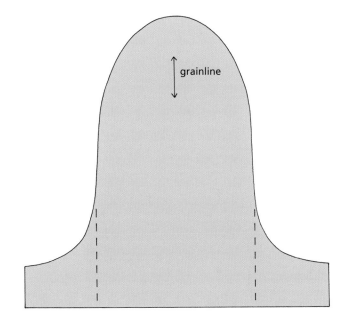

grainline

Above: Café-style curtains are a good choice where privacy and good natural light are required in a room.

Left: Enlarge the template to the desired size, and so that it fits evenly across the width of your fabric.

PATCHWORK

Patchwork was originally made by resourceful women who needed to make warm bedcovers for their homes. They collected scraps of fabric and cut up worn-out clothes, then stitched the pieces together to make a large patchwork cloth. This was filled and backed, then quilted and bound to make a quilt. For many pioneering women, making a patchwork quilt offered an opportunity for creative expression in a bleak world. The activity of quilting, too, became a social occasion involving a whole community of women.

Materials and equipment

A lot of special equipment is required for patchwork and quilting.
This descriptive list will help you choose the correct items.

1 Air- or water-soluble pen
Marks made by these pens wash out or disappear quickly. They are useful for temporarily marking small areas.

2 Beeswax
Running thread over beeswax smoothes the thread and helps prevent knots forming while sewing.

3 Craft knife and ruler
Use a metal-edged ruler when cutting templates with a craft knife. Hold the ruler with the edge facing away from the template. Score the line several times instead of trying to cut through first time.

4 Fabric
Patchwork fabric is often sold in "fat quarters" (45 x 45cm/18 x 18in), but it is usually more economical to determine the colours and quantity required and then to buy long quarters (23 x 115cm/9 x 45in) instead.

5 Freezer paper
Freezer paper (a waxed paper food wrapping) is used for accurate hand piecing or appliqué. It has a non-marking wax coating on one side that can be ironed temporarily to fabric.

6 Fusible bonding web
Fusible bonding web is a mesh of glue used to adhere pieces of appliqué to a background with heat.

7 Graph paper
Use for designing patterns and making templates. Use isometric paper for triangular or diamond patterns.

8 Quilting pins
Long, fine, glass-headed pins are suitable for temporarily pinning layers prior to basting.

9 Pencil and sharpener
Use a sharp pencil for marking paper templates.

10 Protractor
A protractor is used to measure angles when designing patchwork and for marking notches on curved edges. Use a set of compasses to draw curved templates and some geometric shapes.

11 Quilter's quarter
Use this to add consistent 5mm/¼in seam allowances to patchwork shapes.

12 Quilting hoops/frames
These are thick and strong to hold together the multiple layers of a quilt.

13 Quilting thimble
Use a metal thimble on the middle finger of your sewing hand and a quilter's thimble on the index finger of your other hand.

14 Rotary cutting set
Use with a self-healing cutting mat and ruler for speed cutting, to straighten fabric ends and to cut strips and geometric shapes.

15 Safety pins
Use special safety pins for holding quilt layers together. Quilter's safety pins have a deeper bend on one side to accommodate thick layers of wadding (batting) without crushing it.

16 Scissors
Keep separate scissors for cutting fabric and paper because paper dulls the edge of the blade. Use dress-making shears to cut fabric and sharp, pointed embroidery scissors for close work and for snipping threads.

17 Seam unpicker
Use this to cut every third stitch. Pull out the thread from the wrong side.

18 Spray glue
Spray glue is ideal for sticking paper templates to cardboard.

19 Tape measure
Useful for measuring fabric, but not for adding seams.

20 Templates
Accurate templates are essential. Draw templates for hand piecing and appliqué to the finished size. Add seam allowances before cutting out the fabric. Templates for machine piecing should include the seam allowances. Quilting templates are best made from plastic or metal.

21 Template plastic
Use translucent plastic sheeting for cutting re-usable templates. Trace your design directly through the plastic using a soft pencil.

22 Thread
For appliqué, use thread that matches the appliqué or the background or go one shade darker. Use strong quilting thread for hand quilting with beeswax, and invisible thread for machine quilting.

23 Transfer paper and pen
Draw the mirror image of a design on transfer paper and place it face down on fabric. Rub the design line to transfer it to the fabric below.

Looking at fabric colours, tones, shades and values

Most patchwork patterns are created by the contrast between light, medium and dark fabrics. The colours or patterns you choose will affect the overall quilt design. The depth of colour is crucial to some designs such as Tumbling Blocks because light fabrics appear to come forward while dark fabrics recede. Careful placement creates an optical illusion that makes a flat block appear three-dimensional.

The depth of colour is known as the value. It's not difficult to grade one fabric from light to dark, but this value will change when you look at it against other fabrics. Fabrics appear lighter when surrounded by darker shades, and darker when surrounded by lighter shades.

Solid-colour fabrics are used to create bold contrasts in patchwork designs. You can now buy a wide range of fabrics that look solid from a distance but are actually slightly patterned. These fabrics are printed with two subtle shades of the same colour and can be used alongside solid colours to add interest.

Prints

Everyone associates printed fabrics with patchwork. Contemporary prints can be mixed with more traditional patterns for an unusual effect, or an "antique" quilt can be stitched from carefully selected prints.

Small-scale prints tend to look solid from a distance but add interest

Above: Solid colours focus the eye when used in small quantities between patterns.

and create a textured effect when viewed at close hand. Medium prints are perhaps the most popular of the print fabrics used for patchwork. Take care when placing two of these prints together in case the pattern line is blurred and the patchwork effect lost.

Large-scale prints are useful because several different colour-values can be cut from the same fabric. A large-scale print generally becomes an abstract pattern when the patchwork shape is cut. Use a window template to select a particular part of the motif to enhance your patchwork design.

It is difficult to choose fabrics for a quilt from small samples. Visit your

Below: Choose patterns carefully. Large patterns in small areas do not work and small patterns look solid from a distance.

local quilt shop and take out bolts of fabric that you like and arrange them in an order that you find pleasing. By slotting in a new fabric and lifting out an old one, you will soon find a selection of fabrics that work together in terms of colour and scale. When you substitute the right fabric for one that doesn't seem right, the range of colours will appear to "lift". Be brave, try unusual combinations – you may get a pleasant surprise and a most unusual quilt into the bargain.

Using a colour wheel

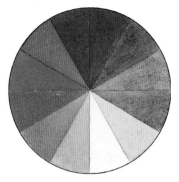

If you find it difficult to choose colours, try looking at a colour wheel. Red, yellow and blue are the three primary colours from which all others are formed. By mixing adjacent primary colours, the three secondary colours, orange, green and purple, are formed. Tertiary colours, such as blue-green, are mixed from two adjacent secondary colours.

Choose three or four adjacent colours to create a harmonious effect or go for colours opposite one another for contrast. Some of the most effective colour schemes use three adjacent colours from one side of the wheel and another from directly opposite for contrast. The primary colours create the most vibrant colour-schemes but three or four tertiary colours produce a more subtle effect.

CHOOSING FABRIC

• Patchwork is often seen as a good way of using up scraps, but in fact you usually need to buy quite a lot of new fabric for a large project such as a quilt.

• The wonderful array of "fat quarters" (45 x 45cm/18 x 18in) lined up in baskets in your local needlecraft shop is very tempting but you will waste money if you buy these small pieces before you have planned your quilt and determined the actual amount required.

• Even if you only need a small quantity of one colour, it may still be better to buy a "long quarter" (23 x 115cm/ 9 x 45in) instead.

• Many quilters buy fabric made for the purpose, but it is also possible to use fabric from other sources such as clothing.

• Always use good-quality fabrics with a similar fibre content for quilt making.

• Thin or worn fabrics will not last and wadding (batting) will work through a loosely woven fabric to produce a surface haze.

• Choose closely woven fabrics, but not with so tight a weave that they will be difficult to sew.

• Visualize and plan the quilt on paper then try out a single block to make sure the colours work well together and that you like them before going on to buy large amounts of fabric.

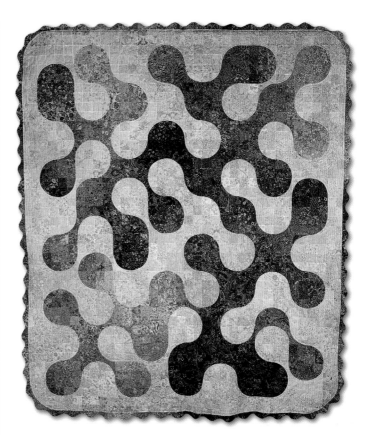

Above: Colours from the whole colour spectrum have been carefully chosen and placed to fade and merge together in this patchwork design. Over 1,500 patches have been used, all with subtle and small-scale patterns.

Preparing the fabric

Some people advocate washing and pressing the fabric before cutting, while others prefer to work with crisp new fabric and like the "antique look" achieved by the fabric shrinking slightly when the whole quilt is washed for the first time. If you choose this method ensure that all your fabrics are colourfast first.

If you want to wash, sort the fabric into light and dark shades and wash each pile separately in warm water with some fabric conditioner. It is not necessary to add detergent if the fabric is clean. Rinse the fabric thoroughly and hang out to dry by the selvages. Press while still slightly damp. Straighten the fabric ends and the grain before cutting.

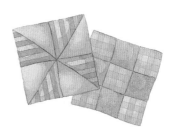

Choosing wadding (batting)

The wadding is the fabric layer that is sandwiched between the quilt top and the backing. Antique quilts were filled with anything to hand from old blankets to worn patchwork quilts. Nowadays, wadding is purpose-made in a range of fibres from polyester, to wool, cotton or even silk. Patchwork suppliers stock a whole range, with each fibre type suitable for a different purpose.

Each fibre has different properties that will affect the finished look of the quilt. The finished thickness or "handle" of a quilt will depend on the type of wadding (batting) used between the layers. Polyester wadding tends to be very bouncy with a padded look, whereas cotton or wool wadding gives a flatter effect that drapes well. Most people choose polyester wadding for their first quilt but this is often rather thick, unwieldy and difficult to quilt. Buy a sample pack of wadding and try out the different types before you make your choice, by sandwiching a piece of wadding between two layers of calico or other cotton fabric. Try hand or machine stitching a small quilting design to see how easily the wadding handles.

Often it may be plain logic that makes the decision for you. If you are making a king size quilt and want to machine quilt it, the wadding will at some stage have to be rolled up, and the roll will have to fit through the sewing machine. Once in the machine you should be able to manoeuvre it.

Types of wadding (batting)

Choose wadding (batting) carefully, because you can't change your mind after it is stitched. On some of the different types of wadding mentioned here you should leave a gap of no more than 7.5–10cm/3–4in between your quilting lines to prevent them from breaking up in the wash. On others you can leave up to 25cm/10in.

1 50g/2oz polyester – a thin wadding (90cm/36in wide) for quilting or padding. It is useful for making padded frames and for backing embroideries to throw the design into relief.

2 115g/4oz polyester – the basic wadding for quilts. It is inexpensive and fairly easy to quilt, but does not drape very well. It is sold off the roll or in quilt-sized pieces.

3 170g/6oz polyester – a bulky wadding that is too thick to sew and is generally used for tie quilting.

4 Firm-needled wadding – a 100 per cent polyester wadding, suitable for making wall hangings and bags. It holds its shape well once quilted.

5 Polydown – a low-loft, soft 100 per cent resin-bonded, polyester wadding that is very easy to stitch.

6 Thermore – a very thin 100 per cent polyester wadding that drapes well and is guaranteed not to beard (the process where strands of wadding work their way through the quilt top). It is ideal for clothing or wall quilts.

7 Wool – this wonderfully soft wadding is very easy to quilt and drapes beautifully. Leave no more than 7.5cm/3in between your quilting lines. A quilt made with wool wadding provides particularly good insulation but needs hand washing or dry cleaning.

8 Cotton – made from 80 per cent cotton, 20 per cent polyester, this wadding has slight bounce from the polyester but the cotton shrinks by up to 5 per cent, which gives an antique look to a quilt.

9 Organic cotton – this environmentally friendly and hypo-allergenic wadding is suitable for hand quilting. For machine quilting, use the scrim-backed version which can be quilted up to 25cm/10in apart.

10 and 11 100 per cent cotton – this wadding is very easy to quilt. The fibres have been needled through a strong, thin base to produce an even, stable wadding that will last for years. Available in different thicknesses, it is suitable for hand and machine quilting and the layers of stitching can be wide apart.

1   2 3   4   5   6   7   8   9   10 11

Getting started

Making a full size quilt is quite a commitment in both time and money. Just knowing where to begin and what design to choose can be daunting. But remember, even the most experienced quiltmaker producing amazing designs started somewhere. And the quilters of the past produced incredible work with few resources except their own creativity.

Today, we have so many gadgets all designed to improve our quiltmaking that knowing what to buy and how to start to make a quilt can become a confusing experience for a novice. The following guidelines will take you through the quiltmaking process one step at a time. Begin by looking at quilts in exhibitions, or ones that friends have made, to establish what kinds of designs and colour schemes appeal to you. If you are working by

hand rather than machine, accept that quiltmaking is a time-consuming business and choose to work on a small-scale wall hanging or cot-size quilt first, before progressing to ambitious bed-sized quilts.

Alternately, making lots of samples of different cushion-sized blocks, then joining them all together into a quilt is a good way to learn many of the basic techniques and which type of blocks and colours appeal to you.

With a design in mind, the next stage is to determine how big the finished piece will be. The box on the next page is a general guide to quilt sizes, but you will need to take into account whether the quilt will sit on top of the bed or will touch the floor on three sides and add on an extra allowance accordingly. Draw a rectangle on graph paper to represent your quilt. Work to a reduced scale and draw a rough diagram first.

Quilt terminology

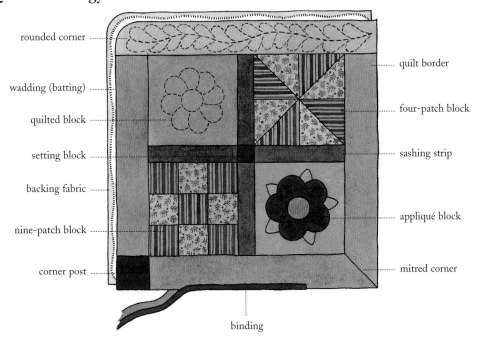

rounded corner

wadding (batting)

quilted block

setting block

backing fabric

nine-patch block

corner post

quilt border

four-patch block

sashing strip

appliqué block

mitred corner

binding

Planning the quilt design

Block quilts are easier to plan than all-over mosaic quilts (one or two patches). Whichever type you are making, it is relatively easy to determine the quantity of fabric needed for a small area and then multiply this to see what is required for a whole quilt.

Quilt composition

Although some quilts have the patchwork extending out to the edge, the majority have a border and others also have strips of fabric, called sashing, which separate the blocks. Borders and sashing alter the size and appearance of your quilt dramatically.

Plan your quilt by drawing a sketch of the blocks that will make up your quilt design on graph paper first, shading them to show the light, medium and dark fabrics. Use photocopies for this stage if there are a lot of blocks. Try out various arrangements and look for border fabrics that will enhance the design.

When you are happy with the arrangement, draw your quilt design on graph paper. This will allow you to check the finished size and determine the fabric quantities. Size is not so crucial for a wall quilt, but the dimensions and overall design are.

Sashing and borders

Sashing and borders are cut on the lengthways grain of the fabric. Add on an extra 5cm/2in to the length of the border pieces and allow 12mm/$\frac{1}{2}$in seam allowance widthways on each strip. First determine how many strips will fit across the fabric width, then find the total number of metres or yards required.

Quilt backing

The quilt back will look best in a fabric that co-ordinates with the quilt front. Determine the total length and width of the finished quilt, then add 5–10cm/2–4in to your measurements. If the quilt back is wider than the fabric it will be necessary to join lengths together, keeping the seams equidistant from the centre.

Binding

You will also need to cut some binding strips to finish off the quilt. Standard binding strips are 5cm/2in wide. Straight binding is cut from the lengthways grain and bias binding is cut diagonally across the fabric. A 1m/1yd length of 115cm/45in wide fabric will provide about 21m/23yd of binding on the straight grain and 19m/20$\frac{3}{4}$yd cut on the bias.

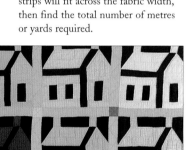

Left: The blocks of this representational school houses quilt design are held together with sashing strips and setting blocks.

CONVERSION CHART

You will find it easier to use the decimal equivalent for imperial measurements when working out quantities with a calculator.

Metric	Imperial	Decimal
3mm	⅛in	0.125in
5mm	¼in	0.25in
9mm	⅜in	0.375in
1.2cm	½in	0.5in
1.6cm	⅝in	0.625in
1.9cm	¾in	0.75in
2.2cm	⅞in	0.875in
2.5cm	1in	1.0in
5cm	2in	2.0in
7.5cm	3in	3.0in
10cm	4in	4.0in
13cm	5in	5.0in
15cm	6in	6.0in

QUILT SIZES

Use this table as a rough guide to the size your quilt should be, but remember the measurements will vary depending on the type of patchwork and size of blocks. You will still need to measure the actual bed to establish the finished quilt size.

Baby	90–115cm/36–45in wide	x	115–137cm/45–54in long
Cot	107–122cm/42–48in wide	x	137–152cm/54–60in long
Single	142–162cm/56–64in wide	x	213–254cm/84–100in long
Double	178–203cm/70–80in wide	x	213–254cm/84–100in long
Queen	193–213cm/76–84in wide	x	228–264cm/90–104in long
King	234–254cm/92–100in wide	x	228–264cm/90–104in long
Jumbo	304–315cm/120–124in wide	x	304–315cm/120–124in long

CALCULATING QUANTITIES: ROAD TO HEAVEN BLOCK

CALCULATING BLOCKS AND PATCHES

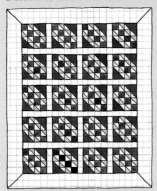

• Draw a rough sketch of your quilt on graph paper, including sashing and borders. Colour or shade the design to distinguish between the different fabrics you will be using.

• Label each shape in the blocks with a different letter and then add up the pieces to determine how many of each shape and colour there are in the block.

For example, this block requires:

Small triangles:
10 Light fabric A
6   Medium fabric B

Large triangles:
2   Medium fabric C

Squares:
4   Dark fabric D

• Multiply the number of fabric pieces required for each shape by the number of blocks in the quilt.

• Determine how many of each shape you can cut from a fabric width, include extra for seams.

• Take off about 5cm/2in wastage across a fabric width to allow for selvages and shrinkage.

• Instead of cutting triangles, cut squares instead and cut them in half across the diagonal.

CALCULATING FABRIC

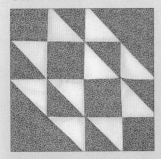

This example shows how to calculate the fabric required to make up a quilt in a Road to Heaven pattern made up of 20 blocks, each 30cm/12in square. Add extra for sashing and borders.

Light fabric A – Each block contains 10 triangles cut from five squares each 9.7cm/3⅞in. For 20 blocks, you will need 100 squares. As 10 squares fit across a 115cm/45in width you will need enough fabric for 10 rows, that is 97cm/38¾in.

Total light fabric required: 97cm/38¾in of 115cm/45in wide fabric.

Medium fabric B – Each block contains six triangles cut from three squares each 9.7cm/3⅞in. For 20 blocks you will need 60 squares. As 10 squares fit across a 115cm/45in width, you will need enough fabric for six rows, that is 58.2cm/23¼in.

Total medium fabric required: 58.2cm/23¼in of 115cm/45in wide fabric.

Medium fabric C – Each block contains two triangles cut from one square 17.5cm/6⅞in. For 20 blocks you will need 20 squares. As six squares fit across a 115cm/45in width, you will need enough fabric for four rows, that is 70cm/27½in.

Total medium fabric required: 70cm/27½in of 115cm/45in wide fabric.

Dark fabric D – Each block contains four squares each 9cm/3½in. For 20 blocks you will need 80 squares. As twelve squares fit across a 115cm/45in width, you will need seven rows each, that is 63cm/24½in.

Total dark fabric required: 63cm/24½in of 115cm/45in wide fabric.

Making and using templates

Different types of template are used for patchwork, quilting and appliqué. Templates for hand piecing and appliqué are cut to the exact size of the finished shape, whereas templates for machine piecing include a 5mm/¼in seam. Some patchwork templates have windows to allow the sewing and cutting lines to be drawn at the same time. Quilting templates have windows to allow you to mark all the quilting lines.

By using a template you can reproduce an exact shape or pattern as many times as you need to. Templates must be made from a material that will stand up to repeated use, such as firm cardboard, plastic or metal.

Plastic has several advantages over cardboard: it is transparent, allowing you to trace shapes directly, and it is hard wearing which means that templates can be re-used. If you are using cardboard, paint the edges of the template with varnish to protect them. Ready-made templates are generally made from metal or plastic.

1 Trace the shape through the plastic with a sharp, soft pencil. It may be easier to mark a dot at each corner and join them up with a ruler. Measure and mark a 5mm/¼in border all around for a machine-stitching or window template if this is required.

2 To cut out your template, use a metal-edged ruler and score along the pencil line several times. Hold the ruler very firmly to prevent it from slipping, with the edge facing away from the template. Make sure you cut the outside line on a machine-stitching or window template.

3 To make a window template, score very carefully along the inside lines of the template. Turn the plastic around and repeat until you have cut out the middle of the template. You may have to score along each line several times to cut right through.

Marking fabric

Try to be as accurate as you can when marking fabric to make it easier for you to join the pieces accurately later. A small discrepancy in each piece can make quite a difference over a whole quilt. Use a sharp pencil on the wrong side of the fabric and keep straight edges along the fabric grain where possible.

To avoid wasting fabric, mark any borders and sashing pieces in a particular colour before cutting the patches. Mark the patchwork pieces in rows rather than dotting them about the fabric.

1 Hand-sewing, quilting and appliqué templates are cut to the exact finished size and are used to mark the stitching line only. Place the template on the fabric with the edge along the straight grain. Mark as many squares as required, leaving enough room between each shape for the two seam allowances.

2 Measure 5mm/¼in out from each edge and join the marks. A quilter's tape or a quilter's quarter tool are useful for adding the seam allowance.

The rotary cutting set

Rotary cutting is a quick and accurate way to trim fabric and cut it into simple shapes. Squares, triangles and rectangles are particularly suitable, but with practice, diamonds can be cut. You will need a rotary cutting tool, a self-healing mat and a special grid-marked ruler. These are an investment, but save hours of work since multiple layers can be cut without pre-marking. Reverse the instructions if you are left-handed.

1 Fold the fabric in half, matching selvages. Steam press the layers. Fold in half again and press. Place the folded fabric on the mat. Align a crossways marking on the ruler with a fold. Roll the blade of the rotary cutter up and down the ruler edge.

2 Turn the fabric around so that the cut edge is to the left. Use the markings on the ruler to cut the width of strip you require with 12mm/¹⁄₂in extra for seam allowances. Cut as many strips as required. Remember that each strip has four layers.

3 Turn the first strip around and align a crossways marking on the ruler with the bottom edge. Trim off 9mm/³⁄₈in at one end. Cut the strip into squares. Each square should be the same as the finished size plus 12mm/¹⁄₂in seam allowance.

4 To cut triangles from squares, add 2.2cm/⁷⁄₈in to the size of the finished triangle, measured down a straight side, and cut the square that size. Cut in half diagonally to make the triangles. For quarter-square triangles, cut the square 3cm/1¹⁄₄in larger than the finished triangle and cut diagonally across in both directions.

5 To cut a short diamond, cut strips the width of the diamond plus 12mm/¹⁄₂in for seams. Align the edge of the strip with the 60° line on the ruler and trim off the end. Keeping the 60° line along the edge of the strip, cut the diamonds the same width as the strips using the grid lines on the ruler or the mat as a guide.

6 Cut a long diamond in the same way, lining the edge of the strip with the 45° line on the ruler.

USING SCISSORS

• Always cut fabrics with a sharp blade, cutting exactly along the pencil line.

• Scissors are useful for intricate shapes and curves.

• Keep the fabric as close to the table as possible. Cut with long strokes along the main lines before cutting into separate shapes. For better accuracy, cut single layers.

Making mosaic quilts

When fabric was a precious commodity and people were reluctant to waste even the smallest scrap, fabric from old clothes and furnishings were set aside until there were sufficient pieces to join together to make a patchwork quilt.

One- and two-patch quilts

The patchwork cloth was lined with thin wool blankets to make bedcovers. The patches were originally sewn together in a random fashion or in strips, but as fabrics became more available, geometric shapes and intricate patterns were devised by quilt-makers to show off their skills and expertise.

Mosaic quilts were one of the most popular early patchwork quilt designs. These are made up from one or two shapes pieced together to create an all-over pattern and are known as one- or two-patch quilts. These quilts were usually made from hexagons and diamonds and hand pieced over papers. Grandmother's Flower Garden is probably the best-known example of this traditional type of hand-sewn patchwork. Sometimes the papers were left in the patchwork and this can help to accurately date an old quilt.

Tumbling Blocks and Trip Around the World are two examples of modern one-patch mosaic quilts.

one-patch block

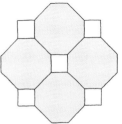

two-patch block

Below: This Tumbling Blocks quilt is a mosaic quilt made from thousands of tiny silk diamonds. Try looking at it from different directions to see the effect of the optical illusion.

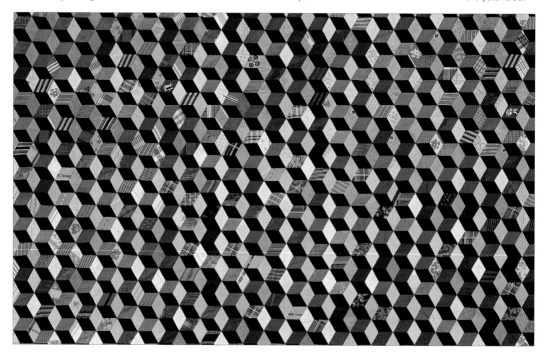

Hand piecing a one-patch block without papers

Tumbling Blocks is a popular one-patch pattern that uses three short diamonds, that are all the same size, sewn together at different angles to make a hexagon. By using different shades of fabric in each block a fascinating optical illusion is created. Each diamond in the hexagon is a light, a medium or a dark fabric.

In this simplest form of Tumbling Blocks patchwork all the hexagons are identical in size – it is the way they are put together which affects the overall appearance. The dark fabric can appear to be on the left, right or on top of the blocks depending on which way the patchwork is viewed. You can make a more complicated pattern by using different colours and keeping the light, medium and dark fabrics in the same position as you sew the hexagons together.

1 Use a window template to draw the diamond shape on the wrong side of the fabric, keeping two opposite sides parallel to the straight grain of the fabric. Make sure the seam allowance is clearly marked on the fabric. Cut the pieces out carefully along the outside lines. Add a 5mm/ ¼in seam allowance if using an ordinary template.

2 Pin two different patches with right sides together. Make sure that the pencil mark corners match exactly by pushing a pin through from one side to the other. Begin with a couple of back stitches and sew small running stitches along the pencil line. Stop at the first corner and work another two back stitches to secure the thread.

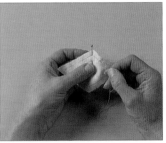

3 Fold the third diamond in half and insert it between the two layers. Pin the seam on two sides to complete the hexagon. Pin the point where the three pieces come together and secure this with a back stitch.

4 Sew across the two sides, making sure you keep to the marked line and finishing off with a couple of tiny back stitches.

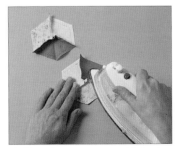

5 Press the seams to one side in the same direction so that the seams swirl open in the centre. Make six hexagons for each tower block.

6 Arrange the hexagons with the dark diamond in the same position on each one. Sew the hexagons together matching the inset points carefully. Press the seams to one side.

Hand-piecing a one-patch block with papers

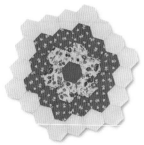

This Grandmother's Flower Garden patchwork takes its name from the way the hexagons are arranged to create flower borders surrounded by a garden path. The "path" around the outside edge is traditionally cream to represent stone, or green for grass. Although it is a simple single patch quilt, there are a multitude of different ways to arrange the patches and colours. In this arrangement two dark fabrics (blue and deep pink), one medium (the cream floral), and one light fabric (the cream path) are used.

The easiest way to stitch hexagons is by piecing them over papers. Cut the papers to the exact finished size and baste the fabric in place. You can also use freezer paper to achieve very crisp edges.

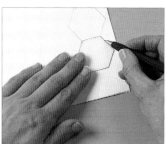

1 Cut a hexagonal template and use it to draw and cut out 37 hexagonal paper shapes for the patchwork. Use thick paper so that the fabric can be folded over accurately.

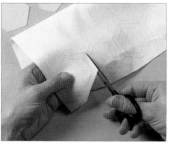

2 Draw out the hexagon on the wrong side of the fabric, adding a 5mm/¹⁄₄in seam allowance around each one. Cut the required number of patches from each colour.

3 Pin a paper shape in the centre on the wrong side of the fabric hexagon. Fold over one edge at a time and baste in place. Take a small basting stitch across each corner to hold the overlapping folds flat. It is best to begin with a knot and finish with a back stitch to make the basting threads easy to remove.

4 Hold two patchwork shapes with right sides together and the corners matching to join them along the required edge. Start with two tiny back stitches into the seam allowance, then oversew the edges together. Use a fine needle to keep the stitches very small. Make sure the needle is straight going through the fabric so that the two shapes will open out flat.

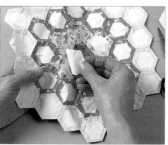

5 Build up the design, working outwards in rings. Once complete, take out the basting threads by undoing the back stitch and pulling the knot gently. Lift out the papers carefully in case they are caught in the stitching. Press the patchwork on the wrong side and on the front with a pressing cloth. The garden motif can be appliquéd on to a cushion cover or joined to other motifs to make a quilt.

Above: This simple one-patch cot quilt has been machine quilted and small buttons added for decoration.

Left: This traditional Grandmother's Flower Garden has been stitched entirely by hand.

Below left: A drawing from a Roman pavement was the basis for this two-patch quilt, made using the same method of working over paper. Squares and elongated hexagons have been used.

Below: A diamond and a square form the basis of this two-patch design.

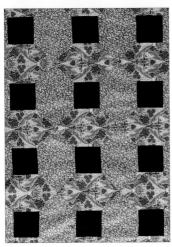

Joining patchwork by machine

Machine stitching is a quick and accurate way to join patchwork. As the seam allowances are included on templates for machine piecing they do not need to be marked on the fabric. Instead, use the side of the presser foot as a guide for sewing a 5mm/¼in seam.

It is a good idea to test your machine first by positioning the fabric exactly on the edge of the presser foot and stitching a test piece in order to measure the seam allowance. It may be easier to adjust the needle position than to guide the fabric farther in or out. A slight discrepancy won't be noticeable when stitching strips or squares, but will be obvious when you come to match triangles or diamonds to the square.

If the fabric was steam pressed and cut with a rotary cutter, pins should not be necessary, although beginners may feel happier using them. Use pins when matching different shaped pieces, curved edges and patchwork seams.

Sewing squares together

Place the two pieces with right sides together and position under the presser foot. Turn the hand wheel to take the needle into the fabric a seam allowance' width from the raw edges and then machine stitch the seam, stopping a seam allowance' width from the raw edge of the fabric.

Chain piecing

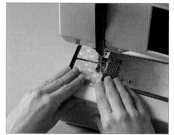

Patchwork pieces can be chain stitched. Stitch to the end of a patch and bring the needle out of the fabric to its highest point. Raise the presser foot and place the next patch under the foot. Continue leaving small gaps between patches then cut apart and press.

Sewing diamonds

It is advisable to secure the edges of seams that will be set in with others by reverse stitching at each end of the seam. Mark the point where the seam allowances will meet with a dot before sewing. Join shapes with slanting sides, such as triangles and diamonds, with the corners offset by 5mm /¼in so that the edges align perfectly when pressed flat.

Sewing right-angle triangles

1 A large patchwork block is made from small shapes that are sewn together. Determine the stitching order before you start, such as sewing triangles together to make squares first. Press the seam to one side and trim the points off the seam allowance as shown.

2 Use pins to hold seamed patchwork pieces together while sewing. Try to sew across the pressed seam to ensure the presser foot runs smoothly over the top. Stitch slowly over the pins to prevent the needle hitting one and breaking.

Pressing seams

While pressing is never a favourite part of making up a patchwork quilt, it is essential. The iron and ironing board should be constantly set up while you are sewing and every single patch should be pressed as it is sewn to another. Miss this step and you may well have uneven seams.

Finger pressing

Small pieces of patchwork can be opened out and creased temporarily with the side of your thumb. Work from the right side of the fabric, keeping both seam allowances to one side. Only ever do this with squares or rectangles. Press curved seams with an iron.

Pressing straight seams

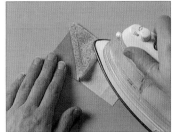

Always press patchwork seam allowances to one side. This makes the seam stronger and prevents it from bursting open. Press the seams towards the dark side if possible or away from an area to be quilted. Use a pressing cloth to prevent unwelcome glazing when pressing from the right side.

Pressing curves

To press fabric, lift the iron up and place it down again, rather than moving it over the fabric. Use a steam iron or a damp pressing cloth. Press curved seams so that the seam allowances lie flat. If this seam had been pressed the other way, the excess patterned fabric would have formed folds on the underside.

Pressing multi-seams

1 When pressing multi-seam joins in hand-pieced patchwork, swirl the seam allowances to open them out and reduce bulk. Press on the wrong side and again from the right side with a pressing cloth.

2 Press seams in the opposite direction where they join to reduce bulk. Press the whole block from the wrong side. In this block all the seam allowances have been pressed away from the light fabric where possible and the seams pressed in opposite directions where two seams meet.

3 No matter how carefully you piece the patchwork, there will always be one or two puckers where seams join. Blocks made from cotton fabrics can be steam-pressed from the right side to smooth out the wrinkles before proceeding to quilt.

Speed-piecing a one-patch block

The square is the simplest shape to sew. Trip Around the World, also known as Sunshine and Shadow, is a simple block made from squares. The pattern is formed by careful arrangement of light, medium and dark fabrics. Depending on where you place the dark squares, you can produce a chequerboard effect or diamonds in bands of light and shade which create a sunshine and shadow effect.

Trip Around the World

Draw out and colour in different patterns on graph paper in light, medium and dark shades. Use the designs below as a guide. Once you have decided on the arrangement, determine how many squares you require in each colour to complete a row the required length. Add up the number of squares in each colour for the complete quilt. Allow extra fabric for seams and for the sashing, borders and binding. When working on a large scale, arrange the blocks on a flat surface before stitching.

Below: Just a few of the different combinations for this design are show here.

1   Place the different fabrics one on top of the other and steam press the layers together. Lift the fabric on to a cutting mat. Trim the edge and then cut strips of the required width allowing 12mm/¹⁄₂in for seam allowances. Turn the strips around and cut into squares.

2   Arrange the squares into the block pattern. Take the first two squares from the top row and sew together. Chain sew the first two squares from each row to save time.

3   Press the seam of the first two squares to one side. Continue adding a square at a time until the top row is complete. Sew the other rows together in the same way. Press the seam allowances in adjacent rows in opposite directions.

4 Pin the first two rows together at each join making sure the seams are aligned exactly. If the seams have been pressed correctly they should lie in opposite directions. Stitch the remaining rows to complete the block. Press all these seams in the same direction. Press all the row seams in the same direction. This creates a strong join.

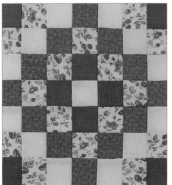

Above: The squares in the Trip Around the World block can be cut small to make a series of blocks that can be set together with sashing strips or larger to make a whole quilt finished off with wide borders in the Amish style.

Above: The blocks of this quilt have been arranged in the Amish style. Pennsylvanian Amish community quilts have one overall design rather than a block construction and are made by working from the centre out towards the edges. This design has the characteristic wide borders typical of Amish quilts but the shape and fabrics are not authentic. The Amish quilts were usually a square shape made of solid colour fabrics as patterned material was considered too worldly. The Amish preferred dark, sombre plain fabrics that reflected their simple way of life.

Working with right-angle triangles

Many patchwork patterns are created from two or four right-angle (or half-square) triangles stitched into squares. Hopscotch, Magic Triangles, and Port and Starboard, for example, are all one-patch designs made up entirely from right-angle triangles. These can be machine stitched and chain pieced or worked by hand in the traditional way.

To make a 30cm/12in block, use 9.7cm/3⁷⁄₈in squares cut in half. It is important when cutting and sewing triangles to create perfect points. The best way to achieve this is by using crisp fabric, cutting accurately and then sewing exactly 5mm/¹⁄₄in from the edge or marked line. If your fabric is flimsy, spray it lightly with starch and press it before cutting.

For half-square triangles (made up of two different coloured triangles), cut two squares 2.2cm/⁷⁄₈in larger than the size of the finished block. For quarter-square triangles (made up of four triangles usually with at least two colours, cut two squares 3cm/1¹⁄₄in larger than the finished block.

Hopscotch

Margaret's Choice

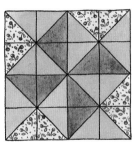

Electric Fan

Magic Triangles

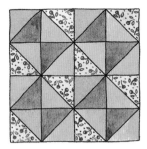

Port and Starboard

Dutchman's Puzzle

Half-square triangles

Steam press two contrasting colour squares right sides together. Draw a diagonal line joining two corners on the wrong side of the lighter fabric. Stitch 5mm/¹⁄₄in to each side of the drawn line. Cut along the drawn line.

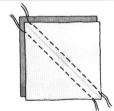

Above: Just two simple blocks make up this stunning quilt design. A plain black block is surrounded by ten pink and black half-square triangles. The blocks are joined together and set on-point to represent fish. The design looks deceptively difficult, but is infact a good example of how simply constructed patches can be arranged to appear complex.

Quarter-square triangles

Make two half-square triangles from contrasting colours. Place right sides together, alternating the colours. Press the pieces together. Draw a diagonal line joining opposite corners. Stitch and cut as before.

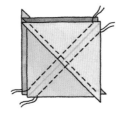

Speed cutting and sewing half-square triangles

If you want to cut down on the amount of drawing around templates and chain piecing, use this method of speed cutting and sewing half-square triangles. Make each square 2.2cm/⅞in larger than the finished triangle. Mark the squares on the wrong side of the lightest coloured fabric and draw a diagonal through each square. You can also buy a special template for marking the stitching lines, which will make this part easier. Take care over cutting and sewing rows of triangles and you should get perfect points each time.

Above: Speed piecing saves hours of laborious cutting.

1 With right sides together, place the lightest colour fabric on top of the darker one. Match the grain lines and steam press. This seals the layers together and makes cutting easier.

2 Place the template on top and mark through the slots on the grid. Alternately, draw the grid and then mark a diagonal line through two corners. Stitch 5mm/¼in to each side of the diagonal line.

3 Machine stitch along the marked diagonal lines, extending the stitching beyond all marked lines. For every square drawn you will get two pieced patchwork squares.

4 Place the stitched fabric on a cutting mat. Cut along the middle of the stitching lines and then along the square grid lines to make half-square triangles. Press the seam allowances to the dark side.

5 Pin and stitch two half-square triangles together. Press the seam towards the dark side. The pieced squares can be chain stitched together, but make sure you leave a long enough chain between the patches to cut them apart easily.

6 When half-square triangles are sewn together in strips the points do not go right to the edge. This is known as a "hung point". Make each point exactly 5mm/¼in from the raw edge and you should get a row of perfect points when stitched.

7 Pin the rows of triangles together, matching the seams and raw edges carefully. Machine stitch 5mm/¼in from the edge. Where possible press the seam away from the light fabric.

American block quilts

The English settlers took patchwork to America, but over the years a distinctive American tradition emerged. In the nineteenth century, quilts were made to commemorate special events. Some of the earliest patterns were in the form of stars created to celebrate the founding of a new state, such as the Ohio Star. These stars were pieced together from simple shapes into square blocks, which were sewn together with sashing strips.

Block-style patchwork became the mainstay of American quilt-making. Patchwork shapes were pieced together to form patterns and given names depending on what the pattern resembled. The names varied depending on where the quilt was made, but often it reflected the lives and surroundings of the people who created the pattern. Frequently the same block design can be known by many different names.

Block quilts are designed on a grid of squares. The most common designs are based on four or nine patches making up the block. Many quilts also depend on blocks being joined together to form an overall pattern.

Types of block quilt

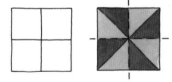

Four patch

A four-patch block can be divided into four equal squares. Each individual patch does not necessarily contain the same pattern, but on some, like the Windmill block, the same patch is rotated to form the pattern. The four-patch block is quite simple to make as the individual pieces tend to be quite large, and easy to sew together. It is a good first block to try.

Nine patch

A nine-patch block is created on a three-by-three square grid. A variety of simple patterns can be created from just one or two shapes, with the most simple being nine squares joined together. The complex nine-patch design illustrated is known as Puss in the Corner. It is created from different size triangles and a square.

Five patch

The five-patch block is less common. It is designed on a five-by-five grid. The pieces are not necessarily all small as some shapes run over two or three squares of the grid. Here the large triangles at the corner of the centre patch could be cut as large triangles or as a square and two smaller triangles. Determine a stitching order before beginning to

Seven patch

Seven-patch blocks are drawn out on a seven-by-seven grid. The most popular seven-patch block is a pattern called Bear's Paw, also known as Hands All Around or Duck's Foot in the Mud. The block resembles four paws facing out from the centre. It is effective when made up in two contrasting plain fabrics. Cut the shapes as large as possible, using strips rather than squares between the paws.

Four-patch blocks

Traditional patchwork blocks are still one of the most popular methods used to piece together a quilt. The same block can be repeated over the whole quilt or different blocks can be made in co-ordinating colours and joined together with sashing strips. Today we have much less time for quilt-making and look for ways of speeding up the process. There are many books on the market containing templates for different block patterns, but it is much quicker and more accurate to cut the patchwork shapes with a rotary cutter. Below you will find cutting plans for making 30cm/12in square four-patch blocks in many popular patterns, along with a suggested diag-rammatic stitching plan. Although the different sizes may seem awkward at first, you will soon become familiar with some measurements.

Cutting plans will work for traditional hand or machine sewing. Once you have cut all the pieces, analyse the block to establish the best stitching order. It is a good idea to sew straight sides together where possible and avoid having to set in pieces. As a rough guide, sew triangles together to form squares, then sew the squares into rows before sewing the rows into blocks. If you intend to speed piece any of these designs, select your fabric carefully. Speed-piecing methods work well on plain or small patterned fabrics that do not have a definite direction. Directional patterns may turn out the wrong way in the block.

Double Pinwheel

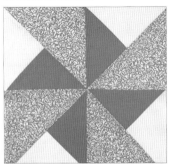

Cutting

1   From cream, cut one square 18.4cm/7¼in. Cut across the diagonals into four triangles (A).

2   From blue, cut one square 18.4cm/7¼in. Cut into four triangles (B).

3   From patterned fabric, cut two squares, each 17.5cm/6⅞in. Cut each into two triangles (C).

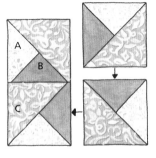

1   Cut all the pieces required for the block. Pin the small triangles together along one short side and machine stitch 5mm/¼in from the edge. Press the seam towards the darker coloured triangle.

2   Pin the long edge of the large triangle to the pieced triangle. Machine stitch and press the seam away from the lightest fabric. Trim any points that are jutting out from the square.

3   Arrange the squares in the pinwheel pattern. Pin and sew the two left-hand squares together, then join the other two. Press the seams in opposite directions then pin and stitch both rectangles together to complete the block.

Windmill

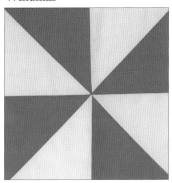

Cutting

1 From cream, cut two squares, each 17.5cm/6⅞in. Cut each across the diagonal into two triangles (A).

2 From blue, cut two squares, each 17.5cm/6⅞in. Cut each across the diagonal into two triangles (B).

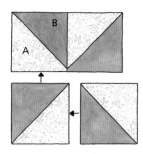

Road to Heaven

Cutting

1 From cream, cut five squares, each 10cm/3⅞in. Cut each into two triangles (A).

2 From blue, cut one square 17.5cm/6⅞in. Cut into two triangles (B).
• Cut three squares, each 10cm/3⅞in. Cut each into two triangles (C).

3 From navy, cut four squares, each 7.5cm/3in (D).

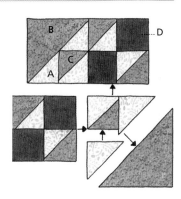

Flower Basket

Cutting

1 From cream, cut one square 17.5cm/6⅞in. Cut into two triangles (A). Discard one triangle.
• Cut two rectangles, each 9 x 16.5cm/3½ x 6½in (B).
• Cut eight squares, each 10cm/3⅞in. Cut each into two triangles (C).

2 From blue, cut three squares each 10cm/3⅞in. Cut each into two triangles (D).

3 From navy, cut one square 17.5cm/6⅞in. Cut into two triangles and discard one (E).
• Cut one square 10cm/3⅞in. Cut into two triangles (F).

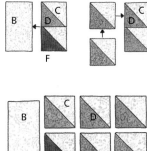

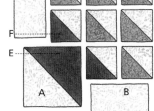

Flock of Geese

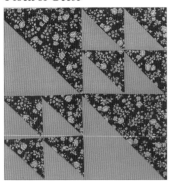

Cutting

1 From pink, cut one square 17.5cm/6⁷⁄₈in. Cut into two triangles. (A).
• Cut four squares each 10cm/3⁷⁄₈in. Cut each into two triangles (B).

2 From patterned fabric, cut one square 17.5cm/6⁷⁄₈in. Cut into two triangles (C).
• Cut four squares each 10cm/3⁷⁄₈in. Cut each into two triangles (D).

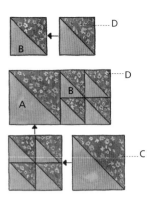

Crockett Cabin

Cutting

1 From cream, cut two squares, each 10cm/3⁷⁄₈in. Cut each into two triangles (A).
• Cut eight squares, each 8.9cm/3¹⁄₂in (B).

2 From pink, cut two squares, each 10cm/3⁷⁄₈in. Cut each into two triangles (C).
• Cut four squares, each 8.9cm/3¹⁄₂in (D).

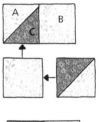

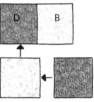

Crosses and Losses

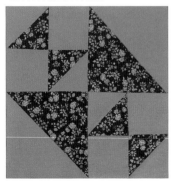

Cutting

1 From green, cut one square 17.5cm/6⁷⁄₈in. Cut across the diagonal into two triangles (A).
• Cut two squares, each 10cm/3⁷⁄₈in. Cut each into two triangles (B).
• Cut four squares, each 8.9cm/3¹⁄₂in (C).

2 From patterned fabric, cut one square 17.5cm/6⁷⁄₈in. Cut across the diagonal into two triangles (D)
• Cut two squares, each 10cm/3⁷⁄₈in. Cut each into two triangles (E).

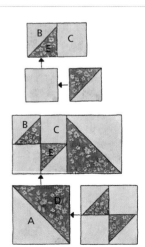

Spool and Bobbin

Cutting

1 From cream, cut two squares each 16.5cm/6¹⁄₂in (A).
• Cut two squares each 10cm/3⅞in. Cut each across the diagonal into two triangles (B).

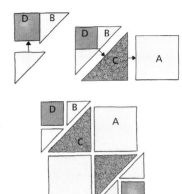

2 From pink, cut one square 17.5cm/6⅞in. Cut across the diagonal into two triangles (C).
• Cut two squares each 8.9cm/3¹⁄₂in (D).

Right: Panels in this sampler quilt feature the following nine designs: 1, 3, 13 and 15 Bear's Paw; 2, Honey Bee; 4 and 11 Churn Dash; 5, Dutchman's Puzzle; 6 and 10 Patience Corner; 7 and 12 Star of Hope; 8 Le Moyne Star; and 9 Jenny's Star.

The design features four-, seven- and nine-patch sample blocks. Though the blocks appear random, they have been arranged so that colours and corners are symmetrical. The sashing strips are made of three strips pieced together, and the corner posts are all small nine-patch blocks.

Making a sampler quilt is a good way of trying out lots of new designs. Just keep the colour scheme co-ordinated and the finished blocks a uniform size.

1	2	3
4	5	6
7	8	9
10	11	12
13	14	15

Nine-patch blocks

If you enjoy working with small units, working with nine-patch blocks is a good way to learn to accurately match seams. Many of the designs shown here could be further divided to make the piecing sequence challenging.

Contrary Wife

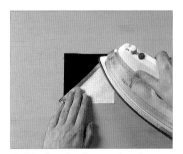

Cutting

1 From cream, cut two squares, each 12.4cm/4⁷⁄₈in squares. Cut each into two triangles (A).

2 From blue, cut five squares, each 11.4cm/4¹⁄₂in (B).

3 From navy, cut two squares, each 12.4cm/4⁷⁄₈in. Cut each into two triangles (C).

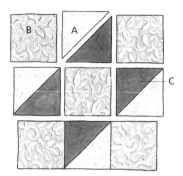

1 Pin the triangles together along the longer edge and machine stitch 5mm/¹⁄₄in from the edge. Press the seam towards the dark coloured triangle. Trim any points that are jutting out from the square.

2 For the top and bottom rows, pin a blue patch on to each side of the pieced square. Machine stitch 5mm/¹⁄₄in from the edge and press the seam away from the lighest colour.

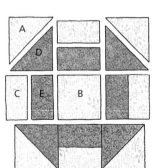

3 For the middle row, pin and sew a pieced square to each side of a plain square, making sure that the pieced squares all face in the right direction when opened out. Join the rows together and press the seams to one side.

Churn Dash

Cutting

1 From cream, cut two squares, each 12.4cm/4⁷⁄₈in. Cut each into two triangles (A).
• Cut one square 11.4cm/4¹⁄₂in (B).
• Cut four rectangles each 6.4cm/2¹⁄₂in x 11.4cm/4¹⁄₂in (C).

2 From blue, cut two squares, each 12.4cm/4⁷⁄₈in. Cut each into two triangles (D).
• Cut four rectangles, each 6.4cm/2¹⁄₂in x 11.4cm/4¹⁄₂in (E).

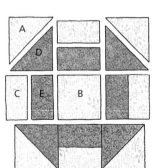

Jacob's Ladder

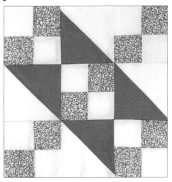

Cutting

1 From cream, cut two squares, each 12.4cm/4⁷⁄₈in. Cut each into two triangles (A).
• Cut ten squares, each 6.4cm/2½in (B).

2 From blue pattern, cut ten squares, each 6.4cm/2½in (C).

3 From solid blue, cut two squares, each 12.4cm/4⁷⁄₈in. Cut each into two triangles (D).

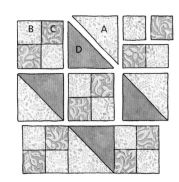

Puss in the Corner

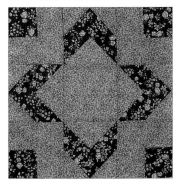

Cutting

1 From pink, cut one square 13.3cm/5¼in. Cut into four triangles (A).
• Cut two squares, each 12.4cm/4⁷⁄₈in squares. Cut each into two triangles (B).
• Cut one square 11.4cm/4½in for the centre (C).
• Cut eight squares, each 7.3cm/2⁷⁄₈in. Cut each into two triangles (D).

2 From dark fabric, cut one square 13.3cm/5¼in. Cut into four triangles (E).
• Cut four squares, each 7.3cm/2⁷⁄₈in. Cut each into two triangles (F).
• Cut four squares each 6.4cm/2½in for the corners (G).

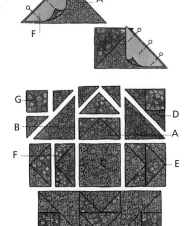

Darting Birds

Cutting

1 From cream pattern, cut three squares, each 12.4cm/4⁷⁄₈in. Cut each into two triangles (A).
• Cut one square 11.4cm/4½in (B).

2 From pink, cut two squares, each 12.4cm/4⁷⁄₈in. Cut each into two triangles (C).

3 From green, cut one square 12.4cm/4⁷⁄₈in. Cut into two triangles (D).
• Cut two squares, each 11.4cm/4½in (E).

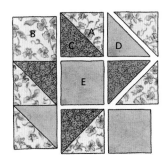

Steps to the Altar

Cutting

1 From cream, cut six squares, each 6.4cm/2½in (A).
• Cut three squares, each 7.3cm/2⅞in. Cut each into two triangles (B).
• Cut two squares, each 11.4cm/4½in (C).
• Cut two squares, each 12.4cm/4⅞in. Cut each into two triangles (D). Discard one D triangle.

2 From pink pattern, cut nine squares, each 6.4cm/2½in (E).

3 From dark pattern fabric, cut one square 12.4cm/4⅞in. Cut across the diagonal into two triangles (F).

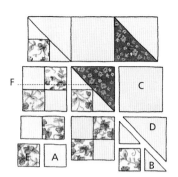

Eccentric Star

Cutting

1 From cream pattern, cut four squares, each 12.4cm/4⅞in. Cut each into two triangles (A).

2 From pink pattern, cut one, 11.4cm/4½in square for the centre.

3 From red, cut four squares each 12.4cm/4⅞in. Cut each into two triangles (C).

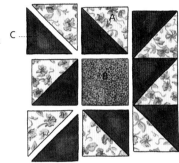

Shoo Fly

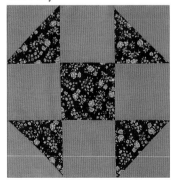

Cutting

1 From pink, cut two squares each 12.4cm/4⅞in. Cut each into two triangles (A).
• Cut four squares each 11.4cm/4½in (B).

2 From dark pattern fabric, cut two squares each 12.4cm/4⅞in. Cut each into 2 triangles (C).
• Cut one square 11.4cm/4½in (D).

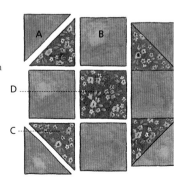

Cat's Cradle

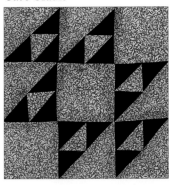

Cutting

1 From blue pattern fabric, cut three squares each 12.4cm/4⅞in (A).

• Cut three squares each 11.4cm/4½in and cut each in half across the diagonal (B).

• Cut three squares each 7.3cm/2⅞in squares. Cut each in half across the diagonal (C)

• From navy, cut nine squares each 7.3cm/2⅞in. Cut each in half across the diagonal (D).

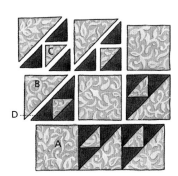

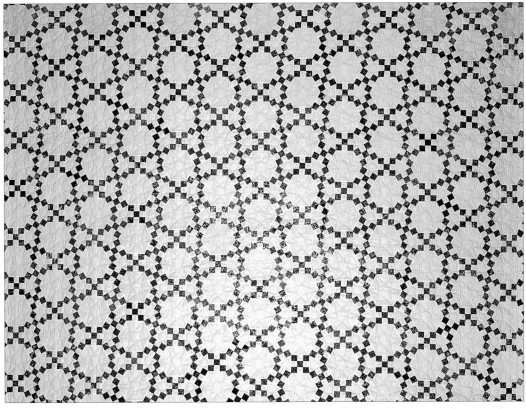

Above: This exquisite geometric design has been entirely hand stitched. The nine-patch blocks are made of 2.5cm/1in squares of cream and small floral prints. Hexagons and triangles form the remainder of the design. When viewed from a distance this mosaic-like composition appears to be formed of interlocking circles.

Piecing star designs

One of the most popular patchwork motifs, the star has been used throughout history as a divine symbol in the decorative arts of all civilizations. The simplified star appears in hundreds of different forms throughout the world with varying numbers of points.

The star was a very popular motif in colonial America. Some patchwork star motifs were designed to commemorate the creation of a state, such as the Ohio Star or the Virginia Star, and others like the Le Moyne Star were named after famous people.

Patchwork stars normally have six, eight or 12 points and are generally made from triangles or diamonds. The easiest stars to make are based on a block pattern. The Ohio Star is a nine-patch design as is the more unusual 54/40 or Fight Star. Other stars, such as the Le Moyne Star, are created from diamonds using an eight-seam join.

Right: Echoing and interlocking stars pieced in vibrant and muted colour silks make up this Star of India design.

54/40 or Fight Star

Women weren't supposed to have a political opinion in the nineteenth century but often used their quilt making to express their views. The 54/40 or Fight Star was created in response to the dispute between the British Hudson Bay Company and the United States of America over the northern boundary of the United States in 1818. The numbers refer to the degree of latitude that the Americans wanted to establish as the boundary between Canada and the USA. After a bitter dispute a treaty was signed in 1846 which established the boundary where it is today.

1 Using the template provided, trace the patchwork pieces on to template plastic and cut them out. Calculate the number of pieces required and draw them on to the different fabrics. Mark 5mm/¼in seam allowances around each piece and cut out.

2 Put the middle-sized corner of a dark triangle and the point of the light triangle together. Use a pin or the needle to match the corners of the seam allowances exactly. Sew the pieces together along the marked line on the long edge with tiny running stitches. Join the second dark triangle to the other side.

Right: Half- and quarter-square triangles and single patches made into different-sized star blocks form the basis of this design. The collage-like design is an exercise in using a restricted colour palette of cleverly placed blues, greys and pinks.

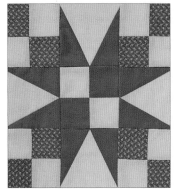

3 Press the seam allowances towards the dark side, then join four small squares together to form five blocks. Press the centres open, spiralling the seam allowances to reduce bulk. Pin and stitch the pieced squares together in rows in the correct order. Press the seams to one side and the seams in adjacent rows to the opposite side.

4 Pin the rows together, matching the seams carefully. Stitch the rows together and press all the seams to one side.

Above: The Fight Star, a nine-patch block, looks complicated to piece, but five of the nine blocks are made of a simple four-patch design in which small single patches are joined together.

Le Moyne Star

The Le Moyne Star is made from eight diamonds that meet in the centre in an eight-seam join. This representational design takes practice to master and accurate cutting and piecing are essential.

The star can be made by hand or by machine. The centre of a hand stitched, eight-seam join is pressed in a spiral to reduce bulk. The finished star can then be made into a block by insetting squares into the corners and triangles along each side.

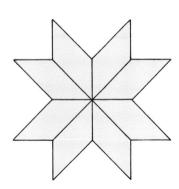

1 Cut eight diamonds from fabric and mark a dot in the corners of the seam allowances on the wrong side. Pin and stitch pairs of diamonds together between the dots, reverse stitching at each end to secure the threads. Press the seams to one side. Pin two pairs of diamonds together matching seam allowances.

2 Place the pieces under the presser foot. Turn the hand wheel to make sure the needle goes in exactly at the point of the seam allowance. Sew the seam and press to one side. Pin the two halves of the star together. Check that the centre point matches by inserting a pin through all the layers. Stitch slowly over the pin.

3 When the star is machine-pieced, press the final seams to one side. If the star has been hand-pieced, spiral the seam allowances and open out the centre. Press the seams to one side and then press the centre rosette flat.

VIRGINIA STAR

The Virginia Star is a complicated block made from a large number of diamonds.

• Although the star can be stitched by machine, it is probably safer to sew it by hand, as diamonds may need careful adjustments to get the points absolutely accurate.

• Use the template provided.

Setting in patchwork pieces

When used to fill in angles such as the spaces between the points of a Le Moyne Star, patchwork pieces have to be "set in". Pieces can be set in by hand or by machine, but take care that the seams on the star are stitched accurately along the seam allowances and stop 5mm/¼in from the edge. Secure the ends of the eight-point seam by tying off the threads or with a few back stitches.

1 With right sides together, pin the patchwork piece to be inset along one side of the angle, matching the corners. Stitch from dot to dot.

2 Pin the inset patch down the other side of the angle. Insert the needle exactly at the point and stitch the seam. Press the seam to one side.

Right: This hand-stitched basket block is made of four diamonds, stitched into pairs. A right-angle triangle is inset between the points of the diamond at each side. The two halves of the basket top are stitched together and a square is inset between the points. The base of the basket is a large triangle set above a half-square triangle. The block is completed with two rectangular units and the whole block is set on point.

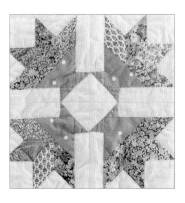

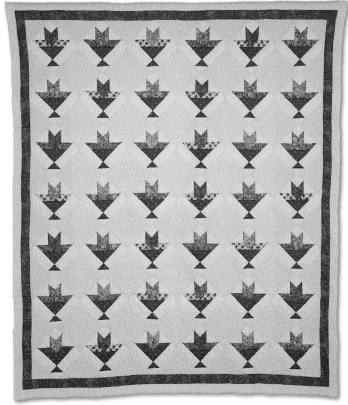

Left: This basket design is similar to the one above, except here the base of the basket is made of three half-square triangles.

Joining curved seams

Curvilinear designs are more difficult to sew than straight seams because the two edges of the curved seam do not lie flat for sewing. One seam has to be pinned and eased on to the other. To make this process easier the curved edge should be cut on the bias. Place the straight sides of the template on the straight grain of the fabric and the curve is likely to be on the bias.

Drunkard's Path

This is one of many patchwork designs made from the same two-piece patch. It is made from 16 identical squares, each with a small contrasting quarter circle in one corner. The patches can be arranged to create different patchwork designs, (see below and right). In the United Kingdom the patches are traditionally arranged to make the design called Robbing Peter to Pay Paul.

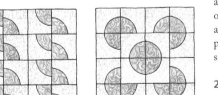

1 Trace and cut out the template provided. Cut the template into two along the marked arc. Fold the pieces on the diagonal through the curved arc and mark the centre line on each piece. Mark the quarter points to each side of the centre line.

2 Place each template on a different colour fabric.

3 Keeping the straight edges along the grain of the fabric, draw around each template. Add the seam allowance and cut out. Cut notches at each mark along the curves to make matching easier.

4 With right sides together and the quarter circle to the top, match the notches and pin, easing the fabric to fit. Use as many pins as necessary to get a smooth line.

5 Work two or three tiny back stitches and then sew tiny running stitches along the curved line. Cut the rest of the pieces and stitch them together to make 16 squares.

Right: "Flowers on the Drunkard's Path" combines machine piecing, machine appliqué and machine quilting.

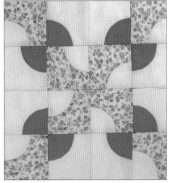

6 If stitching by machine, pin the curved edge with the larger piece on top as this makes the fabric easy to control. Work slowly, removing the pins as you reach them. Press the seam towards the larger piece.

7 Arrange the squares to form the required pattern. Sew the squares into rows. Press the seams in adjacent rows in opposite directions. Pin the rows with right sides together matching the seams carefully. Stitch together to form the completed block.

Above: The Drunkard's Path design is more complicated to piece together because of the curved patches.

English crazy patchwork

Crazy patchwork is unlike any other form of patchwork because it does not use a template. Irregular patchwork pieces are simply arranged in a pleasing way on a foundation fabric and stitched down. As a result, no two crazy patchwork quilts are ever the same.

The origin of crazy patchwork is uncertain, but most people believe it evolved from the practice of patching worn bedcovers. Eventually, after many patches had been added, the effect was like an irregular patchwork quilt. Crazy patchwork reached the height of its popularity in Britain and America in the late nineteenth century when furnishing styles were decorative and very opulent. Irregular pieces were cut from exquisite silks and velvet and the finished patchwork was richly embellished with beads, ribbons, lace and embroidery.

Crazy patchwork quilts are rarely padded and never quilted because of the difficulty of sewing through the foundation fabric. Instead, the patchwork is lined and tied, then bound. Large crazy patchwork quilts are difficult to handle while sewing. It is easier to make small blocks that can be set together to make a large quilt.

Above: Crazy patchwork is always embellished with traditional hand embroidery stitches.

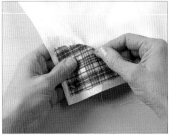

1 Cut a piece of calico slightly larger than required for the foundation. This can be the size of the finished piece or about 30cm/12in square for a block as shown here. Cut the first irregular-shaped piece of fabric and baste it in one corner of the foundation. Choose fabrics of a similar weight and avoid scraps that are beginning to show signs of wear.

2 Pin on a second piece of fabric, overlapping the first by 5–12mm/ ¼–½in. The amount of overlap will depend on the thickness of the fabric and whether it frays easily. Turn under the raw edge of the second piece where it overlaps the first. Hem stitch the folded edge to the foundation through all layers. Continue to add pieces until the entire area is covered.

3 Work an embroidery stitch such as herringbone, feather or chain stitch along each seam of the patchwork. Use an embroidery thread such as stranded cotton or coton à broder on cotton fabrics, and crewel wool (yarn) or coton perlé for velvet and other heavy fabrics.

4 Embroider the individual patchwork shapes with isolated stitches and small, ornate embroidery motifs. The patchwork can also be embellished with beads, lace and other small treasures.

Above and left: Crazy patchwork reached the height of its popularity in Victorian England, when opulent velvets, brocades and thick, silk fabrics were fashionable. It is unlikely that these quilts would have been used as bedcovers, since the highly elaborate nature of their surface decoration would render them unsuitable. Instead they would be used as throws for furniture.

Crazy patchwork can be totally random, with the entire surface covered with a hodge podge of patches, or it can be worked in small block size pieces, and the blocks stitched together at the end. Old examples of crazy patchwork frequently have other well-known blocks such as Log Cabin designs incorporated into their scheme. These quilts may well have been samplers used to test out ideas or to learn how to stitch a block.

Log Cabin designs

This design represents the wall of a cabin built from logs. The centre square is usually red to signify the fire glowing and is often known as the chimney. The light and dark sides of the block represent sunshine and shade on the cabin walls.

Even if you decide not to use red for the centre square, use the same colour throughout to unify the quilt design. Log Cabin patchwork has infinite variations, not only in the way the strips are cut and pieced, but also in the way the blocks are sewn together. Always stitched together without sashing, the most common variations are Light and Dark, Barn Raising and Straight Furrow.

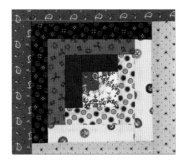

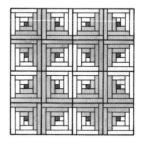

Light and Dark is formed by sewing together groups of four blocks with the dark corners to the centre.

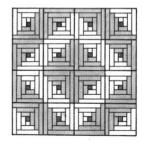

Barn Raising radiates out from the centre in alternating light and dark diamonds.

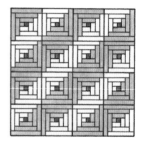

Straight Furrow is a strong diagonal pattern with light and dark bands.

Above: This Barn Raising quilt has been made from 100 log cabin blocks. Each block is made of folded strips of satin, silk and cotton.

Top: A single log cabin block. Choose small-scale patterns or solid colours in light and dark tones for the best effect.

Piecing the Log Cabin block

The size of the finished block will depend on the width of strips that you use. Add a 12mm/½in seam allowance on each strip. A standard strip is cut 4cm/1½in wide.

The most common way to sew Log Cabin is on to a foundation fabric. Choose a fabric similar in weight and fibre content to the patchwork fabric so that they will wash and handle in the same way. A medium-weight calico is a suitable fabric. A standard block has nine strips across the block, so if your finished strips are 2.5cm/1in wide, cut a 24cm/9¾in square.

1 Plan the block by cutting 9mm/³⁄₈in strips of light and dark fabric in a mixture of toning shades. Cut equal numbers of light and dark shades for each block. For a standard block you will need four different light and dark shades, which are cut into different sizes and arranged around the centre.

2 Cut the foundation fabric square. Fold it in quarters diagonally, then baste along the crease lines. Cut a 4cm/1½in square from the fabric for the centre and baste it, right side up, in the centre of the foundation. The corners of the centre square should touch the basted crease lines.

3 Pin the first light fabric strip on top of the centre square, with right sides together, matching the right-hand raw edges. Machine stitch carefully over the pins 5mm/¼in from the edges. Trim the strip level with the left-hand side of the centre square, open flat and press.

4 Pin the second strip of this fabric along the top edge of both the first two pieces. Machine stitch 5mm/¼in from the edge to the end of the squares and trim off the excess.

5 Continue in this way, alternately adding two dark and two light strips. Trim and press open the strips every time you sew and turn the foundation fabric square around ready to add the next strip. The diagonals of the Log Cabin block will only line up when it is a square, but they are a useful guide to make sure the strips are being sewn on to the foundation fabric accurately.

6 Make sufficient blocks to complete the quilt and arrange as required before sewing together. Sew the finished blocks together without sashing strips. Hand quilting is rather difficult with the foundation fabric method because of the extra layer of fabric. Instead, use tie quilting at each corner and in the centre of each block, and finish with a simple binding. Alternatively Log Cabin can be machine quilted "in-the-ditch" between each log.

Pineapple Log Cabin

Unlike the other types of Log Cabin patchwork, Pineapple Log Cabin is easier to sew from templates than from strips. This design is also known as Windmill Blades. The strips are cut in the shape of a triangle with its top sliced off, and radiate out from the centre, in light and dark bands.

Plan the order of the different fabrics and trace pattern pieces for each one. If you are stitching by machine, add a 5mm/¼in seam allowance all around each strip before cutting out the templates. Draw around the pattern pieces on the wrong side of the fabric and cut them out. Keep the pieces in order and label them if you are making a lot of blocks, so that you know which strip to add next.

1 Pin the first two triangles to opposite sides of the square, with right sides together and stitch using 5mm/¼in seam allowances. Open out the triangles and press flat. Pin the other two triangles to the other sides of the square and stitch. Open out the triangles and press flat to form a square. Trim the seam allowances at each stage as required.

2 Pin two matching triangles from the next layer to opposite sides of the new square. Use the edges of the square as a guide when pinning and stitching the triangles in place to keep the pieces exactly in line. Stitch as before and press flat. Pin and stitch the other two triangles, then press flat.

3 Begin to add the strips, sewing two strips to opposite sides and press them flat before adding the other two. Use the previous join as a guideline as well as the raw edge to keep the block as straight as possible while sewing.

4 Continue building up the block in this way, adding the cut pieces in the correct order and alternating between light and dark shades in each group of four. Finally, add a large triangle to each corner and press flat.

5 For the best effect, join the pineapple blocks without sashing. The complete design only becomes obvious once several blocks have been stitched together. Quilt each seam with "in-the-ditch" or outline quilting and finish with a simple binding.

Above: The effectiveness of the Pineapple Log Cabin block can only be seen when it is pieced together with a number of other blocks.

Above: The pineapple log cabin looks effective when worked in just two contrasting colours.

Below: This multi-coloured silk courthouse steps design has no wadding or quilting.

OTHER LOG CABIN-TYPE DESIGNS

The appearance of the basic log cabin block can be altered by changing the stitching order of the strips or by varying the width of the logs.

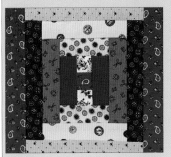

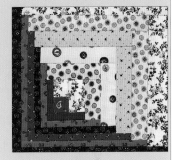

COURTHOUSE STEPS

This design is built up by sewing the two light and two dark strips on opposite sides of the central square instead of adjacent to each other.

OFF-CENTRE LOG CABIN

This design is formed from strips cut in two different widths. Cut one set of strips 4cm/1½in wide and the other set 2.5cm/1in wide. Set the blocks together so that they form wavy lines.

Seminole patchwork

Around the beginning of the twentieth century, traders supplied the Seminole Indians of Florida with hand-wheel sewing machines. Using this new equipment the Seminole people devised a unique strip patchwork that can only be worked by machine. Seminole patchwork uses vivid colours with strong contrasts which make even tiny pieces quite distinct.

The basic technique of Seminole patchwork is to sew strips of fabric together. These stitched panels are cut straight or diagonally into strips. The new strips are then rearranged and stitched to form intricate panels.

Above: Strips of Seminole patchwork can be sewn together without sashing for a very dazzling effect or they can be broken up by sashing strips. Black fabric sets off the bright colours and patterns very effectively.

Cutting the strips

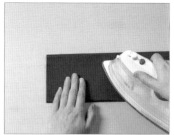

1   Fold the fabric in half lengthways, matching the selvages and steam press the layers. Place the fabric on the cutting mat. Line one of the crossways markings on the ruler with the top folded edge. Hold the ruler firmly and hold the blade of the rotary cutter against the ruler edge. Roll the blade up and down to trim the raw edge of the fabric.

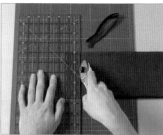

2   Turn the fabric around so that the cut edge is to the left. Use the markings on the ruler to cut the width of strip you require plus 12mm/¹⁄₂in seam allowance.

3   Keep moving the ruler across the fabric to cut as many strips as required, remembering that each strip has four layers.

The chequerboard

1   From each of two contrasting fabrics, cut one strip 4cm/1¹⁄₂in wide. Sew the strips together. Press the seam to one side. Cut the strips into pieces 4cm/1¹⁄₂in wide.

2   With right sides together, pin the pieces together so that the seams face in opposite directions and one colour is on top of a different colour. Sew the pieces together into a chequerboard.

Joining three strips

1 Cut one strip from each of three colours, making the centre strip narrower than the other two. Join the strips together and press the seams in one direction. Cut the strip at an angle and then cut diagonal strips of equal width from the band of fabric.

2 Pin the pieces together with right sides facing. Pin carefully so that the top edge of one centre strip touches the bottom edge of the next. Stitch with a 5mm/¼in seam allowance and press the seams in the same direction.

3 Place the panel on the cutting mat and trim a long edge straight. Turn the strip around and line the grid lines up against the raw edge to cut a straight panel.

Joining five strips

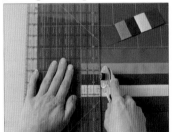

1 Cut five differently coloured fabric strips the same width and stitch them together. Press the seams in the same direction. Cut the panel into strips the same width as the original strip.

2 Pin the strips right sides together. Stagger the strips and match the seams. Stitch, then press the seams in the same direction.

3 Place the panel flat on the cutting mat and trim the triangles from one edge. Turn the strip around and line the grid lines up against the raw edge to cut a straight panel.

Joining two sets of strips

1 Cut five strips – three wide and two narrow – from two fabrics. Stitch together alternating the colours. Trim the raw edges and cut into fairly wide strips. Press the seams flat.

2 Cut two wide strips and one narrow one from two contrasting fabrics. Sew them into a second panel the same width as the first. Trim the end and cut into narrower strips.

3 Pin the strips together, staggering them so that the second seam of the first panel matches the first seam of the second panel. Sew the seams and press in one direction. Trim the edges.

Hand stitched appliqué

Appliqué takes its name from the French verb "appliquer" meaning to apply. The technique involves cutting fabric to shape and sewing it on to a background fabric. Appliqué has evolved into a highly decorative art and is used in various forms all over the world. The people of Hawaii and Laos, for example, stitch intricate forms of reverse appliqué, and in North America wonderful pictorial appliqué is sewn.

Raw-edge appliqué

Use this method for non-fray fabrics such as felt, or to give a ragged look to raw edges. Iron light-weight interfacing to the wrong side of woven fabrics before cutting out, or iron the appliqué to the main fabric with fusible bonding web.

Felt appliqué looks particularly effective if blanket stitch or another embroidery stitch is worked around the edge of each piece.

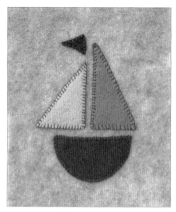

Above: Felt always has a neat trimmed raw edge that does not fray. For this reason it is a good choice for beginners.

Alternately, you may choose to make a feature of frayed raw edges, choosing fabrics such as scrim or other loosely woven fabrics that fray easily.

1   Cut templates to the size of the finished shape. Pin each to your choice of fabric. Cut out shapes without seams and pin them to the main fabric.

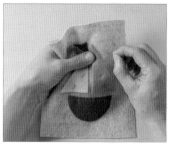

2   To stab stitch around the edge of the appliqué, bring a threaded needle up through the fabric next to the appliqué. Take it back down catching the edge of the appliqué.

Traditional appliqué

Choose simple shapes for appliqué because it is difficult to turn under raw edges on intricate shapes and keep lines smooth on tight curves. Cut motifs so that the grain matches the main fabric. Appliqué can be worked with or without an embroidery hoop. Sew the appliqué carefully to avoid fabric distortion.

1   Cut a template to the finished size and draw around it on the right side of the fabric. Cut out, adding a 5mm/¹/₄in seam allowance all around.

2   Clip into the seam on inward-facing curves, and notch outward-facing curves. Cut up to the marked line, but not beyond it. Straight edges do not need clipping.

3   Pin the appliqué in place. Baste 12mm/¹/₂in in from the raw edge. Turn under the raw edge with the needle tip so that the pencil line disappears. Hem stitch along the fold.

Using freezer paper

Freezer paper is a wax-coated paper that is used to wrap food. The paper sticks firmly, but temporarily to fabric if pressed with a medium iron. It is non-stain and can be peeled off easily.

1   Cut a template the exact size of the appliqué and draw around it on the dull side of the freezer paper. Cut out the shape along the lines.

2   Iron the shape to the wrong side of the fabric and cut out, adding a 5mm/¹⁄₄in seam allowance all around.

Above: Strips and squares of brightly coloured fabric have been applied to a dark ground. The appliqué squares have been frayed and overstitched with free-style machine embroidery.

3   Snip inward-facing curves close to the paper and make a notch in the seam of outward-facing curves. Turn under the raw edge and baste. Press again. The wax on the freezer paper will help the shape retain a crisp, neat edge.

4   Pin the shape in place on the main fabric and hem stitch in place. Use a small, fine needle threaded with a colour to match the appliqué or background fabric.

5   Hem most of the way around the shape and then remove the basting stitches. Slide your finger between the freezer paper and the appliqué and ease it out carefully. Hem the last section of the appliqué in place.

Machine appliqué

Machine appliqué is a quick and easy way to apply shapes to a background fabric. For a smooth, unpuckered finish, the fabric shape must be fixed in place before sewing. The easiest way to do this is with fusible bonding web, which will give a neat fixed shape without pin or needle marks. Machine appliqué can be worked with the presser foot in place or by free machine stitching.

Using fusible bonding web

Before beginning machine appliqué using a presser foot, back the background fabric with light- or medium-weight interfacing or fabric stabilizer to prevent puckering. The excess stabilizer can be torn away when the appliqué is complete. The interfacing will remain in place.

Fusible bonding web is sold in narrow strips or in large sheets. It is a thin mesh of glue backed with paper that is used to attach the pieces of fabric smoothly and cleanly.

1 Cut a piece of interfacing to fit the background fabric. Fix to the wrong side using a hot iron. If the fabric is unsuitable for interfacing, use fabric stabilizer instead.

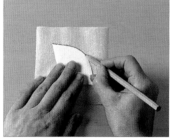

2 Place the appliqué template right side down on the shiny paper side of the fusible bonding web. Trace around the template.

3 Place fusible bonding web, shiny paper side up on the wrong side of your fabric choice. Press with a medium-hot iron. Allow to cool, then cut out the shape along the lines.

4 Peel the paper backing off and press in your chosen position on the background fabric using a hot iron.

5 Set the width to medium satin stitch and loosen the top tension slightly. Stitch around the edge of the shape. For a wider line, stitch on top of the first narrow zigzag.

6 Add details such as stems and veins. Here, the stem is worked in satin stitch and the veins with a straight stitch.

Above: This clever design is made of plain and patched blocks set on-point. The blocks have been carefully planned to create a three-dimensional effect. The cyclist has been appliquéd to the pieced ground and attached with very closely worked machine satin stitch.

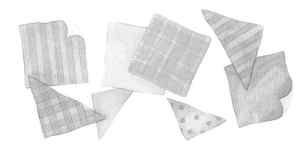

Baltimore quilt

An appliqué quilt was kept for best because of all the work that went into it and also because it wasn't as hard wearing as a patchwork quilt. The finest quilts were made by women in the Baltimore area. The beautiful wreaths, garlands and baskets of flowers that adorned these nineteenth-century quilts have become standard appliqué designs. These are built up in stages because pieces overlap and are generally complex.

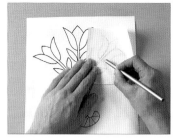

1   Enlarge the design provided and transfer it by your choice of method to the right side of the centre of the fabric. Trace the various shapes on to the shiny side of freezer paper. (To reverse the design, trace it on to the dull side instead.) Cut out the shapes.

2   Iron each freezer paper shape to the wrong side of the required fabric. Cut each shape out adding a 5mm/ ¼in seam allowance all around. Notch outward-facing curves and snip inward-facing curves. Trim points carefully to reduce bulk.

3   Determine the stitching order for each section of the design. All pieces in the background are stitched first.

4   Slip stitch the shapes in place, using the point of the needle to turn under a 5mm/¼in hem. Match the thread to the appliqué or use a dark neutral shade such as grey.

5   The Cornucopia is formed from 12mm/½in strips of fabric sewn together in bands of light, medium and dark fabric. Cut out and pin in position on the background fabric. Turn under the edge and slip stitch in place. Press from the right side with a damp cloth.

Above: The Cornucopia is a traditional favourite design. Use your choice of appliqué method to attach it neatly and accurately to the background.

Broderie perse

Broderie perse is a technique of cutting motifs from one fabric, rearranging them, and stitching them on to a new background fabric. The technique developed in the seventeenth and eighteenth centuries as a means of making precious fragments of fabric last longer.

Above: A hand appliquéd and hand quilted Baltimore tablerunner.

Designs were originally made using the brightly coloured chintz fabrics imported from India. When the English government imposed a ban on these fabrics to protect its own textile industry, the technique increased in popularity. In nineteenth-century America special fabrics were printed with suitable motifs for Broderie perse.

1 Wash and press the fabric. Cut around your appliqué shape leaving a 5mm/¼in seam allowance. Do not cut tiny details – these can be added at a later stage. Clip into the seam allowance to make it easier to turn under the edge. Notch outward-facing curves. Do not cut more than 3mm/⅛in into the seam allowance.

3 Sew all the pieces of appliqué in place and press from the right side with a damp cloth. Embroider any details needed to complete the design.

2 Pin the shape in position on the background. Thread a needle with a colour to match the appliqué. Use the point of the needle to turn under the edge and slip stitch in place with small, almost invisible stitches.

Below: Traditionally broderie perse designs incorporated exotic floral motifs.

Shadow appliqué

Shadow appliqué is simple to work. Brightly coloured fabric is sandwiched between a sheer top layer and a base fabric. The sheer top and base are traditionally white, but subtle and unusual effects can be achieved by using different colours instead. The appliqué design needs to be strongly coloured to allow for the way it dulls when the sheer top layer is placed over the top.

1 Make a template of the design provided. Trace each shape on to fusible bonding web. Draw the shapes in groups according to the colour of fabric that will be used.

2 Iron the bonding web on to the wrong side of the fabric following the manufacturer's instructions. Cut out the shapes along the lines. Peel off the backing paper.

3 Place the background over the template. Position the shapes on the fabric using the template as a guide. Cover the shapes with a muslin cloth and carefully press to secure them.

4 Place a sheer fabric such as voile, organdie or organza on top and pin in place. If you want to quilt the appliqué, add wadding and backing under the base fabric at this stage.

5 Work small running stitches close to the appliqué, through all layers. Stitch around every shape even if it is overlapping or sitting on top of another. Once the appliqué is complete, details such as leaf veins can be worked in running stitch.

Above: Shadow appliqué can be as simple or as complex as you make it.

Hawaiian appliqué

This colourful and intricate form of appliqué has been practised by the people of Hawaii since the early nineteenth century. Several distinctive features set Hawaiian appliqué apart from other reverse appliqué designs. It is created using a paper cut-out and when complete, it is always quilted with rows of echo quilting, which are said to resemble the waves lapping on the shore of the people's island home.

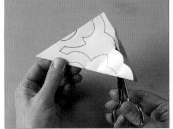

1 Choose the size for the appliqué, then cut a paper square the size of the appliqué plus 9mm–2.2cm/³/₈–⁷/₈in. Fold it in quarters, then in half diagonally so that the folded edges are together. Draw a snowflake pattern between the two folded edges. Draw the border pattern across the edge. Cut out the pattern, but do not discard the outside piece.

2 Hawaiian appliqué quilts are traditionally made in two solid colours, typically vivid hues of red, blue, green or orange on a white ground. Cut one piece of coloured fabric and one piece of white fabric slightly larger than the template. Place the coloured fabric on top of the white fabric and position the opened template in the centre.

3 Carefully draw around the edge with a sharp, soft pencil. Draw the border outline in the same way using the other piece. With small stitches, baste 5mm/¹/₄in inside the marked lines of the main motif through both layers of fabric. Baste 5mm/¹/₄in outside the border line.

4 Cut out the appliqué from the top fabric, one section at a time, along the marked lines using small, pointed scissors. To make the fabric easier to turn under, snip into any corners and along deep curves. Make these small cuts no deeper than 3mm/¹/₈in.

5 Use the point of the needle to turn under 3mm/¹/₈in along the raw edge. Sew the folded edge of the appliqué to the main fabric with tiny, close slip stitches. Work around all the edges until the entire appliqué is stitched in place. Stitch the inside edge of the border in the same way.

6 Remove all the basting and press the right side of the panel with a damp cloth. Add a thin layer of wadding (batting) and a backing to the back and work a row of outline quilting around the appliqué. Echo quilt the entire design with lines 5–15mm/¹/₄–⁵/₈in apart.

Stained glass appliqué

The bright, bold colours and the simple shapes used in stained glass windows are ideal for appliqué design. With this technique, shapes are held together with a narrow fabric strip. In recent years stained-glass appliqué has become so popular that narrow sticky-back bias binding has been produced especially for this task. This tape is available in a range of colours as well as the traditional black.

The finished appearance of stained glass appliqué relies on the distinct contrast between the shapes and the bias tape. Plain fabric in bold colours is guaranteed to work, but you can use fabrics with a subtle pattern. There are many new patchwork fabrics that have a self-coloured print in a slightly darker shade that are suitable. These fabrics can be used to emulate the rough texture of old stained glass windows. There are many books with hundreds of stained glass designs to give you inspiration or choose a simple design such as this Charles Rennie Macintosh rose for your first attempt.

Right: Choose designs with strong lines and clear colours for stained glass appliqué.

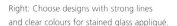

1 Make a template on tracing paper and transfer to the right side of the background fabric using your choice of methods. Draw curves in an outward motion to produce a smoother line.

2 Decide where all the colours will go and mark this on a copy of the template. Cut the template along the lines to separate the pieces.

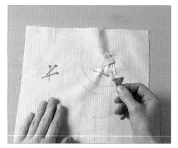

3 Pin the template shapes on the right side of the appropriate colour fabric and cut out. Beginning in the centre of the design, pin the first few pieces of appliqué on the background.

Above: This classic Arab seven pointed star pattern has been worked in traditional colours. Over 230 metres/250 yards of handmade bias binding outlines the stars.

Below: Stylized designs are a good source of inspiration for stained glass techniques.

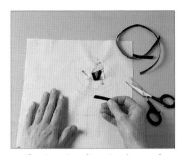

4 Cut lengths of bias binding to fit over the edges of the appliqué and pin in place. Fold under the end of each piece of binding and cover the end of the last piece. Continue in this way, pinning and basting the appliqué.

5 Cover the appliqué with a muslin cloth and press with a steam iron to secure the binding. If the design is to be used as a picture, stitching is unnecessary. Otherwise slip stitch along both sides of the binding.

Reverse appliqué

With reverse appliqué, instead of adding pieces of fabric, sections of fabric are cut away from the right side to create a design. Extra colours can be added into sections of the design to prevent the fabric layers from becoming unwieldy.

The best known reverse appliqué is the brightly coloured Molas worked by the women of the San Blas islands. These maze-like designs feature simplistic animals, birds and plants.

1 Draw and cut out a template. Choose a simple design and make narrow sections no smaller than 5mm/¼in. Transfer the design to the right side of the fabric. Draw an outline 5mm/¼in away from the design.

2 Arrange the fabrics together. In this case there are three layers: the patterned top fabric, a plain cream fabric and a white base fabric. Baste between the lines of the appliqué and around the outside of the design. Keep the lines at least 3mm/⅛in away from the marked lines.

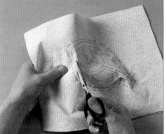

3 Using the template as a reference, cut between the lines of the appliqué motif, through the top layer of fabric only. Snip into the corners without cutting through the marked lines.

4 Find the areas that should have cream showing and turn under the cut edge with the point of the needle and slip hem the folded edge. Notch or snip the deeper curves if required so that the fabric lies flat. If the area is wider than 12mm/½in, trim the excess fabric in the seam allowance to 5mm/¼in.

Right: Hand-worked appliqué and reverse appliqué feature in this quilt design, which has been pieced together and quilted by machine.

Left: Although only made from between two and four layers of fabric, Mola quilts are multi-coloured because the bottom layer is often pieced from several colours and other colours inserted as required.

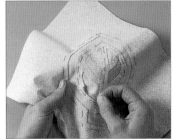

5 In areas you want to be white, cut through the cream fabric as well to reveal the white beneath. Trim and clip the seam allowances and clip carefully into the corners.

6 Turn under both fabrics together and slip hem along the fold. Press the finished appliqué on the wrong side and then press again with a damp pressing cloth.

Above: Start with simple designs and few layers when learning reverse appliqué.

Putting it together

Patchwork and appliqué blocks can be joined together in many different ways. They can be sewn directly together, separated by strips of fabric or by both strips and setting squares. The same set of blocks will look quite different made up in these three ways.

Joining blocks

Some patchwork blocks, such as Log Cabin, are joined directly together so that the wonderful shading can be seen to full effect. Album or sampler quilts, where each block is quite distinct from the others, are usually sewn together between strips of fabric called sashing. The different blocks may be in co-ordinating fabrics and the right sashing fabric can "pull" the colour scheme together. Often the sashing is self-coloured, but a quilt can look striking with the sashing in a busy, colourful print that contains all the colours used in the blocks. Blocks that are in similar colours or all the same design can benefit from extra setting squares as well as sashing strips. Setting squares are the same width as the sashing and sit at the corners of each block. They are usually in a contrasting colour. Piece smaller squares and narrower strips together to make more unusual setting blocks and sashing strips.

Side by side

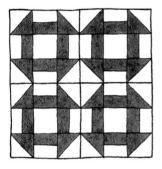

1 Arrange the blocks for the first row on a clean, flat surface in the correct order.

2 With right sides together, pin the first two blocks. Match the seams if possible and ease the edges to fit if required. Machine stitch the seam.

3 Continue adding blocks one at a time to complete the row. Press the seams in the same direction.

4 Complete all the rows in this way, pressing the seams of adjacent rows in opposite directions.

5 Pin the first two rows right sides together. Match the seams carefully, inserting pins along each seam line and easing the fabric in between if required. Stitch over the pins.

6 Press the seams and trim the outside edges before binding.

Using sashing

1 Determine the sashing width, and add 12mm/¹/₂in for seams. Cut sashing the length of each block. Pin and stitch horizontally between blocks.

2 Cut sashing strips to fit vertically between the quilt panels. Pin and sew the sashing in place.

3 Add sashing strips to the outside edge of the quilt before the binding.

Sashing strips and setting blocks

1 Add sashing between the horizontal rows of blocks. For the vertical rows, cut more sashing the same length as the blocks. Cut squares for setting blocks the length and width of the sashing width. Sew a square between each piece of sashing. Press the seams in to the square.

2 Pin the pieced sashing to the quilt panels, matching the seams carefully. Machine stitch using the straight edge of the sashing as a stitching guide. Add setting blocks and sashing strips around the outside edge before adding the binding.

The quilt sandwich

Once you have pieced the blocks together into a patchwork cloth, press the design carefully from the wrong side. Measure the design to make sure it is the correct size. At this point decide whether or not you will add a border all around the design. Borders can be pieced or plain, and can incorporate corner posts. They can be used to pull the whole colour scheme together, or to add accent colours.

Decide on the border width, then cut border strips the length of each side plus seam allowances. Add to opposite sides of the quilt. Measure the quilt width. Cut, then stitch the borders in place top and bottom.

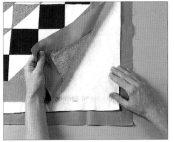

2 Cut the quilt backing 5–10cm/ 2–4in larger than the quilt top, stitching lengths together as required. Cut the wadding slightly smaller than the backing. Centre the quilt top on the wadding. Smooth out any ripples with your hands.

4 If you are hand quilting in a frame, baste the layers together. Begin in the centre and stitch out in radiating lines.

1 Press the quilt top from the wrong side, making sure that all the seams lie flat. Trim any loose threads. Turn the quilt right side up and press thoroughly with a pressing cloth to remove any puckers. Determine and transfer the quilt design at this point.

3 The quickest way to secure the layers is with pins. Ordinary safety pins are suitable, but the quilt will lie flatter with special quilting pins that have a deeper curve on the underside. Insert pins every 5–10cm/2–4in, working out from the centre.

5 If you are quilting in a hoop or by machine, sew horizontal and vertical basting lines at 5–10cm/2–4in intervals to hold the layers securely.

Transferring the quilting design

Quilting adds the final decorative touch to a patchwork quilt, but it takes skill to make the pattern fit. If you are quilting a pattern, it is best to transfer the quilt design to the right side of the patchwork cloth before you make up the quilt sandwich.

Prick and pounce

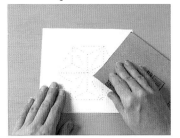 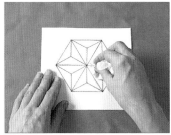 

1 Draw the quilting design on a sheet of firm paper. Remove the thread from the sewing machine and stitch along these lines with a long stitch. Lightly rub the wrong side of the paper to remove the rough edges and help the pounce to go through.

2 Place the template on the fabric. Make a pounce bag by putting a tablespoonful of corn flour (corn-starch) in the centre of a double layer of muslin. Draw the edges together and dab the bag all over the design.

3 Check that the design has been transferred to the fabric before lifting the template off carefully. To make the lines more permanent, mark with a sharp, soft pencil.

Dressmaker's carbon

Choose a sheet of dressmaker's carbon that closely matches the colour of the fabric but still allows you to see the design's lines once they have been transferred. Check that the marks can be removed on a spare piece of fabric.

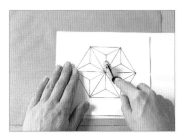

1 Place the dressmaker's carbon, coloured-side down, on the right side of the fabric. Position the template on top and trace over each line.

2 Carefully remove the dressmaker's carbon. The lines of the design should be clearly marked on the fabric.

TIPS

• Transfer the quilt design on to the right side of the fabric before you make up the quilt sandwich. That way you can press on to a hard surface and mark a clear design on the quilt top.

• Quilting "in-the-ditch" does not need marking on the surface.

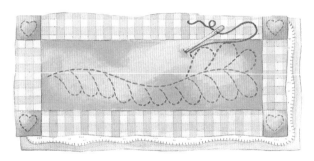

Quilting template

There are many different quilting templates you can buy. Choose one made from translucent plastic because it will be the most hard-wearing and will allow you to see exactly where you are marking.

1 Position the template with the slots exactly where you want to quilt. Check that the design is positioned to go around the corner and then mark with a soft pencil. Use a colour that will just show up on the fabric or one that you can wash out.

2 Small templates can be used to mark a repeating border on a quilt. Cut two notches to show where the template must be placed each time to create the same repeat. Mark with a sharp, soft pencil in a similar colour to the fabric that will wash out.

Quilter's tape

It is not always necessary to mark out quilting lines on the quilt top. On patchwork quilts, for example, you can use the seam lines as a guide for the stitching.

This 5mm/¼in wide sticky-backed tape is useful for adding seam allowances around patchwork shapes before cutting and also for marking straight quilting lines. Stick one edge of the tape exactly where you want to stitch and use it as a guideline. The tape can be lifted and re-used several times.

1 For outline quilting, where each shape is outlined with a row of running stitches 5mm/¼in away from the seam line, stick the tape along the seam line.

2 Sew a line of small running stitches along the other edge of the quilter's tape.

3 For echo quilting, lift the tape and move it to the other side of the quilting stitches. Sew along the far side of the tape. Keep moving the tape further in to produce equally spaced quilting lines.

Above: The basket quilt above has been echo quilted with concentric lines around the basket handle.

Quilting

Quilting is the stitching technique used to hold layers of fabric and wadding (batting) together. You can quilt by hand or machine or simply tie the layers together. Quilting takes place after the quilt sandwich is made up and before the binding is added.

Decorative quilting

Although all quilting embellishes the surface of a quilt in some way, most people associate quilt-making with creating patterns and motifs. Amish quilts, which are made from large pieces of fabric, are famous for their intricate quilting. Decorative quilting patterns are most effective when stitched on larger pieces of plain fabric, rather than on small patchwork or appliqué squares. They are usually transferred to the quilt top with a template.

There are three types of decorative quilting patterns: medallions, borders and corners. Medallions are large, ornate motifs used mainly as a centrepiece for a quilt. Traditional patterns include the Lover's Knot and the Feather Wreath. Border patterns are narrow, linear patterns that fit along borders and sashing strips.

Small shapes such as diamonds and single feathers can be repeated to make a border pattern. Templates for borders often include a corner, to allow you to complete a border all around the quilt top.

Corner motifs are intricate, ornate motifs that often match the style of the central medallion on the quilt top. Feathers and fans are popular corner motifs.

Wholecloth quilts

For those who love hand stitchery, wholecloth quilt are an excellent way to show off quilting technique. Traditionally made from cotton sateen, the surface sheen on the fabric brings out the textures formed by the quilting patterns. Traditional whole-cloth patterns, handed down through the generations, can give us an idea about who owned the quilt. Wedding quilts usually feature hearts in the border but it was considered unlucky for someone to stitch hearts in a quilt until they were at least engaged. Wholecloth quilts take careful planning. The patterns are usually symmetrical and feature medallion, border and corner motifs in an attractive design. Wales has a strong tradition of making wholecloth quilts. The Welsh wedding quilts are particularly distinctive, made in bold-coloured sateen with a different colour on the underside.

Left: Wholecloth quilts will appeal to those who love hand stitching. This intricate design is worked entirely in running stitch.

Quilting by hand

Hand quilting may be time consuming but it is very relaxing and produces the softest finish on a quilt. Quilting needles are very fine and can pierce the skin quite easily, so you will need a thimble to protect the middle finger of your sewing hand. Some people also use a leather or quilter's thimble on their other hand to guide the needle back through the fabric. Whether you are using a hoop or a frame, make sure you are sitting comfortably and in good light before you begin.

Below: This Carpenter's Square design is hand pieced and hand quilted.

1 Thread a small betweens needle (size 8) with a single length of quilting thread and tie a knot in the end. The knot must be small enough to pull through the fabric, yet large enough to catch in the wadding (batting). Take a small stitch into the quilt top and through the wadding.

2 Pull the needle through and tug the thread sharply to pull the knot through the quilt top to catch in the wadding layer.

3 Use the thimble to guide the needle at an angle through the layers and then bring the needle back

through to the surface. Take several stitches at a time along the needle before pulling the thread through. Try to make the stitches all the same size (with practice you will be able to make them smaller). The stitches will probably come out smaller and more irregular on the wrong side.

4 End the quilting with a knot tugged into the wadding. Wind the thread twice around the needle and insert it through the quilt top and wadding. Bring the needle back out on the surface and tug the thread sharply to sink the knot into the wadding. Trim the thread end.

Machine quilting

Machine quilting is much quicker than hand quilting but the preparation should be more thorough. If the layers are not basted together carefully unsightly folds will be caught in on the underside.

1 Use a size 90/14 needle in the machine and set the stitch length to sew about 12 stitches per 2.5cm/1in. Stitch a small sample first to check the tension, using the same quilt layers. You may need to loosen the top tension so that the stitches lie flat. Fit a clear-view presser foot in the machine. This can be made of perspex or have a cut-away section at the front that allows you to see exactly where you are stitching.

2 When stitching a large quilt, you will have to roll the basted layers quite tightly and evenly to fit in the sewing machine. Machine stitch as much of the flat area as possible, then unroll the quilt ready to stitch the next section.

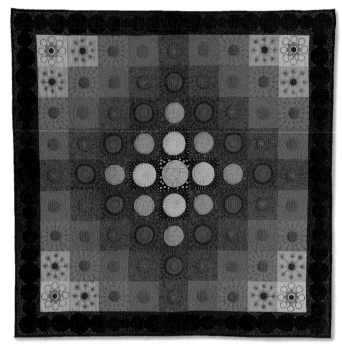

Above: Appliqué circles on a simple one-patch design have been heavily quilted using free-motion quilting.

Methods of quilting

There are many different quilting designs and most are suitable for both hand and machine stitching.

Choose a stitching pattern according to the amount of time you can spare, the type of wadding (batting) you are using and the effect you want to create. For example, patchwork quilted "in-the-ditch" is almost invisible, whereas filling patterns (such as those used in wholecloth quilts) will be a major feature of the overall design. The lines of stitching on some types of wadding should be spaced as close as every 7.5–10cm/3–4in to prevent the wadding from breaking up in the wash. Other types only need to be tied or stitched every 25cm/10in.

In-the-ditch

This technique is almost invisible when stitched in a matching or neutral thread. Work hand stitches in the centre of the seam line. If quilting by machine, stitch slowly and flatten the top fabric on either side of the seam so that the stitches fall exactly "in the ditch". Stop when you reach a corner, making sure the needle is in the fabric, lift the presser foot and turn the quilt to face down the next seam.

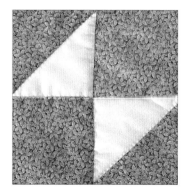

TIP

To make the stitches almost invisible, nylon thread can be used on the top of the machine and a 100 per cent cotton thread in the bobbin.

Selective

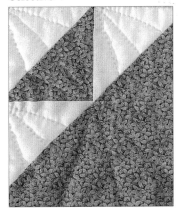

This method is most suitable for patchwork or appliqué quilts and is used to highlight certain areas by quilting them and leaving other areas unstitched. Stitch across the seam lines to create a distinctive pattern.

Outline

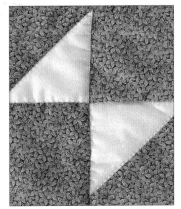

Lines of outline quilting should be stitched 5mm/¼in away from the seam lines and worked around every shape on the design. Use quilter's tape or a 5mm/¼in ruler to keep the lines straight.

Echo

Begin echo quilting in the same way as outline quilting, and stitch further lines every 5mm/¼in until the whole quilt is covered. Match the thread to the background or use a contrasting colour for a decorative effect.

Parallel lines

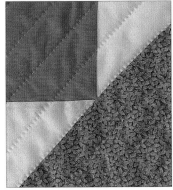

This is a quick and easy method especially if worked by machine. Score lines on the fabric with a blunt point or use a spacer bar on the machine to stitch all the lines the same distance apart.

Shell-filling pattern

Curved filling patterns are more suitable for quilting by hand. They look best stitched on sashing strips and borders, or plain fabric areas of a quilt rather than on patchwork.

Diamond-filling pattern

Straight filling patterns are ideal for machine stitching. Mark the design lines carefully. When you reach a corner, leave the needle in the fabric, lift the presser foot and turn the quilt to face along the next seam. Lower the presser foot and continue. On more complicated patterns, determine a stitching route before you begin to ensure the lines are stitched with as little stopping and starting as possible.

Trapunto quilting

This method of quilting makes use of loose stuffing rather than wadding (batting). Two layers of fabric are stitched together using a quilt design. The backing fabric is slit and the stuffing added. The padded areas stand out in relief and, for contrast, the flat areas can be covered in filling stitch. This is one of the oldest forms of quilting and was used to decorate clothes and furnishings in the seventeenth and eighteenth centuries.

Trapunto quilting was introduced to America by the early settlers and originally worked on linsey-woolsey or cotton. In the early-nineteenth century, the stitching of large, intricately patterned, all-white quilts became popular among the wealthy women in the north east and southern parts of the United States.

Use a glazed cotton or satin fabric for the top layer to emphasize the relief areas and a closely woven fabric such as calico for the wrong side. You can use a loosely woven fabric if you prefer, and use a bodkin or similar tool to stuff the padding between the woven threads, but this will not give such high relief.

1 Trace the design directly through the backing fabric. Place the design face down and place the main fabric on top.

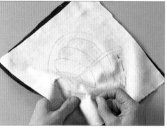

2 Baste around the design to hold the two layers together. Sew along all the design lines by hand or by machine. Sew or tie off the ends on the wrong side.

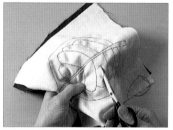

3 Using sharp embroidery scissors, cut a small slit in the first area to be stuffed. Be careful to cut only through the calico and not to cut into the main fabric.

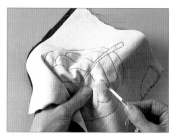

4 Using a bodkin or similar blunt tool, push small pieces of stuffing into the slit. Use the tool to ease the stuffing into the corners and to spread it into an even layer.

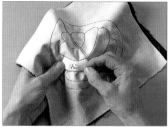

5 Sew the two cut edges together with herringbone stitch. Do not try to pull the edges close together as the raw edges will fray. Stitch into the stuffing for extra security.

Above: Padding large areas creates relief in a design, but to stop the fabric around it from puckering you will need to pad areas of the whole fabric.

Italian quilting

Italian or corded quilting is a purely decorative form of quilting. No wadding (batting) is used to make the quilt extra warm, which explains why it became popular in places with a warm climate, such as southern Italy. Wool (yarn) or cord is pulled through narrow stitched channels to produce thick raised lines on the right side. Italian quilting was very fashionable in the seventeenth and eighteenth centuries.

1 Trace the design on to the backing. Place it right side down and position the main fabric on top. Baste around the design to hold the layers together. Stitch along all the design lines. Sew or tie off the ends on the wrong side.

2 Thread the needle with cord or wool (yarn) without knotting the end. Insert the needle into the backing only between two rows of stitching. Be careful not to puncture the main fabric with the needle.

3 Push the needle along the channel as far as it will go and bring it back out through the backing fabric. Pull the wool (yarn) through to leave a 12mm/½in tail. Insert the needle back in the same hole and take another stitch, leaving a small loop on the wrong side.

4 Work around corners by taking small stitches around the curve, leaving loops on the wrong side.

5 Once all the channels have been filled, pull the fabric on the bias to even out the cord and remove any puckers.

Above: Traditionally bedcovers and clothing such as waistcoats and caps were richly embellished with corded channels. Italian quilting is often worked alongside Trapunto quilting, with the corded channels used to echo the high relief areas of padding.

Choose a soft, medium-weave fabric for the backing to allow you to pull the needle and wool (yarn) through the weave fairly easily.

SHADOW CORDING

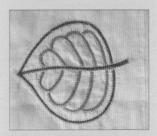

Shadow corded quilting is worked in the same way as Italian quilting. Choose a firm sheer fabric such as organdie or organza for the top layer. Insert brightly coloured cord or wool (yarn) through the channels.

Sashiko quilting

This traditional Japanese quilting technique became widely known in the early eighteenth century, when women made warm outdoor jackets by sewing two layers of indigo-dyed fabric together with rows of neatly worked running stitches.

Initially Sashiko quilting stitches were purely functional, but later they were stitched in complex geometric patterns. Although it incorporates a traditional embroidery stitch, Sashiko is ideal for quilting with a thin layer of wadding (batting) between the main fabric and backing. As with all things Japanese, the patterns are formal with strict guidelines for stitching. Use special Sashiko thread, coton à broder or fine coton perlé for stitching, and keep to the same number of stitches per 2.5cm/1in – usually just five, six or seven evenly-sized stitches

1 Transfer the design to the top fabric. Try to sew the pattern in continuous lines instead of stopping and starting. Look closely at the pattern before you start to determine the best route to take.

2 Two stitches should never come together at a point. Leave spaces at corners and stop lines short of each other if they finish at the same central point.

Above: Sashiko worked on the traditional blue ground but with shades of white and pale blue stitching.

TRADITIONAL SASHIKO PATTERNS

Maru Bishamon (a Buddhist symbol) is an intricate design of interlocking circles.

Higaki (a Cypress fence). Cypress screens were a decorative feature in traditional Japanese houses.

Asanoha (a hemp leaf). Hemp was one of the five basic crops grown in ancient Japan.

Matsukawabishi (pine bark diamond) – a symbol found in all forms of Japanese decorative art.

Tied quilting

Tied quilting is the quickest way to bind the three layers of a quilt together. It is used when the wadding (batting) is too thick, or the top layer too firm, to stitch through easily. Patchwork quilts worked on a foundation fabric, such as Log Cabin, are traditionally tied. The ties can be knotted at the front or back of the quilt, or even tied in a bow. Buttons, beads or charms can be added as a decorative feature.

1   Use long quilting pins rather than safety pins so that you can tie over the pin. The space left between the ties depends on the type of wadding (batting) used, but generally, a spacing of 7.5–15cm/3–6in will be enough. Put the ties closer together if the quilt will be washed often. If the border on the quilt is wider than 7.5cm/3in, it needs to be tied, too.

2   Thread the needle with strong thread: fine crochet cotton, coton à broder or coton perlé are all suitable. Take a back stitch directly over the pin leaving a 7.5cm/3in tail and then work a second back stitch on top. Trim the end leaving the same length of tail.

3   Tie the ends in a reef knot (square knot) working left over right and then right over left. Pull the knot tight and trim the tails neatly.

4   For speed, instead of sewing and tying each knot individually, move to the next pin without cutting the thread. Work across the quilt until you run out of thread and then snip the threads and tie as before.

5   As a decorative finish, tie short tufts of cotton into the reef knot before you trim the tails. Cut small bundles of thread about 5cm/2in long and place them on top of the first knot. Tie a second knot on top and pull tight. Trim the tufts and tails evenly.

Above: Tied quilting has been used to decorate the back of a quilt, which has been pieced using the same colours, but a different design to the quilt front.

Binding the quilt

Binding is the final stage in the quilt-making process and the last opportunity to add colour and definition. There are different ways of binding a quilt. Square or rectangular quilts have binding that is cut on the straight grain while binding for curved quilts is cut on the bias.

Adding separate binding

1 Trim the wadding (batting) and backing level with the quilt top. Cut binding strips 5cm/2in wide along the lengthways grain of the fabric. Cut four strips each 2.5cm/1in longer than each side of the quilt. Piece the lengths together as required, joining the lengths on the diagonal. Along one long edge of each, turn in and press a 5mm/¼in seam allowance.

2 Pin one longer length of binding to the quilt side with right sides together and raw edges aligned. Just 12mm/½in of binding should overhang at each end. Begin stitching a seam allowance' width from the edge. Reverse stitch to secure the ends, then stitch the binding to the quilt. Stop 5mm/¼in from the corner and reverse stitch to secure the ends.

3 Pin and stitch the other pieces of binding to the quilt in the same way, stopping the stitching 5mm/¼in from each corner. Reverse stitch to secure the ends.

4 Fold the binding over the raw edges of the wadding and backing. Pin, then slip stitch the folded edge of the binding in place to the backing. The binding will be much wider on the wrong side than on the quilt front. Stitch down the binding on the sides first and then along the top and bottom edges.

5 To reduce bulk in the corners trim excess fabric to 5mm/¼in. Fold the next binding strip over at the corner and pin in place. Slip stitch along the next edge.

Adding a fold finish

1 This simple finish is suitable for quilts that have sashing strips added around each side. Fold back the top layer of the quilt and trim the wadding (batting) by 5mm/¹/₄in.

2 Fold the raw edges of the backing fabric over the wadding only and baste in place.

3 Turn under 5mm/¹/₄in along the raw edges of the quilt top and pin so that the folded edges are together. Slip stitch the edges neatly.

Adding self binding

1 If the quilt back is at least 2.5cm/1in wider all around than the quilt top and cut in a co-ordinating fabric, a self-binding will add a very neat, slim finish. Trim the quilt top and wadding (batting) evenly. Trim the backing 2.5cm/1in larger all around. To prepare the mitred corner, fold one corner of the backing over until it touches the quilt top at the corner. Fingerpress the fold, then trim across the diagonal.

2 Turn in a 5mm/¹/₄in seam along the trimmed diagonal, then all around the backing. Fold the backing over again to enclose the quilt top and wadding. Check that the mitres meet neatly and pin.

3 Slip stitch the folded edge to the quilt front. Slip stitch the slit in the mitred corners to finish.

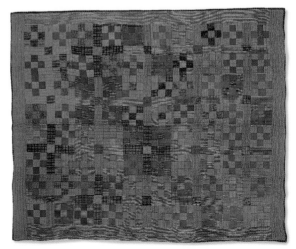

Right: This simple nine-patch railroad design, made around the turn of the twentieth century is made from the cotton shirts of the railroad workers. It is bound with a separate contrast colour.

Making continuous binding

Bias binding is cut across the diagonal of the fabric to enable it to stretch smoothly around curved edges. As you need long lengths of binding for a quilt, it is easier to stitch and cut a continuous binding rather than piecing together numerous strips of fabric.

Mitring is a very neat way to finish square corners because it reduces excess bulk and covers all the raw edges. Mitring is easier on light- or medium-weight fabric that can be pressed with a crisp foldline.

1 Cut a square of fabric with the edges on the straight grain. Cut the square in half diagonally. Pin two short edges with right sides together. Stitch 5mm/¼in from the raw edge, reverse stitching at each end.

2 Press the seam open. Place the pieced fabric right side up on a flat surface. On the right side, draw parallel lines, 5cm/2in apart. Use a wide ruler and press down hard to prevent the fabric from stretching.

3 With right sides together, pin the diagonal edges to make a tube. Offset the edges so that the first line below the corner is level with the opposite edge of fabric. Stitch 5mm/¼in from the raw edge. Press the seam open.

4 Cut the fabric tube into a continuous strip beginning at one corner and cutting along the marked lines. Press the bias binding with a steam iron, pulling it slightly to remove excess stretch.

Mitring corners

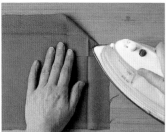

1 Turn over and press the fabric on the hem line along both sides of the corner, keeping the fold along the straight grain if possible. Turn over the corner exactly where the crease lines cross and press.

2 Open out the corner and trim across the diagonal 5mm/¼in away from the pressed line. Turn over 5mm/¼in along all the raw edges and press.

3 Turn the hem over along the crease lines. Check that the mitre matches and adjust if necessary, then pin and baste. Stitch close to the turned edge of the hem. Slip stitch the mitred corner.

Adding a bias binding edge

1 Trim the corners of the quilt top into a curve if required or simply tidy the raw edges. Pin the bias binding along the edge of the quilt top, easing it around the curves. Stitch in place 5mm/¹⁄₄in from the raw edge.

2 Trim the wadding (batting) and backing to the same size as the quilt top. Clip carefully into any points on a decorative curved edge.

3 Turn the quilt over. Turn under 5mm/¹⁄₄in along the raw edge of the binding and pin in place. Slip stitch the binding to the backing.

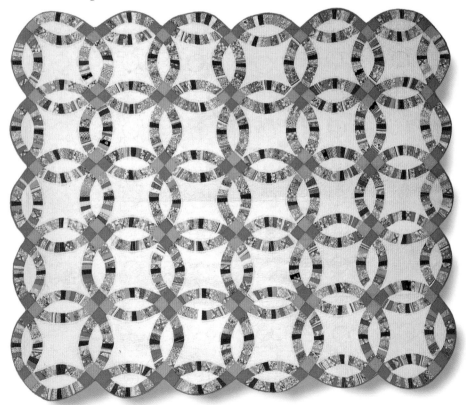

Above: This Double Wedding Ring design incorporates curved seams and is traditionally finished with a scalloped edge. This type of edge requires a separate binding cut on the bias.

Bias binding is used when the quilt has a decorative curved edge or where a quilt is curved at the corner to hang neatly over a bed. Unlike other binding techniques, bias binding is pinned and stitched to one side –

usually the quilt front – before the wadding (batting) and backing are trimmed level. The binding has to be folded into small tucks to lie flat over the points along the edge of this Double Wedding Ring Design.

EMBROIDERY

Embroidery embraces a wealth of different historical and contemporary techniques. All over the world people continue to develop traditional and innovative methods to decorate garments and soft furnishings, or to create an art form that re-interprets the traditional skills, thus ensuring that embroidery is a constantly growing and developing craft. Here the basic techniques of hand and machine embroidery are described. Once you've mastered the basics, move on to create your own designs.

Materials and equipment

For those new to hand embroidery, the pleasure of this craft lies in the simplicity of the equipment. For little outlay, and a bit of imagination, you can decorate and embellish furnishings and clothes. Simply learn the skills and practise them. The basic equipment – needles, threads (floss), fabric and an embroidery hoop – is readily available. If your interest lies in machine embroidery, a basic zigzag machine will suffice.

1 Beads

Many different bead sizes and shapes can be used for embroidery. They can be sewn on individually or couched in rows. Seed beads can be used to add texture to canvas work, cross stitch and other flat embroidery techniques.

2 Fabric

Fabrics as diverse as plain calico and luxurious as silk dupion are suitable for embroidery. The choice depends on the finished look you want to achieve. Even very delicate fabrics can be used with a backing fabric.

Use an even-weave fabric such as canvas, linen, Hardanger and Aida for all types of counted-thread embroidery. These techniques require fabrics that have a distinct weave which allows you to work even, regular stitches. Freestyle embroidery and ribbonwork can be stitched on almost any ordinary fabric.

3 Hoops and frames

Hold your fabric in a frame or hoop while you are embroidering it. The most popular frame used for hand embroidery is the wooden hoop, available in a number of different sizes. A medium sized 18–20cm/ 7–8in hoop is comfortable to hold and you can move it across the fabric as the embroidery is completed.

For machine embroidery, use a wooden hoop upside down or a purpose-made plastic hoop that fits easily under the darning foot.

4 Needles

Crewel needles are the best needles to use for embroidery. They have large eyes that make threading easy and come in various sizes. Chenille needles look like crewel needles but are much larger. They can be used to take thick couched threads through to the wrong side of the fabric. Tapestry needles have a blunt point which makes them ideal for even-weave fabrics.

For machine embroidery use a heavier needle (80/12 or 90/14) to prevent the needle bending and breaking. For thicker, fancy threads use an embroidery needle that has a much larger eye and each time you change the thread, change the needle.

5 Scissors

Embroidery scissors are essential for fine, hand embroidery. They have short blades for accurately cutting threads or trimming small pieces of fabric. The long, thin, pointed blades can be used to remove stitches without damaging the background fabric. Never use sewing scissors for cutting paper because this will soon blunt the blades.

6 Silk ribbon

Use either synthetic or silk ribbons for embroidery. They are available in a wide range of colours and in three widths, 2mm/$^1/_{16}$in, 4mm/$^3/_{16}$in and 7mm/$^5/_{16}$in, and are suitable for a wide range of different embroidery stitches.

7 Threads (Floss)

You can buy some wonderful threads (floss) for hand embroidery in many different colours, textures and weights. The most popular one, stranded cotton, is a versatile thread made up of six strands of twisted cotton. It is used for cross stitch and hand embroidery. Coton à broder and soft cotton are both single-strand cotton threads. Coton perlé is a twisted round thread with a deep shine used for canvas work and hand embroidery.

Viscose rayon threads are also becoming more popular. These are stranded threads with a silky sheen available in rich, luxurious colours. Flower or Nordin thread is a rustic single-strand thread that works very well on homespun fabrics. For really special embroidery try using silk threads. There are a great many specialist embroidery threads, some plain and others fancy or metallic.

Machine embroidery thread is finer than sewing thread with a loose twist so that the threads will shine. Some fancy threads can be wound on to the bobbin and stitched with the fabric upside down.

Preparation for hand stitching

With a beautiful collection of threads to hand and an idea of the finished piece in your mind's eye, curb your enthusiasm to start work until your preparation is complete. Ensuring that the fabric is painted or coloured exactly as you want and is dry enough to begin, that the design has been transferred accurately and that the fabric is held taut in a hoop will ensure your progress is not hindered and better results are achieved.

Colouring the fabric

There are many ways you can embellish fabric for embroidery: by adding pieces of appliqué or by colouring it with dyes or paints before you start. The entire piece of fabric can be dyed using techniques such as space- or tie-dyeing. Sections of the design can be coloured using wax or gutta to restrict the flow of the dye.

You can also use temporary masking techniques, templates and masking tape to spray-paint, sponge or stencil a design on to fabric. Water-based fabric paints are available in many colours for home use. Splatters can be washed off easily and the dry paint can be set using a household iron.

Right: 1 brushes, 2 silk paints, 3 sponge, 4 fabric paints, 5 gutta, 6 oil sticks.

Resist techniques

Resist-dyeing methods such as batik, tie-dye and gutta all use the same principle to create a wide variety of effects.

Batik is a traditional dyeing technique that uses wax to resist the dye. Hot wax is applied with a brush or a tool called a tjanting so that after the fabric has been dyed the waxed areas remain unchanged in colour. Several colours can be added, waxing each time, to build up the design.

Tie-dye is another technique that can be used to create a wide range of patterns. Wonderful bold and delicate designs can be achieved: rolling a piece of fabric over a piece of thick cord and tying the ends before dying can produce an amazing mottled snakeskin appearance. Tritik is another simple technique that creates a variety of patterns. For this, pieces of fabric are gathered with strong thread and tied up before dyeing.

Gutta is a resist medium that you can buy ready to use in tubes fitted with a nozzle for easy application. Once dry, it prevents the silk paint or dye in adjacent areas of the design from running together as you apply them. Gutta is a thin, glue-like substance that is available in a few different colours. Clear gutta washes out of fabric, but coloured lines will remain on the fabric and must be incorporated into the design.

Left: The background of this landscape has been hand-dyed, then sympathetically hand and machine embroidered.

Stamping techniques

Blocks used for stamping are available in different shapes and sizes. Many of the larger stamps are made from a firm foam material which is available from craft stores. It can be cut to any shape and glued to a wood block ready for use.

Try the stamp out on spare paper and fabric first. It may help to wash the background fabric before stamping to remove any fabric finish or you can try adding a drop of detergent to the paint.

1 Use a paintbrush or sponge roller to apply a thin layer of acrylic paint over the stamp surface. Paint parts of the stamp in different colours or blend paint over the stamp.

2 Place the stamp face down on the fabric and press. Avoid agitating the stamp as this will produce a blurred edge. Once dry, press the fabric on the wrong side to set the paint.

Colour washing

This is a simple method of applying colour to a background fabric with a sponge or brush. The finished result is difficult to control because the colour spreads over the fabric very much on its own accord.

However, wonderful effects can be achieved as one colour merges into another. Either apply the paint straight from the bottle or water it down to a paler shade before use. Colour washing can also be used to colour canvas for counted-thread embroidery. When coloured to match the wool (yarn), the canvas will be less obvious behind loose or openly worked stitches.

1 Wash the fabric to remove any sizing. Either apply the dye to wet fabric or iron the fabric dry before use. The moisture will help the dye to spread but will also dilute the colour. Apply the dye with a small sponge or paintbrush. Experiment with differently sized brushes for different effects.

2 Apply the next colour in the same way. Paint directly over the edge of the previous colour or allow the colours to merge across a small gap. Colour washing is particularly suitable for creating the sky, landscapes and garden designs.

Masking techniques

Using a media such as plastic or tape will prevent paint or dye from penetrating defined areas of the fabric.

1 Stick the strips of masking tape to the background fabric to create the shapes you want. Make sure the tape is firmly stuck down to prevent the paint from seeping underneath.

2 Use stencil crayons or paints to fill in the uncovered areas between the tape.

3 When working with a stencil brush or small sponge, make sure the excess paint is blotted off before applying it to the fabric.

Transferring a design

Embroidery designs can be transferred on to a background fabric in several ways. Which method you choose will depend on the fabric and thread you are using and the type of design. Some designs are simply outlined and then developed as you stitch, whereas others need all the fine details included from the start. Make sure that all marked lines will be covered with embroidery even if you are using a vanishing-ink pen.

Direct tracing

This is the easiest way to transfer a design on to fabric but will only work on thin, light-coloured fabrics.

1   On light colour paper, draw your choice of design using a black felt tip pen.

2   Place the fabric over the design on a clean, flat surface. Re-draw the lines with a soft pencil.

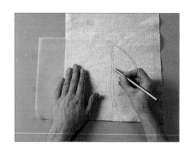

Transfer pen

1   Ink from a transfer pen will not show up on dark fabrics so it is only suitable for lighter fabrics. This special pen is sold in kit-form with the transfer paper. Using the pen, trace a mirror image of the design directly on to the transfer paper.

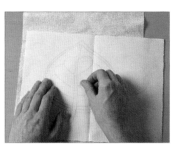

2   Place the fabric right side up on a hard surface. Position the transfer paper drawing side down on the fabric and rub along the lines with the edge of your thumb nail. (Some transfer pens need the heat of an iron – use the manufacturer's instructions.)

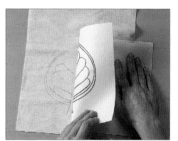

3   Lift one corner of the transfer paper to check that the design has been transferred. If not, go over the lines again, pressing slightly harder.

Dressmaker's carbon

This method is best for firm, smooth fabrics. Choose a carbon colour to match the fabric – white carbon will show up on white fabric as a dull line.

1   Place the fabric right side up, on a hard surface. Cover with a piece of dressmaker's carbon, coloured side down. Position the design on top and draw along the lines with a blunt pencil.

2   Check that the lines have been transferred clearly before removing the paper.

Prick and pounce

This traditional transfer method is suitable for all fabric types. It works best with simple designs.

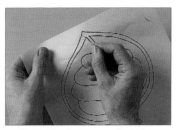

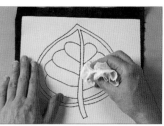

1 Draw the design on a firm sheet of paper. Make small holes along the lines with a thick needle or stitch along the lines using an unthreaded sewing machine. Place the fabric right side up on a hard surface.

2 Rub the muslin bag over the surface to push the cornflour (cornstarch) through the holes. Check that the design has transferred. Baste or draw along the lines to make the design more permanent.

Using a frame or hoop

For most embroidery you will need to stretch the fabric in a frame or hoop to get the best result. The wooden hoop is the most popular. It is ideal for all types of embroidery except those worked on canvas because canvas is damaged when crushed between the rings.

Bind the inner hoop with tape before you begin.

Binding a hoop

Wrap a length of 5mm/¼in wide seam tape round the inside ring at a slight angle so that the tape overlaps all the way round. Fold the raw edge to the inside of the hoop and hemstitch in place.

Fitting the fabric in the hoop

Remove the outer frame and place the stitching area of the fabric right side up, over the inner hoop. Hold the outer ring in place and push down to secure the fabric between the rings. Loosen the tension ring slightly on a thicker fabric before pushing it into place. If the fabric isn't taut in all directions, tighten the screw slightly and re-fit. Use a screwdriver to tighten the outer hoop to keep the tension taut. If the fabric works loose or needs moving, lift the hoop off without loosening the screws and re-fit. Avoid permanently stretching the fabric. Fine fabric can be stretched over a firm light-weight backing fabric and then stretched in the hoop and worked as a single fabric.

Outline and composite stitches

Contemporary techniques use traditional embroidery stitches in an innovative way. But before experimenting with different stitches you need to know how to work a whole range of stitches.

Many outline stitches will be familiar to you as they are the basic stitches used in hand embroidery. Composite stitches are made up of two stitches. These are outline stitches with further embellishment added.

Feather stitch

The Victorians often used this delicate stitch on their crazy patchwork because its light, feathery line contrasted beautifully with the heavy, ornate fabrics they used. It can be worked as a straight or a gently curving line.

Work slanting stitches alternately to the left and to the right as shown. Tuck the working thread under the needle before pulling it through.

Double feather stitch

Double feather stitch forms a wide branched line that can be worked in a soft curve. It creates a delicate lacy effect when used as a filling stitch.

It is worked in the same way as feather stitch except several stitches are made to each side before changing direction. You can either work an equal number of stitches on each side or vary the amount to create an undulating line.

Closed feather stitch

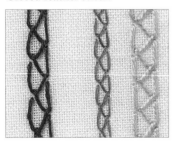

Closed feather stitch is worked in a straight line singly or in multiple rows. It is effective when used to couch narrow ribbon or braid.

Bring the needle out on one side, near the top of the stitching line. Take a straight stitch across to the opposite stitching line. Bring the needle out slightly further down this stitching line, pulling the working thread over the previous stitch as shown. Work from side to side in this way.

Coral stitch

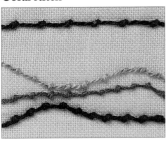

Coral stitch is a thin line stitch that has tiny knots evenly spaced along its length. Change the spacing and position of the knots in each row to create different textural effects.

Work from right to left. Take a small stitch where the next knot is to be formed. Loop the thread (floss) around the needle and hold the knot in place with your thumb as you pull the needle through the fabric.

Knotted cable stitch

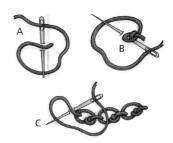

Knotted cable stitch is a combination of cable and coral stitches. Although it looks quite complicated, it is stitched in stages and the coral stitch holds the chain loop in place while the next stitch is worked.

Begin by making a coral stitch (A). Push the needle into the fabric under this stitch and work a chain stitch (B). Continue alternating between coral and chain stitches (C).

Scroll stitch

Scroll stitch looks like tiny waves. It is ideal for intricate shapes. The closer the scrolls are worked, the tighter the curve. Use a round thread for a raised effect or stranded cotton for a wide, flat line.

Work the stitch from left to right. Take a small stitch and loop the thread around the needle. Pull the needle through and begin the next stitch further to the right.

Double knot stitch

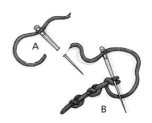

Double knot stitch makes a beaded line and is best worked in a round thread to make neat raised knots. Use it to create areas of surface texture.

Working from left to right, make a small diagonal straight stitch across the stitching line (A). Slip the needle under the previous long straight stitch and pull the thread through. Feed the needle under and over the stitch threads and bring the needle out over the working thread ready to begin the next double knot (B).

Chain stitch

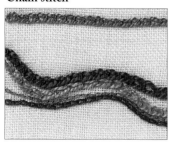

Chain stitch is one of the most popular embroidery stitches. It can be worked in a single line, in a spiral or in multiple rows to fill shapes.

Work the stitch as shown in the diagram, making each loop a similar size. Any embroidery thread (floss) suitable for the fabric can be used, but a smooth thread shows the loops well. Finish the chain by making a tiny straight stitch through the last loop.

Chequered chain stitch

Chequered chain stitch is a decorative line stitch worked in two colours.

Thread the needle with two colours and bring them out on the right side. Work a chain stitch looping only one of the colours to form the chain under the needle. Pull the needle through until the chain is formed. Tug the other colour thread gently to pull the excess thread to the wrong side.

Twisted chain stitch

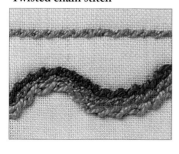

Twisted chain stitch is simple to stitch and looks effective when the stitches are small and compact. A round thread produces a raised line and stranded cotton has a flatter look.

Bring the needle up through the fabric and hold the thread down with your left thumb close to where it emerges from the fabric. Work a small chain stitch over the thread using the illustration as a guide.

Double chain stitch

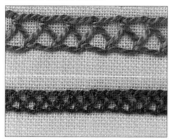

Double chain stitch is a simple variation of chain stitch that forms a wide band. It is generally worked in a straight line or in rows to fill large spaces, but can be stitched in a gentle curve. You can also alter the width of the double chain stitch to fill the space between two wavy lines. Perfect the chain stitch first before trying this more decorative stitch.

Begin at the top left. Work wide chain stitches alternately to the left and to the right as shown.

Feathered chain stitch

Feathered chain stitch is a variation of chain stitch. Rows of feathered chain stitch can be worked side by side as a diamond or irregular filling stitch or overlapped in a random fashion to build texture.

Make a diagonal chain stitch then make a small diagonal stitch downwards from right to left ready to work the chain stitch on the other side. Continue down the fabric.

Heavy chain stitch

Heavy chain stitch makes a bold line that is ideal for heavy outlines.

Make a straight stitch and bring the needle out further down the line. Thread the needle under the straight stitch and back through the fabric where it emerged. Bring the needle out further down and work a second loop through the straight stitch. Continue down the row, but thread the needle under the previous loops.

Whipped chain stitch

Whipped chain stitch makes a heavy raised line that is useful for strong outlines. The stitch will be bolder if whipped in both directions. You can also whip each side of the chain with more than one colour.

Work a row of chain stitches. Thread a tapestry needle with a contrasting or matching thread (floss) and whip under each chain stitch without sewing into the fabric.

Cable stitch

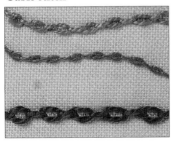

Cable stitch works equally well as a line or a filling stitch. The stitch can easily be worked along a curve. Rows of cable stitches can be joined with small straight stitches or whipped together.

Begin with an ordinary chain stitch, then wrap the thread around the needle as shown before making a short straight stitch and bringing the needle back out of the fabric to make the next chain. Pass the thread under the point of the needle before pulling it through to form the loop.

Back stitch

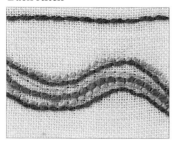

Back stitch is a fine line stitch that can be curved or angular, depending on the length of the stitches. Try using different weights of thread.

Work back stitch from right to left, inserting the needle into the fabric at the end of the previous stitch. Bring it back out at the start of the next stitch. Keep each stitch the same size and avoid pulling the thread tight or leaving it too loose.

Whipped back stitch

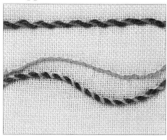

Whipped back stitch can be worked in one colour to create a heavy line resembling fine cord or in contrasting colours for a decorative effect. Try using a different weight of thread for the back stitch and the whip stitch.

Work a row of 5mm/¼in long back stitches. Thread a needle with another colour and slip the needle under each back stitch without going into the fabric.

Threaded back stitch

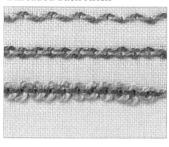

Threaded back stitch can be worked in one or several different threads. Choose a smooth thread (floss) for the back stitch and fancy or metallic threads to weave through.

Work a row of small back stitches. Thread a needle with the second colour and slip the needle under each back stitch, alternately up and down, without going into the fabric. Work a third thread in the opposite direction.

Stem stitch

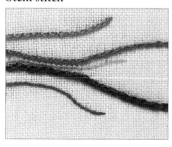

Stem stitch is one of the most common line stitches. It is used to fill in small areas of a design if the stitches are small and evenly sized.

Stem stitch is worked in a similar motion to back stitch, only from left to right. Work up the thread line keeping the thread loop to the right of the needle, and bringing the needle back out half way down the previous stitch. Aim to make the stitches look like a smooth line and all the same size.

Split stitch

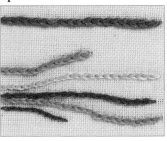

Split stitch is used for creating lines or when worked in rows, as a filling stitch. It is best suited to stitching details such as hands, feet and faces. When stitched correctly, split stitch looks like a fine chain stitch.

Split stitch is worked in a similar way to stem stitch except the needle is brought up through the middle of the previous stitch using the point of the needle to split the thread.

Pekinese stitch

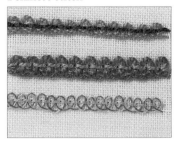

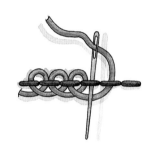

Pekinese stitch can be worked as a line stitch or as a solid filling stitch. Use a fine thread for the foundation row and lace with a heavier-weight thread to create a braid-like effect.

Work a row of back stitches loosely across the fabric. Thread a tapestry needle with the second colour and loop it through each back stitch as shown. Tighten each loop as it forms and keep them even along the rows.

Running stitch

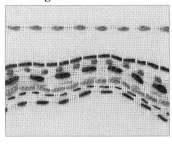

Running stitch can be a tiny prick stitch, a line of basting or a near solid line, depending on the length of the stitches and the spacing between each. In embroidery, running stitch is worked as a single line or in multiple rows to fill larger areas.

Take the needle in and out across the fabric. Several stitches can be "run" on the needle at one time before it is pulled through the fabric.

Whipped running stitch

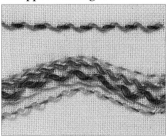

Whipped running stitch or cordonnet stitch is a raised line stitch used for outlines and fine details. Work a subtle line in two shades of the same colour or create a decorative line with two contrasting colours and yarns.

Work a line of even running stitches leaving a gap between each stitch. Aim to make the gaps the same length as each stitch. Use a blunt tapestry needle to whip a second thread neatly and evenly through each stitch.

Cretan stitch

Cretan stitch is a long-armed feather stitch that is often used as a border pattern. It can be used singly or in rows as a filling stitch.

Begin at the top of the centre stitching line. Make long stitches down the fabric slanting them alternately to the left and to the right. Loop the thread (floss) under the needle each time before pulling it through.

Open Cretan stitch

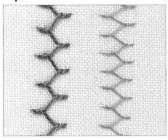

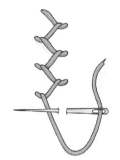

Open Cretan stitch can be worked in a straight or a gently curving line. Several rows side by side form a delicate honeycomb pattern.

Work in the same way as Cretan stitch. Keep the needle horizontal and take a small stitch towards the centre line. Pull the needle through over the working thread. Work a series of stitches alternately to the left and to the right down the fabric.

Closed Cretan stitch

Closed Cretan stitch is generally used to fill small shapes such as leaves. It can also be worked between two straight lines as a heavy, braid-like border stitch. A flat thread (floss) such as stranded cotton gives the best coverage when working solid shapes but a round thread is better for the border stitch.

Draw out the shape on the fabric with a vanishing-ink pen. Working from alternate sides, take small stitches in towards the centre of the shape as shown. Pull the needle out over the working thread.

Left: Cretan stitch would traditionally be used as a border on soft furnishings items such as tablecloths, or on clothes.

Cross stitch

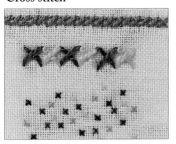

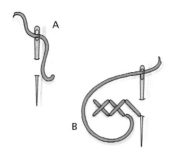

Cross stitch is one of the oldest and most common embroidery stitches. It can be worked individually or in rows, but it is essential to make the top half of each stitch slant in the same direction for an even result.

To work a row of cross stitches, first sew a line of diagonal stitches (A), then complete each cross with a second diagonal stitch on the return journey (B).

Couching

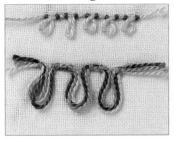

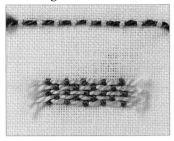

Couching is used to attach groups of thread to fabric.

Hold the thread (floss) to be couched with your thumb. Working from right to left, take small stitches across the bulky thread. Make the couching stitches close together when working a curve and secure a corner with several stitches. Use a large-eyed needle to take the couched thread through to the wrong side.

Pendant couching

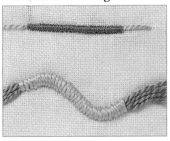

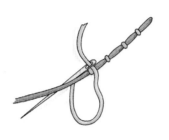

Rows of pendant couching stitched one above the other form a loop-pile filling stitch. Try cutting the loops to create a tufted texture.

Working from right to left, hold the thread to be couched with your left thumb. Work a small stitch across it, then form the base thread into a loop. Couch the other side of the loop. Continue along the stitching line, forming small loops between pairs of couching stitches.

Satin stitch couching

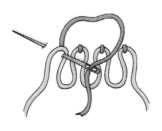

Satin stitch couching forms a neat raised line that is ideal for strong outlining. Here the couched threads are completely hidden by the embroidery thread.

Place a thick thread or a bundle of threads across the fabric and couch it down with small touching stitches that completely cover the threads. Use a large-eyed needle to pull the couched threads through to the wrong side at the end.

Band and border stitches

These are usually worked in straight lines or gentle curves to create borders or fillings, but there is plenty of scope for innovation. Traditionally they were used to bind the edges of items such as blankets and tablecloths. Experiment using different threads (floss) or work parts of the stitch in a different scale to change the appearance. Stitch several different bands together to create an unusual and wide border.

Buttonhole stitch and blanket stitch

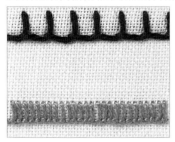

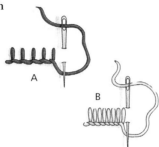

Buttonhole and blanket stitch are essentially the same, except for the way they are spaced. The space between each blanket stitch matches the length of the vertical stitch (A). With buttonhole stitch, the stitches are worked close together (B).

Work both types of stitch from left to right. Space the stitches as required, pulling the needle through over the top of the working thread.

Double buttonhole stitch

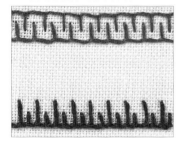

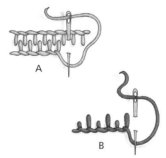

This should more correctly be called double blanket stitch because it consists of two facing rows of blanket stitches worked as a band (A). Long and short buttonhole stitch is another variation in which the stitches are alternately long and short (B).

Work a row of blanket stitches from left to right, then turn the fabric around and work a second facing row from left to right. Position the vertical stitches in the gaps between those of the previous row.

Knotted buttonhole stitch

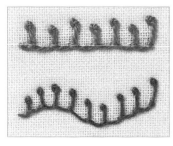

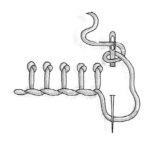

Knotted buttonhole stitch is a pretty variation of blanket stitch. Use a round thread to enhance the raised appearance of the stitch.

Working from left to right, wind the thread over your left thumb and drop the loop on to the fabric so that the tail is underneath. Push the needle through the loop and make a blanket stitch. Tug the loop tight before pulling the needle through.

Closed buttonhole stitch

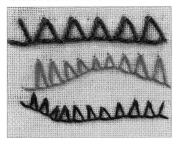

Closed buttonhole stitch is a variation of blanket stitch. Rows of stitching can be worked back-to-back or interlocking, to form a range of borders or filling patterns.

Work the first blanket stitch at an angle and then work the second stitch into the same hole to make a triangle. Try working three or even four threads into the same holes for a more complex result.

Ladder stitch

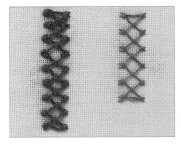

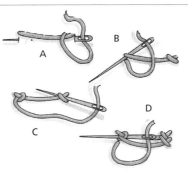

Use ladder stitch for straight borders and filling long, straight shapes.

Bring the needle out at the top left, take it across to the right-hand side and make a small stitch (A). Stitch back across from right to left as shown. Without stitching through the fabric make a knot on the left-hand side (B) and again on the right-hand side (C). Work down the fabric in this way to form a ladder (D).

Diamond stitch

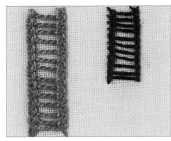

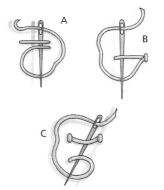

Diamond stitch forms a wide lacy border between two parallel lines.

Make a stitch from left to right and then bring the needle out just below on the right-hand side. Make a knot at the end (A). Take the thread (floss) across and make another knot on the left-hand side (B). Insert the needle just under the knot and bring it out further down the line. Make a knot in the centre (C). Take a small vertical stitch on the right-hand side and continue to form the diamond.

Vandyke stitch

Vandyke stitch is wide ladder stitch that has an attractive plaited (braided) line down the middle.

Bring the needle out on the left-hand side and take a back stitch in the centre, slightly higher up. Work a stitch from right to left through the fabric. Then take the needle back under the previous stitch at the centre. Continue stitching through the fabric and under the stitch as shown.

Herringbone stitch

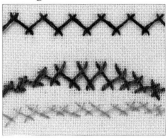

Herringbone stitch forms a crossed zigzag and makes an open border.

Working from left to right bring the needle up through the fabric. Make a small stitch from right to left slightly ahead and above. Move down to the lower line and work a second small stitch from right to left, ahead of your last stitch. Continue alternating between the upper and lower guidelines.

Threaded herringbone stitch

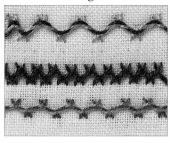

Threaded herringbone stitch produces a zigzag or solid border. Multiple rows of this stitch can be used as a very ornate filling stitch.

First, work a row of herringbone stitch. Then starting on the left-hand side, use a tapestry needle to slip the second thread first under and then over at the point where the herringbone stitches form a cross. Do not pull the thread tight.

Fancy herringbone stitch

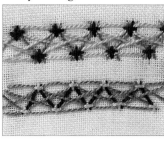

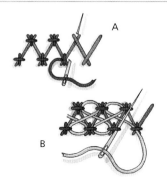

Fancy herringbone stitch is an elaborate border stitch.

Mark parallel lines on plain fabric. Make a foundation row of herringbone stitches, widely spaced. Work an upright cross stitch over each of the top and bottom intersections, making the vertical bar of the cross before the horizontal bar (A). Work the interlacing loops (B) using the illustration as a guide.

Laced herringbone stitch

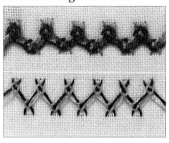

Work laced herringbone stitch in a hoop to prevent the foundation row from being pulled out of shape.

Work a row of herringbone stitches 2cm/³⁄₄in wide. Turn the work upside down. Working from left to right around the crossed part of the herringbone stitch, lace the thread (floss) under and over the foundation and the stitching thread as you cross it. Make two circles around the top crosses and one-and-a-half times around each lower cross.

Tied herringbone stitch

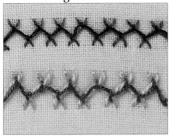

Tied herringbone stitch makes a knotted zigzag line and is usually worked in two contrasting colours. It is used as a border design or in multiple rows as a filling stitch.

Work a row of herringbone stitches. Without picking up the background, use a different thread (floss) to sew a row of coral stitches over the foundation. Place the stitch where the herringbone stitches cross.

Double herringbone stitch

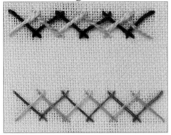

Double herringbone is also used as a foundation for more complicated border stitches.

Work a row of herringbone stitches. Work a second herringbone row on top in the gaps between the stitches. You can interlace the stitches if preferred by threading the needle under the foundation row on the upward stitch and running the thread over it on the downward stitch.

Interlaced herringbone stitch

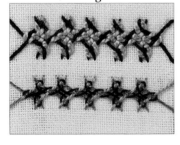

Interlaced herringbone stitch makes an elaborate border stitch.

Work a foundation row of double herringbone stitches as shown. Bring the interlacing thread up on the left and take it around the first top cross. Lace across the top half of the herringbone stitches. Take the thread around the centre cross at the end of the row and then work back along the lower half to complete the stitch.

Chevron stitch

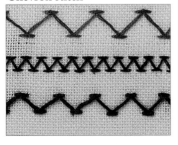

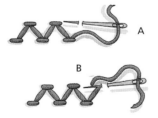

Chevron stitch looks similar to herringbone stitch. It is commonly used in smocking to make diamonds.

Bring the needle out through the fabric. Make a diagonal stitch bringing the needle out a short distance back (A). Take a stitch along the line, ending ahead of the diagonal. Work a back stitch bringing the needle back out next to the diagonal (B). Work the next diagonal stitch across to the lower line, bringing the needle out further back along the line as before.

Raised stitches

These stitches are usually made up of two or more stitches to create height. They are used in three-dimensional stumpwork and other ornate embroidery techniques. The stitches illustrated here are composite band stitches, meaning that they each travel in a line and are made up of more than one stitch or layer of stitching. These stitches are ideal for making use of different threads and colours.

Raised chevron stitch

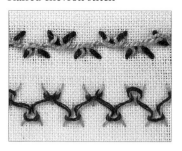

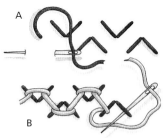

Raised chevron makes a strong, raised line and is used for borders and in multiple rows to make deep bands.

Stitch a foundation row of v-shaped stitches from right to left in a back stitch motion (A). Thread a needle with the second thread (floss) and bring it through at the top left of the foundation (B). Work the stitches across the foundation without catching the background fabric.

Raised chain band

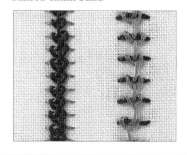

Work raised chain band in a hoop. Try making the bars and chains in different weights of thread.

Work a row of small horizontal stitches. Bring the needle out just above the centre of the top horizontal stitch. Slip the needle over the bar to emerge at the left. Insert the needle under the bar at the right to form a loop. Take the needle under the bar below and pull it through the loop.

Raised stem stitch band

Raised stem stitch band is a dense raised band that forms a distinctive long oval shape and is used as a feature on heavy embroideries.

Sew a foundation block of long straight stitches close together, and to the required width. Work a series of parallel straight stitches across the foundation. Thread a tapestry needle with thread, and bring it out at the base of the block. Work stem stitches over the horizontal threads. Continue until the foundation is covered.

Striped woven band

This stitch is used for filling and borders. Work with two differently coloured threads (floss).

Work a band of evenly spaced horizontal straight stitches. Thread two needles and bring both threads through at the top left above the first stitch. Weave the threads alternately over and under the foundation. Begin each row with the same colour.

Raised lattice band

This is a pretty compact border stitch. It can be worked in different weights and colours of thread. Work with your fabric held in a hoop or a frame.

Work a foundation of long straight stitches, putting more in the centre to create a rounded appearance. Cover the foundation layer with closely worked satin stitches. Work a row of threaded herringbone stitches over the satin stitches.

Sheaf stitch

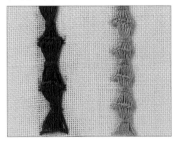

A B

This is an unusual border stitch.

Stitch a foundation of pairs of horizontal straight stitches. Work satin stitches over the bottom two pairs. Work subsequent vertical satin stitches taking the needle between the previous stitches (A). Sew between the first two satin stitches, one from above and one from below. Slip the needle through the loop. Tighten to make a knot. Work a knot between each pair of stitches. Sew two satin stitches to gather the sheafs.

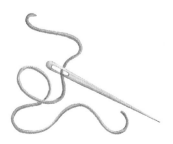

Right: This stitch sample makes innovative use of traditional band stitches and is an inspirational way of displaying stitches.

When learning new stitches, rather than working rows and rows of neat lines, add interest to your work with different weights of threads and unusual textures.

Edging and insertion stitches

Edging stitches are used to finish hemmed edges or to add a decorative border to appliqué. Insertion stitches are used to join two pieces of fabric to make an open decorative seam. The technique was originally used to make larger pieces of table linen from long narrow strips of fabric. Insertion stitches are traditionally worked in white on white and make a delicate feature on christening and bridal wear.

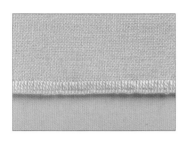
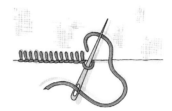

Work looped edging stitch from left to right over a small turned edge. This stitch looks like buttonhole stitch.

Secure the thread (floss) close to the edge on the wrong side. Insert the needle from the back of the fabric at the edge. Pull the thread through and take the needle through the loop from the back, going over the working thread. Pull the knot tight.

Venetian picot

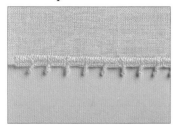
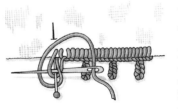

Venetian picot stitch is used to decorate a plain buttonhole edging.

Make a few buttonhole stitches. Insert a pin through the fold next to the last stitch. Loop the thread under the pin and begin another buttonhole stitch carrying the thread around the pin. Weave the needle under the loop thread, over the pin and under the other loop thread. Make sure you go over the working thread. Pull to tighten the knot. Work buttonhole stitch all the way down the loop.

Antwerp edging stitch

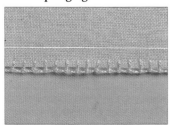
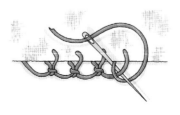

Antwerp edging stitch is worked on plain fabric as a loose decorative knotted edging.

Work the stitch from left to right. Bring the needle through on the fold. Make a buttonhole stitch. Hold the working thread under your thumb next to the stitch. Slip the needle behind the stitches and over the working thread. Pull the knot tight and continue along the edge.

Interlaced insertion stitch

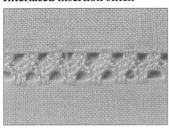

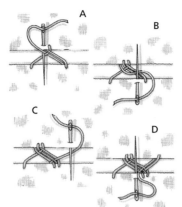

This stitch has a pretty, lacy look.

Hem stitch two fabric strips, then baste the two pieces on to a strip of paper leaving at least a 5mm/¹⁄₄in gap between them. Bring the needle through the bottom fold at the left-hand side. Take a small stitch diagonally to the right through the front of the upper fold. Take another stitch to the right along the bottom fold, then back to the top fold. Loop the needle around the previous stitch to make a twist before inserting it along the top fold from behind.

Knotted insertion stitch

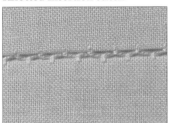

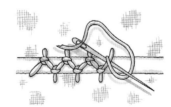

Knotted insertion stitch is slightly heavier than interlaced and has pretty knots instead of twists. The gap between the two fabrics can be slightly wider.

Prepare the fabrics by hemming and basting them to a strip of brown paper about 9mm/³⁄₈in apart. The knots are the same as those used in Antwerp edging. Begin at the left-hand side, working the stitches alternately on the top and bottom fabric edges. Once complete, remove the basting and brown paper and press gently on the wrong side.

Looped edge insertion stitch

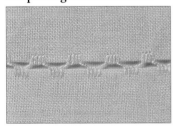

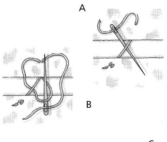

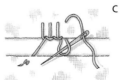

Looped edge insertion stitch makes a firm, narrow join with a delicate appearance. The same effect can be achieved with both knotted and regular buttonhole stitch. The looped edge stitch is simple to work.

Hem and baste the two fabric pieces to a strip of brown paper about 5mm/¹⁄₄in apart. Begin at the right-hand side and work groups of four looped edging stitches alternately on the top and bottom fabric edges. The effect can be altered by using different numbers of stitches or by altering the gap between the fabric edges.

Carefully remove the basting stitches holding the brown paper to the work.

Isolated stitches

Isolated stitches are very versatile. The smaller ones can be used individually to add details such as eyes, berries and flower centres or they can be scattered in a random fashion to fill in a large background. They are also used to create texture on top of other stitches. Larger isolated stitches are useful for heavier embroidery techniques. Experiment with thread (floss) and colour combinations until you get the desired effect.

Bullion knot

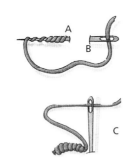

Use a long needle with a small eye to work bullion knots.

Bring the needle out at A and make a back stitch the required length of the knot (B). Bring the needle back out at A. Coil the thread (floss) round the needle seven times and pull the needle through the coil (C). Hold the coil down with the left thumb, pull the working thread to make the coil lie flat, then insert the needle at C.

French knot

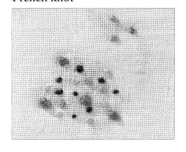

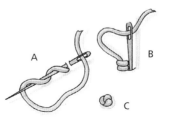

French knots add texture and colour when scattered over fabric and can also be used *en masse* to fill a shape with subtle shading and rich texture.

Bring the needle and thread up through the fabric. Take a small stitch where the thread emerged. Twist the thread around the needle twice (A) and then gently pull the needle through (B). Stitch back through the fabric at the side of the knot (C).

Straight stitch

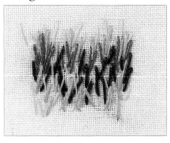

Straight stitch is quick to work and useful for covering large areas with texture and shading. Add shading by stitching in various tones of the same colour or by using several colours of fine thread in the needle at one time.

Work individual straight stitches over the fabric, varying the size and direction at will. Overlap the stitches to create areas of dense texture.

Fly stitch

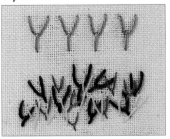

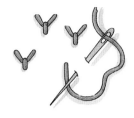

Fly stitch can be worked individually or in rows as an evenly spaced filling. Vary the length of the tail to produce different effects.

Bring the needle through the fabric at the top-left of the stitch and insert it through the fabric diagonally from the top right as shown. Pull the needle through over the working thread (floss) and make a vertical stitch or tail to hold the loop in place.

Lazy daisy stitch

Lazy daisy stitch is a single chain stitch caught down with a small straight stitch at one end. Stitch in rows or scatter the stitches over the fabric to create texture. Most threads are suitable, but varying the weight of the thread will alter the size of stitch.

Work lazy daisy stitch in the same way as chain stitch, but anchor each loop with a small straight stitch before beginning the next loop.

Lazy daisy with straight stitch

This variation of lazy daisy stitch is more solid than lazy daisy stitch and looks like tiny leaves or solid petals. It can be worked alongside lazy daisy stitch to vary the texture, scattered randomly over the fabric, or stitched in a flower shape.

Work a lazy daisy stitch, then add a straight stitch down the centre. Use contrasting colours for leaves or different threads for a solid effect.

Long-tailed lazy daisy stitch

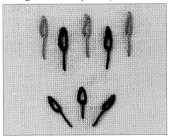

Long-tailed lazy daisy stitch can be worked in a circle with the straight stitches pointing inwards or outwards, to make a flower. Work the stitches side by side or with the loops arranged alternately at the top and bottom of the row.

Work long-tailed lazy daisy stitch in the same way as lazy daisy stitch, but add an extended anchoring stitch to create the tail.

Woven wheel

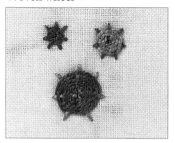

Woven wheels make attractive raised circular motifs for spiders' webs or large flowers.

Work an odd number of evenly-spaced straight stitches, usually seven or nine, radiating from the centre of a circle. Weave a second thread (floss) over and under the straight stitches, starting in the centre and working out. Use a tapestry needle to avoid catching the straight threads.

Ribbed wheel

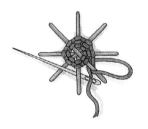

Ribbed wheel stitch is a variation of the woven wheel that forms a textured circle with pronounced radiating bars. It looks best worked in a round thread with a sheen, such as cotton perlé.

Work an even number of straight stitches radiating from the centre of a circle. Eight and 12 are the most common arrangements. Then work back stitches over the spokes, spiralling out from the centre. Use a tapestry needle to avoid picking up the fabric.

Buttonhole wheel

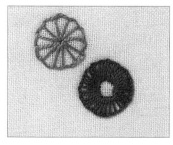

Buttonhole wheel is a circular version of buttonhole stitch. On loose-weave fabrics the stitches can go through the same point in the centre to make a decorative eyelet.

Work buttonhole stitches closely together leaving a small circle in the centre and add French knots to the centre. Alternatively, arrange the stitches so that each straight stitch goes into the same hole in the centre.

Catherine wheel

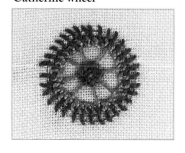

The Catherine wheel was originally an open needlepoint filling stitch. Use a firm round thread.

Work a large circle of blanket stitches, with the straight bars fanning outwards. Work a second row of blanket stitches through the loops of the first circle, using a tapestry needle. Work four straight stitches across the centre to make eight spokes. Work two rings of back stitch over the spokes at the centre.

Raised cup stitch

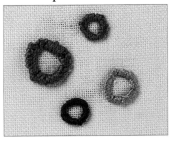

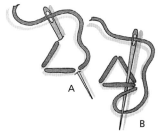

Raised cup stitch forms a heavy raised ring. It is used in stumpwork or Jacobean embroidery.

Stitch an equilateral triangle on the fabric and then bring the needle out at one corner (A). Take the needle under one side of the triangle and loop the working thread around the needle before pulling through (B). Work these stitches along the side of the triangles without catching the fabric. Pack the stitches quite tightly.

Crow's foot

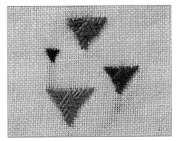

A crow's foot is a tailoring stitch used to strengthen a garment at the top of pleats or pockets. It can also be used as an embroidery stitch. Use a hoop or frame to keep the tension even.

Bring the thread out at the point where you want the base of the triangle to be. Make a long stitch to the top left corner of the triangle. Make a second stitch to the right-hand corner, ensuring it overlaps the first stitch slightly. Each stitch should be the same length. Continue around the triangle, working in to the centre so that the lines of stitching appear to interlock with each other.

Below: This impressionistic flower garden is made up of random isolated stitches in vibrant hues of colour.

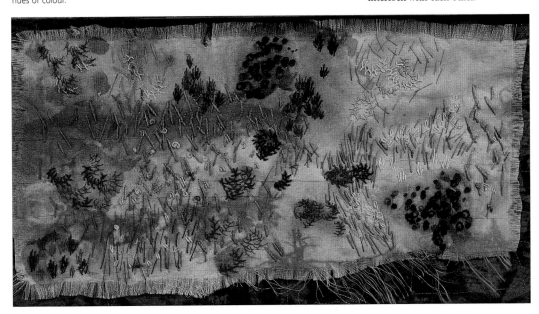

Filling stitches

Filling stitches can either be solid or open. Solid stitches cover the fabric completely and are generally worked over quite small areas. Although the stitches look quite simple, some, such as satin stitch, take practice to work neatly. Open filling stitches cover larger areas in a random or regulated way. Work open filling stitches with the fabric stretched in a hoop to keep the thread at the correct tension.

Brick stitch

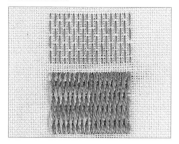

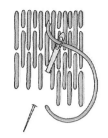

Brick stitch is easy to work and fills large spaces quickly. Rows of "bricks" can be worked in different colours to create subtle shading.

Work a row of straight stitches along the top edge of the area to be filled, making them alternately full- and half-length. Work back across the area, adding full-length stitches under the half stitches. Stagger the full-length stitches until the shape is full.

Basket filling stitch

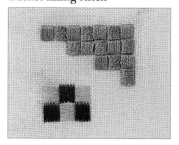

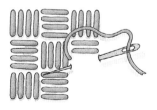

Basket filling is best worked on even-weave fabrics. Although this stitch is traditionally worked in a single colour, an attractive chequerboard effect can be achieved by using two colours.

Basket filling stitch is usually worked by alternating blocks of four horizontal and four vertical satin stitches. The rows can be stitched in any direction, but the stitches should be of an equal size and spacing.

Fishbone stitch

Fishbone stitch is a filling stitch, but can be used as a heavy border. Use stranded thread (floss) and pack the stitches tightly over the background.

Score a line down the centre of the shape to be filled. If it helps, work a small straight stitch down the centre line from the top of the shape. Then make slanting straight stitches from the edge to just over the centre line, working from side to side.

Satin stitch

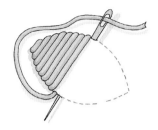

Satin stitch is a flat stitch that looks simple to work – it takes practice to stitch it neatly. Blocks of stitches can be worked in different directions to create areas of light and shade.

Hold the fabric taut in a hoop. Work straight stitches across the shape keeping them close together. Long satin stitches can look untidy, so choose an alternative stitch such as Romanian couching.

Padded satin stitch

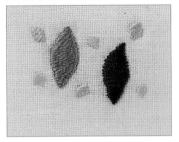

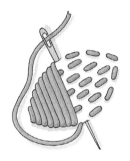

Padded satin stitch has a slightly raised shape. It is used to emphasize shapes by making them stand out from flat areas of stitching. Work this stitch in an embroidery hoop to prevent puckering.

Pad the shape with closely worked rows of running stitches, stem stitches or chain stitches. Then work satin stitch over the padding stitches. Keep the satin stitches close together.

Long and short stitch

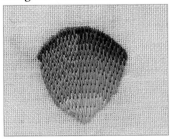

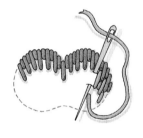

Long and short stitch is worked in the same way as satin stitch, although the finished appearance is completely different. Work the stitch in a hoop or frame.

Work the foundation row in alternate long and short satin stitches that follow the contours of the shape, and completely cover the fabric with tightly packed straight stitches. Work rows of equal sized stitches in this way until the shape is filled.

Right: These charming bird motifs are worked entirely by hand in long and short stitch.

Seeding

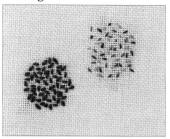

Seeding is a pretty filling stitch. Use single strands of cotton for a light, speckled filling. Seeding can be used as padding under a solid filling stitch such as padded satin stitch. Use a single thread colour or several different colours for a mottled effect.

To work seeding, make tiny straight stitches randomly across the fabric area. Make them all the same length and packed closely together.

Open fishbone stitch

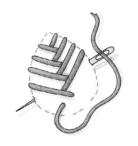

This is a variation of the solid fishbone stitch.

Bring the thread (floss) out just to the left of the centre line near the top and take a slanting stitch to the right edge. Bring the needle out on the left edge and work another slanting stitch that ends just to the right of the centre line. Continue until the shape is filled. An outline stitch around the edge will define the shape.

Roman filling stitch

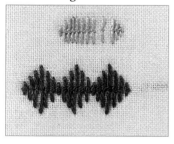

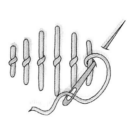

Roman filling stitch can be worked close together or widely spaced. It can also be worked in diamond shapes to create a regular mosaic-like pattern.

Work a long, straight stitch. Bring the needle out at the centre of the long stitch and make a short stitch over it. Either leave a space between each Roman filling stitch or work them close together to cover the fabric area.

Leaf stitch

Leaf stitch is a light open stitch. An outline stitch can be worked around the edge to define the shape.

Begin at the bottom, bringing the needle out to the left of the centre line. Working upwards, make a slanting stitch to the right-hand edge. Bring the needle out again near the centre line, below the first stitch and make another slanting stitch to the left-hand edge. Work slanting stitches until the shape is filled.

Detached wheat-ear stitch

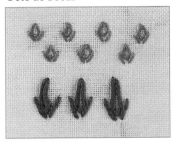

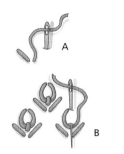

Work detached wheat-ear stitch in rows and grids or as a scattering of isolated stitches. To keep the shape of the stitch in proportion, make larger stitches with a heavy thread. The most striking effect is achieved with a thick, round thread such as coton perlé.

Work two straight stitches at right angles, in a "v" shape. Work a single daisy stitch over the base of the "v".

Tête de boeuf

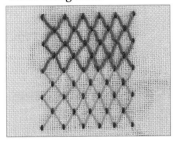

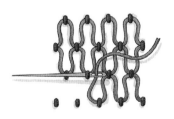

Tête de boeuf or "bull's head" is a pretty stitch that can be used to make regular patterns or for random filling. The size of the stitch can be varied to create different effects. It can be worked very neatly on even-weave fabric if you count the threads.

Work two straight stitches at right angles (A), then place a single daisy stitch above (B). Position the next row between the previous stitches.

Cloud filling stitch

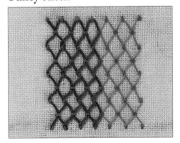

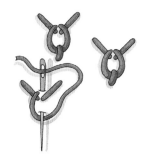

This light, lacy stitch can be used to fill shapes and cover backgrounds. Work the running stitches closer or further apart to alter the effect.

Work evenly-spaced rows of small, vertical straight stitches in a diamond grid pattern as a foundation. Thread a tapestry needle with a contrasting colour and bring it out at the top right. Weave through each row of straight stitches in a zigzag pattern.

Fancy stitch

Fancy stitch is similar to cloud filling stitch, but creates a slightly different lacy trellis. Work it in two colours.

Work evenly-spaced rows of alternate horizontal and vertical small straight stitches across the fabric. Thread a tapestry needle with a contrasting colour and bring it out top left. Weave down the fabric in a zigzag. Go under the working thread at the bottom before coming back up. Subsequent rows share the same horizontal and vertical stitches.

Roman filling burden stitch

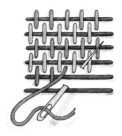

Burden stitch is a couched filling stitch so the long straight stitches can be worked in a range of fancy or decorative threads. The short stitches are best worked in a smooth thread.

Work rows of evenly-spaced long horizontal foundation stitches across the fabric. Couch these threads (floss) down with shorter vertical stitches. These stitches can be staggered in each row to form a brick pattern.

Trellis couching

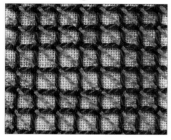

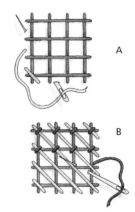

Trellis couching is built up from three layers of straight stitches that can be worked in similar or contrasting threads. It looks very effective when one of the long stitch layers is worked in metallic thread. Use an even-weave fabric for best results.

With the fabric held in a frame, work rows of long, evenly-spaced horizontal straight stitches, then complete the grid with a series of similar vertical stitches. Add a third set of long straight stitches diagonally across the grid (A). Finally, anchor the threads with a small diagonal stitch across each intersection (B).

Square filling stitch 1

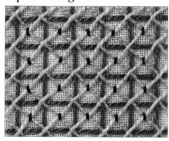

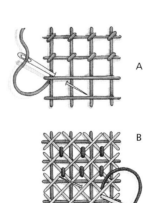

This makes a delicate square trellis pattern. It looks very effective if one of the long thread layers is sewn in metallic thread. This stitch is quite open when complete. Choosing to paint the background first will help this stitch if it is to be used in large quantities. To alter the effect, change the spacing of the stitches and use a different weight thread.

Work rows of evenly-spaced horizontal stitches, then complete the grid with a series of similar vertical stitches. Anchor the threads with a small diagonal stitch across each intersection (A). Sew a third and fourth set of long straight stitches diagonally across the square grid as shown and secure these with a short vertical stitch at each intersection as before (B).

Square filling stitch 2

This is a heavy, textured filling stitch worked on a diagonal grid. For best effect, use a metallic or fancy thread (floss) for the long diagonal stitches.

Work two pairs of long straight stitches to form a diagonal grid as in square filling stitch 1. Work an upright cross stitch at each intersection to anchor the long threads. Complete the pattern by working a French knot in the centre of each diamond.

Griffin stitch

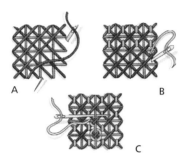

A

B

C

Griffin stitch forms an intricate multi-layered grid. It can be varied by changing the spacing of the stitches or the weight of the threads.

Work a square grid and then long straight stitches to form a diagonal grid as in square filling stitch 1 (A). Secure the diagonal threads by working a short straight stitch at each intersection (B). Thread a tapestry needle with the final thread and lace it around each intersection through all four long stitch layers (C).

Bokhara couching

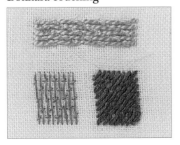

Use Bokhara couching to cover a background or to fill a shape. The same thread is used for both the laid stitches and the couching.

Begin at the left and work straight satin stitches across the area to be filled. Anchor them on the return journey with evenly-spaced small slanting stitches. Stagger these stitches in each row. Only couch satin stitches when they are long enough.

Romanian couching

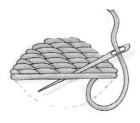

Romanian couching is worked in a similar way to Bokhara couching. Use it to cover a background or fill shapes.

Begin at the left and work long straight stitches across the area or shape. Secure the longer stitches on the return journey with evenly-spaced long slanting stitches. It should be difficult to distinguish between the couched and the laid threads if this stitch is properly executed.

Cretan open filling stitch

This intricate-looking stitch creates a chequerboard effect. Sew the first rows in a firm thread (floss). Use a supple thread for the overstitches.

Work evenly spaced vertical straight stitches across the area to be filled. Bring the second thread out at the top right corner. Sew blocks of Cretan stitches over the straight stitches, without picking up the background fabric.

Chevron stem stitch

Chevron stem stitch looks like appliquéd tweed fabric. The straight horizontal stitches must be worked in a firm thread. Try using two colours.

Make a foundation of evenly-spaced long horizontal stitches. Bring a second thread out at the bottom left. Work stem stitches in a zigzag over the horizontal threads. The needle goes through the fabric at the beginning and end of each row.

Honeycomb filling stitch

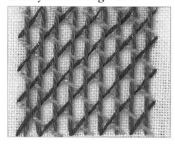
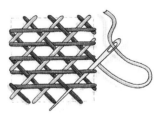

Honeycomb filling stitch is a geometric pattern made of three sets of interlocking straight stitches.

Work evenly-spaced horizontal straight stitches across the area to be filled. Over the top of the work, stitch diagonally from bottom left to top right. Weave a third set of diagonal straight stitches in the opposite direction, passing the needle under the horizontal stitches and over the first set of diagonal stitches.

Ceylon stitch

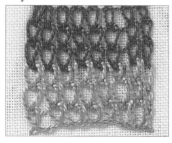

This is a needlelace stitch that can be worked very loosely to create a lacy filling, or tightly to look like knitting.

Make a straight stitch across the top of the area to be filled, and couch it down if it is quite long. Work evenly-spaced loops from left to right over the thread without catching the fabric. At the row end, take the thread down into the fabric and out a short distance below. Work the next row through the previous row.

Battlement couching

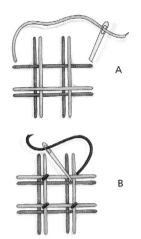

A

B

Battlement couching is an unusual filling for simple shapes. The stitch looks impressively complicated, but it is very simple to work. It can be worked in a single colour, but looks most effective when several shades of one colour are used.

Work two horizontal stitches with two vertical stitches on top in an offset cross formation (A). Continue adding pairs of horizontal and vertical stitches in this way, moving across one or two threads each time to create an overlapping lattice. Once complete, secure each intersection of the top four stitches with a small diagonal stitch (B).

Right: Couched threads and honeycomb filling stitch have been used to effect in this representational work.

Shisha work

Shisha are irregular pieces of mirror glass that are used extensively in Eastern embroidery. There are many different ways to attach shisha. Two methods are described here. Use an embroidery hoop to keep the fabric taut while attaching shisha.

Method 1

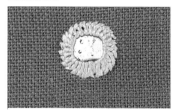

Use a strong thread (floss) that will not fray or break when pulled against the cut glass to work this traditional shisha embroidery stitch.

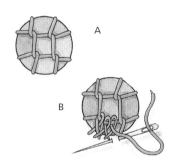

Create a frame for the embroidery stitches by sewing two threads across the shisha from side to side. Sew two more across the shisha, looping the thread around each laid thread (A). Bring the needle through to the right side close to the shisha. Take a stitch under the frame and cross over the first thread. Make a back stitch through the fabric (B). Continue around the shisha, bringing the needle up between the ends of the previous crossed loop.

Method 2

This is a pretty, ornate way to attach shisha. Work all the stitches the same length or make them alternately long and short as shown.

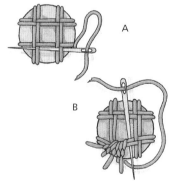

Work eight straight stitches across the shisha, arranged in pairs. Take the last pair of stitches under the first pairs where they cross (A). Make the centre square small. Bring the needle out close to the shisha at the bottom left-hand corner and insert it close to where it emerged. Take a small stitch through the fabric and over the top of the working thread. Pull the thread towards the shisha to "set" the knot close to the edge of the glass. Take a second vertical stitch through the framework only.

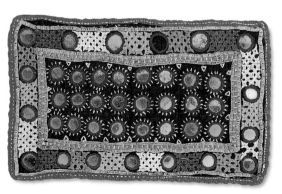

Left: This antique piece of shisha demonstrates the traditional method of applying glass, surrounded by vibrant colours and ornate hand embroidery.

Ribbon embroidery

Ribbon embroidery has existed in one form or another since the Middle Ages, but it was especially popular in Victorian times when frivolous, ornate embroidery techniques or "fancy work" were widely used. Flowers were a favourite theme, as they still are today.

Most embroidery stitches can be adapted for ribbon embroidery, but the stitches will look slightly different as the ribbon opens out on the surface. The simplest stitches are the most effective.

Ribbon embroidery looks deceptively difficult. In fact, the stitches used are either adapted straight stitches or well-known embroidery stitches such as daisy stitch, satin stitch and stem stitch. Narrow ribbon specially designed for

embroidery is available in different widths and a wide range of colours. They are made from either synthetic fibres or silk. Silk ribbons are more expensive but give wonderful results.

Almost any fabric can be used for ribbon embroidery, but it is easier to stitch on a looser weave. Linen and cotton even-weave fabrics are both suitable. Ribbon embroidery is a good technique for beginners, since the ribbon covers large areas quickly, and small designs can be finished quickly.

Threading a needle

Choose a needle that will allow the ribbon to pass through the fabric without fraying. Try out different-sized needles on the fabric to find the most suitable one. Don't worry too much if the needle makes a pronounced hole, because the ribbon should open out to cover it. Use this technique to secure the ribbon to a large needle to ensure it does not pull through the hole as you work.

1 Thread the needle in the normal way and then pierce the end of the ribbon with the needle as shown. Pull the long end to secure it over the eye. Work with short lengths so that the ribbon does not look ragged.

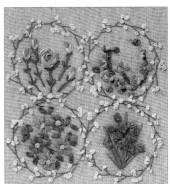

Beginning and finishing

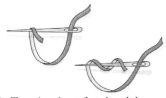

1 To make a knot, first thread the needle in the normal way, then fold the end of the ribbon over the needle. Wrap the ribbon around the needle before pulling through.

2 Ribbon embroidery does not look very tidy on the wrong side, so finish the ribbon by threading under some of the ribbons on the wrong side.

Right: Ribbon embroidery lends itself to floral compositions and can be used with other embroidery techniques.

Garden flowers

Make your own herbaceous border using some of the flowers shown here. Fill in the spaces with simple leaves using straight stitch in different greens.

Cornflower

Work one circle of straight stitches and a second over the top as shown. Stitch straight stitches to fill the centre. The leaves are ribbon stitch on a stem stitch stalk.

RIBBON STITCH

Bring the ribbon out and make a stitch directly through the ribbon.

Hollyhock

Work in a cone shape. Begin at the top with green French knots and change to the flower colour. Make the French knots large towards the base. Stitch thread French knots on top of the larger flower buds.

Iris

Work one ribbon stitch vertically and three others in a fan below. The stalk is worked in stem stitch and the leaves in twisted straight stitch.

Hydrangea

Work four straight stitches for blossoms and a small French knot in the centre.

Periwinkle

Work five short straight stitches and fill the centre with a French knot. The leaves are straight stitches and the flower buds are ribbon stitch.

Pansy

Work five ribbon stitches, two in yellow and three in purple. Add straight stitch stamens and a French knot to complete the centre.

Hollyhock

Hydrangea

Cornflower

Iris

Pansy

Periwinkle

Wild flowers

This pretty wild flower garden has some of the more common wild flowers. All use the basic ribbon embroidery stitches.

Poppy

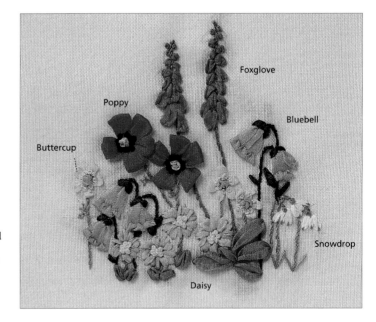

Poppy

Foxglove

Bluebell

Buttercup

Snowdrop

Daisy

Work four to six loop stitches around a centre French knot. Use a plastic drinking straw to make each loop of each petal the same size. Work a ring of black French knots around the centre.

Foxglove

Work a stem up to the top of the proposed flower tip. Work small green floss French knots and then a few flower-colour ribbon French knots. Continue down with straight stitches, changing to ribbon stitch for the lower flowers.

Daisy

Work straight stitches out from a centre area in palest blue. Fill the centre with tiny floss French knots.

Bluebell

Work three ribbon stitches for the flower, only pulling the ribbon until a roll appears at the bottom of each petal. Work two straight stitches on top for the calyx and then work a stem stitch stalk.

Buttercup

Work five loop stitches (over a cocktail stitch) in a circle. Work a large French knot in the centre and surround it with tiny French knots

Snowdrop

Work three straight stitches in a fan shape with a green French knot at the top. Work a green floss straight stitch at the tip of each petal.

Counted-thread embroidery

Cross stitch, blackwork and Assisi work are all counted thread embroidery, and are stitched on even-weave embroidery fabrics such as linen or Aida. Even-weave means that there are an equal number of threads running horizontally and vertically throughout the fabric. Needlepoint, often wrongly called tapestry, is worked on an open-weave

Fabrics

Even-weave fabrics are available in various sizes or counts. The count refers to the number of threads per square 2.5cm/1in.

Linen is a soft, high-quality plain-weave fabric. As the weave is quite fine, stitches are normally worked over two threads. Linen is an expensive fibre and many so-called linen fabrics are actually made from cotton or a mixture of fibres such as cotton, linen and viscose.

Aida is a 100 per cent cotton fabric woven from blocks of four threads with distinctive holes formed between each block. This makes Aida very easy to stitch on. It is available in a wide range of colours in 6- to 18-counts. Many Aida fabrics are only available in 14-count, the most popular size. You can also buy fancy fabrics, such as Lurex or Rustico, that have metallic or linen threads woven through them. The holes in these fabrics are slightly less pronounced than those on regular Aida.

Hardanger embroidery is also worked on an even-weave fabric. It can be stitched on linen or on a 22-count Hardanger fabric that is woven in pairs of weft and warp threads.

Waste canvas, a loose weave canvas is used as a guide for working cross stitch on plain fabric. Once the cross stitch is complete, the canvas threads are loosened by spraying with water or by agitating the threads, and then removing with tweezers.

Plastic canvas is a non-fray material used for counted-thread embroidery. The finer gauge is ideal for cross stitch decorations. Larger gauges are suitable for canvas work and can be made into three-dimensional shapes.

Canvasses for needlepoint

Needlepoint is a type of embroidery worked over a stiff open-weave canvas. Different types of canvas as well as different mesh sizes are available. The mesh or count relates to the number of threads per 2.5cm/1in. Most canvas types are available in white or natural shades.

Single or mono canvas is a plain-weave canvas that is easily pulled out of shape. For best results, stretch the canvas in a frame to work on, and avoid using diagonal stitches such as tent or half cross stitch.

Interlocking canvas looks similar to single canvas, but the warp threads are twisted around the weft threads during weaving. This renders the fabric fairly stable, making it suitable for all types of canvas embroidery including diagonal stitches.

Double canvas is woven with pairs of threads rather than single ones. It is used primarily for tramming, where a thread is laid under the stitches. The sub-divided mesh also makes it easier to work fractional stitches.

Below: 1 Lurex Aida; 2 interlocking canvas; 3 waste canvas; 4 single canvas; 5 Aida; 6 plastic canvas; 7 natural double canvas; 8 coloured even-weave linen; 9 double canvas; 10 Aida; 11 waste canvas; 12 raw linen; 13 single canvas; 14 natural petit point canvas; 15 interlocking canvas; 16 natural single canvas.

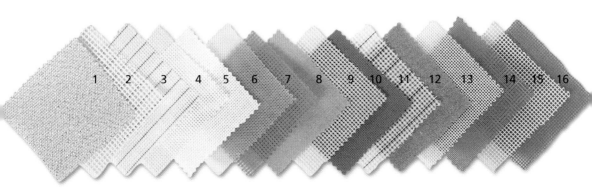

Threads

Tapestry, crewel wool (yarn) or Persian yarns are the traditional threads used for needlepoint, but almost any thread can be used. Embroidery cottons (floss) such as soft cotton and coton perlé are particularly suitable for 10- or 12-count canvas, and new metallic threads have been produced which can be stitched easily without fraying or unravelling. Heavier braids can be used on their own and fine metallic threads and blending filaments can be stitched together with another yarn.

Tapestry wool is a 4-ply, single-strand yarn used on a 10- or 12-count canvas. Use two strands to cover a 7-count canvas with tent stitch. Crewel wool is a 2-ply, single-strand wool. Use three strands to cover a 12-count canvas. Two or three colours of these finer yarns can be blended "in the needle" to produce an interesting effect. Persian yarn consists of three strands of 2-ply yarn. It can be separated to stitch on fine canvas or doubled up for a larger-mesh canvas.

Right: This design makes use of simple stitching and just two colours to convey the impression of a Scandinavian landscape.

Starting and finishing

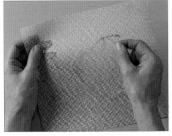

1 The holes in canvas are quite large, so a knot on the wrong side will work through to the right side. Instead, make a knot on the right side 2.5cm/ 1in from where you want to stitch. The thread will be secured by your stitches and the knot can be cut off.

2 Whichever thread (floss) you choose, it must cover the canvas completely, but without being too thick to sew through the canvas. Cut a 45cm/18in length of yarn. A longer length will become thin and frayed before you get to the end.

3 Take the yarn through to the wrong side to finish off. Slide the needle under the stitching for about 2.5cm/1in and then trim the end. Begin new threads in the same way, but avoid running under the same stitches or the work may look uneven.

These are usually worked over two threads of linen or canvas or one block of Aida. You can easily change the scale of the stitches by working over fewer or more threads, changing the thickness of the thread to suit. The fabric should be covered by the stitch without being cramped and bulky. If you are a beginner, choose a fabric where the holes are symmetrical and are easy to see.

Cross stitch

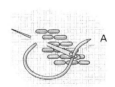

Cross stitch is one of the oldest embroidery stitches. It is worked on canvas or even-weave fabrics so that the stitches are the same size.

Work a row of diagonal stitches in one direction and then cross them with a second row of diagonal stitches slanting in the opposite direction. Make all the top stitches slant in the same direction unless a variation of light and shade is required.

Upright cross stitch

Upright cross stitch is a neat stitch suitable for filling small shapes. It looks like a textured woven fabric. To create a different effect, change the spacing between the stitches and the weight of thread used.

Work rows of evenly-spaced horizontal stitches over two threads, diagonally from left to right until the shape is filled (A). Work vertical stitches over two threads (B). On small shapes, work complete stitches.

Long-armed cross stitch

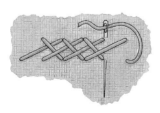

This is a good, textured filling stitch or it can be a border stitch.

Beginning on the left, take a long stitch over eight vertical and four horizontal threads. Bring the needle out four threads down, and cross the stitch with a short stitch over a square of four threads. Bring the needle out four threads down ready to work another stitch. Repeat along the row. Make the long stitches twice the length of the short stitches.

Broad cross stitch

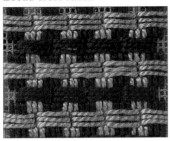
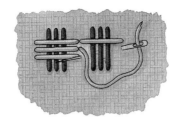

Broad cross stitch is used on single canvas to fill large areas. It makes a smooth, textured pattern. Stranded cotton gives the best coverage.

Work three vertical straight stitches over six threads. Add three horizontal straight stitches of the same length across them. Work the blocks in horizontal rows, fitting subsequent rows of blocks into the spaces in the preceding row.

Half cross stitch

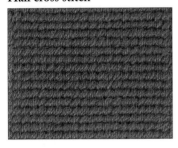
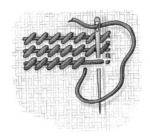

Half cross stitch is stitched on double canvas with tramming. The stitches are worked over a straight thread sewn between the double canvas threads.

Make a long stitch from right to left taking the needle between the double threads of the canvas. This is padding, and helps to cover the canvas. Work diagonal stitches from left to right over the long stitch and the pairs of canvas threads.

Tent stitch

Tent stitch is a small diagonal stitch used mainly on single canvas. The small size of the stitch makes it ideal for working intricate designs from charts or on printed canvas. This stitch is relatively quick to work.

Work across the shape in diagonal rows, as shown, making small half cross stitches over the canvas. Tent stitch can be worked in straight rows but stitching diagonally is less likely to pull the canvas out of shape.

Linen stitch

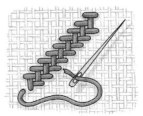

Linen stitch has the appearance of a woven fabric. It is a useful stitch for filling large areas.

Begin at the top right and work a horizontal back stitch over two canvas threads. Work further back stitches diagonally down the canvas, moving one hole behind and down each time. Work vertical stitches over two threads below the horizontal stitches, filling the canvas hole under each one. Repeat to fill the shape.

Brick stitch

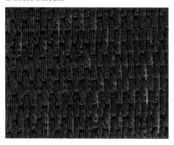

Brick stitch fills a large area quickly and can be worked in different colours for subtle shading. When shading, choose colours that tone so that they merge together.

Work a row of straight stitches, alternately full- and half-length, across the top of the area to be filled. Stagger rows of full-length straight stitches underneath. Fill the last row with half-length stitches.

Gobelin stitch

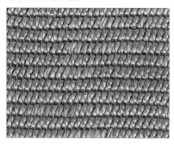

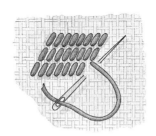

Gobelin stitch can only be worked on single canvas. It produces a flat, ribbed effect. To completely cover the background use a thick thread (floss).

Beginning on the left, work rows of long diagonal stitches over two horizontal and one vertical canvas thread, inserting the needle upwards each time. Turn around and work back in the opposite direction, this time inserting the needle downwards.

Mosaic stitch

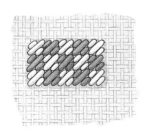

Mosaic stitch is a small pretty block stitch that fills a nine-hole square. The blocks can be stitched in different colours to create intricate designs. Use a thread with a smooth surface to give the stitch definition. This stitch is quick and easy to do and looks very effective.

Each mosaic has a diagonal stitch that covers three holes, with shorter parallel stitches on each side.

Reverse cushion stitch

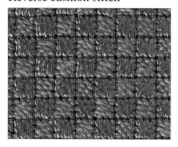

Reverse cushion stitch produces a neat pattern of squares that can be used to fill canvas. The alternating stitch directions give an attractive light-and-shade appearance. For an interesting effect use metallic thread.

Work each reverse cushion stitch block over a square of 16 holes. Work five graduated diagonal straight stitches within the square, starting with a small stitch over two holes. Work the blocks in rows, alternating the direction of the stitches.

Hungarian stitch

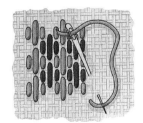

Hungarian stitch can be worked on single or double canvas. It produces a pattern of diamond-shaped blocks.

Hungarian stitch consists of three parallel vertical straight stitches: short ones on each side of a long stitch worked over two and four horizontal canvas threads. Work the stitch in horizontal rows leaving two vertical threads between each block. Work subsequent rows in the gaps.

Diamond straight stitch

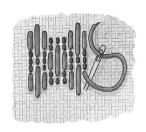

Diamond straight stitch can only be worked on single canvas and can be used to fill a large shape.

Each diamond is made up of five vertical straight stitches worked over one, three or five canvas threads. Work the diamonds so that each row fits neatly into the row above with a single thread space between each one forming a trellis. Fill in the trellis in a different colour.

Plaited gobelin stitch

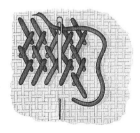

Plaited gobelin stitch produces an attractive interwoven pattern that is quick to work. It will cover a large shape or background if the correct weight of thread (floss) is used.

Begin at the left, and take a stitch over two vertical and one horizontal canvas threads. Stitch with the needle in a vertical position. Complete the next row as shown so that the stitches slant in the opposite direction.

Milanese stitch

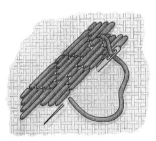

Milanese stitch creates a smooth background that is worked diagonally across the canvas.

Begin at the top right and work a diagonal row of back stitches, making the stitches cover first one then four canvas holes. Work a second row alongside, making the stitches alternately over two then three holes. In the third row make the back stitches alternately over three then two holes. Make row four as row one, beginning with a long stitch.

Knitting stitch

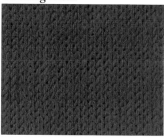

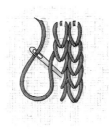

This is a solid filling stitch that looks like knitted stocking stitch.

Work up and down the canvas, beginning at the bottom right. Complete each column in two journeys. Work the right-hand set of stitches slanting upwards over three horizontal canvas threads and across one vertical canvas thread. Work the second set of stitches downwards with a reverse slant.

Star stitch

A

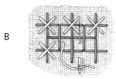
B

Star stitch fills an area with a textured pattern of crosses. It can only be worked on single canvas.

Work upright stitches in horizontal rows, with the four arms of adjacent crosses sharing the same holes in the canvas (A). Over stitch the crosses with two sizes of ordinary cross stitches on alternate rows (B). Work small stitches over two threads and large stitches over four threads.

Rhodes stitch

Rhodes stitch is a decorative filling stitch built up from square blocks.

Work a diagonal straight stitch across five canvas threads from bottom left to top right. Move around the square anti-clockwise (counter-clockwise), working further long diagonal straight stitches until every hole in the square is filled. To make a larger block, work the stitches over six or seven threads not five.

Half Rhodes stitch

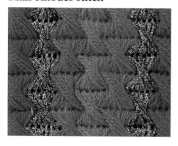

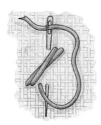

Half Rhodes stitch creates a pattern of bow-tie shapes and makes a stunning textured background or filling when worked in toning colours. This stitch can be worked in any thread (floss) on single canvas and is worked over six threads.

Work Rhodes stitch along only the top and bottom sides of the square. Work the next stitch sharing the same holes. Position further columns so that each one interlocks with the preceding one.

Waffle stitch

Waffle stitch consists of a large square block that has a raised diamond in the centre. This stitch is always worked over an odd number of threads. Use a round thread (floss).

Work diagonal stitches following the stitching diagram as your guide. Bring the needle up at 1, down at 2, up at 3 and down at 4 and continue, following the numbers on the diagram until complete.

Rice stitch

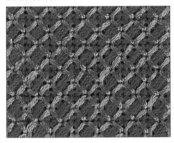

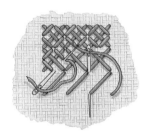

Rice stitch creates an ornate filling stitch when the top layer of crosses is worked in a contrasting thread. The lower layer is usually worked in a thicker thread than the upper layer.

Cover the shape to be filled with a grid of large cross stitches worked over four vertical and four horizontal canvas threads. Work small diagonal stitches across each corner at right angles to make further crosses.

Captive rice stitch

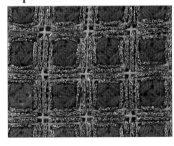

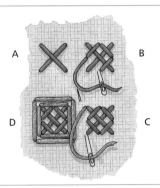

Captive rice stitch is a variation of the previous stitch with a border around each textured square. Try mixing metallic thread and wool (yarn).

Work a rice stitch over four threads (A and B), then surround it with a double layer of four straight stitches so that it fills a square of six canvas threads (C and D). Fill the small unstitched space between each captive rice stitch with a cross stitch.

Cushion stitch

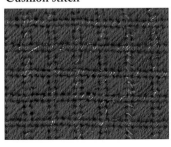

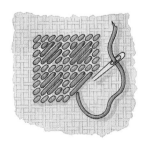

Cushion stitch is a neat textured, square filling stitch. When worked in two colours it creates a checked pattern known as Scottish stitch. This stitch is most effective when worked in two contrasting threads.

Work blocks of five diagonal stitches over one, three and five canvas thread holes. Slant all the stitches in the same direction and leave a gap of one canvas thread around each square. Work a border of tent stitches around each square.

Chequer stitch

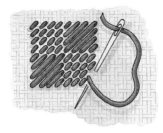

Chequer stitch forms a highly textured square. It is generally worked over a background using one colour, and is best stitched in a shiny thread such as coton perlé or viscose rayon.

Work blocks of 16 tent stitches to form a chequerboard pattern and fill the spaces in between with seven diagonal straight stitches as shown. Work all the tent and straight stitches in the same direction.

Ray stitch

Ray stitch makes a pattern like the sun's rays. Work the rows in alternate directions to create a subtle light-and-shade effect. Work this stitch over a four-, six- or eight-hole square and on a loose-weave fabric.

Make seven straight stitches radiate from the bottom right-hand corner of a four-hole canvas square. Pull the stitches tight so that they form a hole at the bottom corner.

Vault stitch

Vault stitches are worked horizontally and vertically in an interlocking grid.

Begin with a vertical vault stitch. Work a straight stitch over eight horizontal threads down the centre. Work a narrow cross stitch of the same length on top, using the holes on each side. Work a wider cross over the top to complete the rectangle. Work alternate horizontal and vertical vault stitches to fill the shape.

Velvet stitch

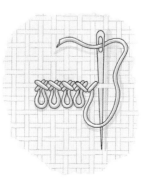

Velvet stitch produces a surface like a long-pile carpet. It looks best worked in wool (yarn) or crewel wool.

Begin at the bottom left-hand corner and work a diagonal back stitch over one canvas thread. Take the needle under the horizontal thread and form a loop as shown. Work another diagonal stitch across the first one to anchor the loop firmly to the canvas. The long-pile loops can be cut and trimmed to look like velvet once complete.

Scallop stitch

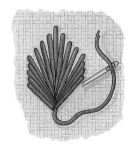

Scallop stitch produces a pattern of interlocking shells that can be used to fill large areas on single canvas.

Work each scallop stitch over eight horizontal and 12 vertical threads. Work a straight stitch over 12 threads down the centre. Work 15 diagonal straight stitches radiating out from the base of the centre stitch as shown. Arrange the shell shapes in horizontal rows and interlock subsequent rows.

Fan stitch

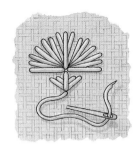

Fan stitch forms an intricate pattern that fills large areas of single canvas.

Work the fan over five vertical and ten horizontal threads. Work 15 straight stitches of different lengths all radiating from the same central hole. Below the fan, work five stitches spanning four horizontal threads and three vertical canvas threads. Below, work a vertical straight stitch over two threads.

Fir (Pine) stitch

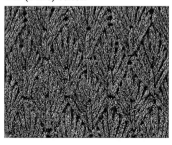

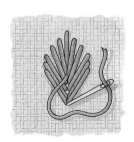

Fir (pine) stitch can be worked individually or as an ornate filling on single canvas. Shade the motifs by using several tones of one colour.

Work a central vertical straight stitch over six threads. Work five diagonal stitches of varying lengths to the left and right, using the five canvas holes below the vertical stitch. To finish, work a vertical stitch over these five holes.

Eyelets

This stitch makes an attractive diamond that can be turned on its side to make a square or be modified to become a circle.

Work each diamond in a block over ten canvas threads. Stitch 18 satin stitches of graduated length, radiating from the same hole in the centre. Frame the block with back stitches. Work each circular eyelet in a block of six canvas threads. Work 16 satin stitches, radiating from the same hole in the centre.

Assisi embroidery

Assisi embroidery is a type of cross stitch originating from Assisi in Italy. For this, the normal principles of cross stitch are reversed so that the design area is left blank and the background filled in with rows of cross stitches. Traditional Assisi designs are heraldic and often featured real or mythical birds, animals and flowers. Assisi embroidery is usually sewn in a combination of blue, red or black threads on white or cream linen.

Holbein stitch

An essential feature of Assisi embroidery is the Holbein stitch used to outline the cross stitch and to create the pretty filigree border that is often the outline for this type of design. Before working any cross stitches, outline the design area with Holbein stitch.

Above and below: Both examples have been worked in the Assisi style, but the example below does not have the traditional Holbein stitch outline.

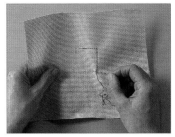

1 To sew Holbein stitch, work a row of running stitches around the outside edge of the cross stitch area.

2 Go back along this line of running stitch, filling in the gaps between the stitches on the return journey.

3 Outline the motifs in Holbein stitch in this way, then fill in the background with cross stitches.

4 Work the details and filigree in very fine gold braid.

Blackwork

As its name implies, blackwork embroidery is worked with black thread. It probably originated among the Muslim communities of the Middle East, where the teachings of the Koran forbade the use of figurative designs. The Moors brought this technique to Europe during their 700-year occupation of Spain. It is thought that Catherine of Aragon made it popular in Britain at the beginning of the sixteenth century.

Blackwork features on many of the garments shown in English court paintings from around the time of King Henry VIII. It is thought that the fashion for blackwork began with the arrival of his wife Catherine of Aragon. One artist in particular, the younger Hans Holbein, painted the ornate blackwork collars and cuffs with such exquisite detail that his name became synonymous with one of the stitches used.

During the Elizabethan era, blackwork was greatly influenced by Jacobean crewel embroidery. Around this time gold began to be used on the designs, too, and they became increasingly extravagant, featuring coiled goldwork stems and beautiful blackwork flowers.

Blackwork is traditionally worked in silk on fine linen but can also be worked on Aida using stranded cotton with the delicate blackwork patterns formed using a single strand of thread. Use a heavier thread (floss) such as coton à broder or coton perlé to outline the design. Use fine metallic thread or very fine braid for any goldwork details.

How to stitch blackwork

Blackwork patterns are worked in two straight stitches: back stitch and Holbein stitch. Use back stitch for broken lines in the pattern and Holbein stitch for continuous lines. Find the shortest route along the design lines so that you can keep stitching for as long as possible with one strand of thread.

Holbein stitch consists of a double row of running stitches. Work a row of running stitches along the design lines (on linen work each stitch over two threads), leaving a gap the same size as the stitches in between. Then work back filling in the gaps with a second row of running stitches. To prevent the line from looking crenellated, bring the thread out above one running stitch and insert the needle below the next one.

Creating a blackwork pattern

Blackwork patterns are fascinating to stitch and amazingly easy to design. These exquisite geometric designs are constructed from simple patterns that are repeated in a linear or symmetrical format. Use graph paper or a basic graphics computer program to produce suitable designs.

A good way to keep a record of patterns for future reference is by stitching them on a sampler. Mark a piece of linen into 4cm/1½in squares and stitch a different pattern in each one. The squares in the sampler shown at the section end are graded from dark at the top to light at the bottom. This makes it easy to select suitable patterns for designs.

Below: Blackwork is ideal for representational pieces where the stitch density effectively creates areas of light and shade.

Creating a blackwork picture

The most effective blackwork pictures are simple in design and have distinctive bold shapes filled with different stitch patterns.

Blackwork patterns are by nature light, medium or dark. The density of the stitches determines the depth of light or shade in the pattern. You can easily adapt patterns to make them darker or lighter by adding or removing some of the lines. Blackwork patterns can be used to create a three-dimensional effect. Choose darker patterns to make parts of the design appear farther away and lighter patterns for the foreground. Plan your design carefully before beginning to stitch.

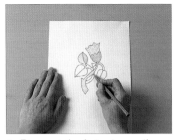

1 Draw out the design in pencil. Decide which parts of the design will be light, medium or dark. The lightest areas will seem further forward than the dark areas. Cross hatch sections of the design to build up the density of shading required. Rub out or darken areas until you have found a pleasing balance.

2 Draw along the lines of the design in black felt pen and trace directly through on to the fabric with a soft pencil. Choose blackwork patterns that will fit the different light, medium and dark areas of the design. Try out the different patterns on graph paper to check the density of colour before beginning to stitch.

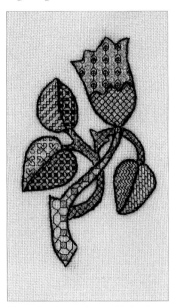

Above: Use the template provided at the back of the book as your design source, then fill in the areas using some of the blackwork designs pictured on the right.

3 Work the blackwork patterns in Holbein stitch or back stitch using a single strand of black stranded cotton (floss). Work the patterns carefully, filling the shapes accurately.

4 Embroider a line of stem stitches along all the design lines using a heavy black thread such as coton à broder. Press on the wrong side.

HOLBEIN STITCH

Work even-sized and spaced running stitches along the design lines. Then work back filling in the gaps with a second row of running stitches.

Right: These are just a selection of the hundreds of patterns that can be created in blackwork. Practise making the stitches neat and even, then develop your own designs either on graph paper or using a computer graphics program.

Hardanger embroidery

This form of cutwork originates from the town of Hardanger in Norway. It consists of blocks of satin stitches known as kloster blocks formed into a geometric outline. The fabric inside the blocks is carefully cut away, except for a few thread bars which divide the space up into additional squares. These thread bars are used to decorate the space with delicate needlelace and weaving.

Making a kloster block

A kloster block consists of five satin stitches worked over four fabric threads. The area around the kloster blocks is usually filled with surface embroidery in a geometric pattern, worked in satin stitch and other simple stitches such as Algerian eye or chain stitch.

Hardanger is traditionally worked on a heavy even-weave linen or on 22-count Hardanger fabric. Use thread (floss) that is slightly heavier than the weave of the linen. A round thread such as coton à broder gives the best effect for Hardanger. Precise stitching is the key to this technique.

1 Work two small back stitches leaving a tail of thread (this will be sewn in later). Stitch the first block of five satin stitches, then take a large diagonal stitch, bringing the needle out four threads to the left of where the thread last emerged.

2 To work blocks on the diagonal, stitch one kloster block, but take a back stitch on the last satin stitch. This will bring the needle out at the corner of the kloster block ready to begin the horizontal satin stitches of the next block.

Completing the cutwork

Baste the shape you wish to create on to the fabric before you work the kloster blocks and use this as a guideline. If the threads inside the blocks are to be cut, make sure the blocks are positioned directly opposite each other. Once complete, run the thread under a kloster block on the wrong side to secure it and trim. Unpick the back stitches and sew this thread in on the wrong side too.

1 Using sharp scissors, cut four fabric threads along the edge of a block. Cut the same four threads at the other side and pull the threads out one at a time with tweezers. Cut the horizontal threads in the same way.

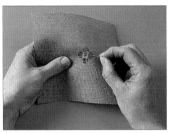

2 Leave the threads in the centre where there are no kloster blocks. These bars left inside the cutwork are covered decoratively. The simplest way to cover them is with closely worked overcasting stitches.

3 The thread bars can be woven or wrapped. Secure the thread on the wrong side and weave under and over two fabric threads until the bar is full. Move to the next bar by weaving through the blocks on the wrong side.

Adding the decorative filling

The following stitch diagrams show just a few of the stitching techniques used to decorate kloster blocks.

Work a small sampler of kloster blocks, then practise filling the areas with the designs here. Leave some blank and fill others with the lacy designs. As you reach the end of each thread, weave it in under and over the fabric and stitching threads on the wrong side of the work.

Above: Detail of a garment showing wrapped, woven and picot bars.

Above: Geometric surface embroidery has been used here to fill areas of fabric in Hardanger embroidery.

Wrapped bars

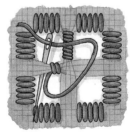

Overcast the thread bars tightly. Sew the end in securely on the wrong side by weaving it in and out of the newly created bars.

Picot

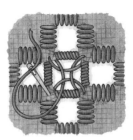

Picots are small decorative knots that are worked half-way down a woven bar. Insert the needle as shown and wrap the working thread around before pulling it through.

Lace stitch

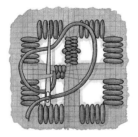

Insertion stitches are used to fill the spaces in Hardanger embroidery. Take a stitch in each corner interlacing the threads (floss).

Woven bars

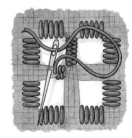

Weave under and over two threads to make a solid bar. Take the thread under the stitches on the wrong side ready to begin the next bar.

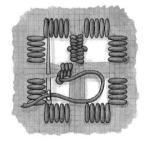

Weave under and over two threads then make another picot on the other side. Complete the bar, then stitch under the blocks on the wrong side to begin the next bar.

Twisted lace filling stitch

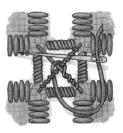

Work a cross stitch across the space and wrap loosely. This insertion stitch produces a star in the centre if worked across the wrapped or woven bars.

Pulled-fabric embroidery

Pulled fabric, also known as punchwork, is a type of counted-thread embroidery that creates attractive lacy patterns on the fabric. The weave of the fabric used and how tightly the stitches are pulled will determine how pronounced the holes in your design will be. Pulled-fabric work began as peasant embroidery, and later developed into an exquisitely fine embroidery, requiring high standards of workmanship.

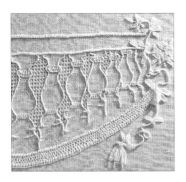

Pulled-fabric stitches are more prominent on an even-weave linen, whereas a scrim or muslin fabric is so easily pulled that the shape and pattern of the holes come to the fore. It is traditionally worked in a thread (floss) that matches the fabric colour so that the lace effect is seen. Stretch the fabric in a hoop for best effect.

Left: This Caselguidi balustrade has pulled fabric worked in select areas of the design.

There are several types of pulled-fabric stitches. Diagonal stitches such as diagonal square stitch create a lacy effect. Isolated stitches can also be grouped together to form a filling. Surface stitches, such as coil filling stitch, are worked with different groupings of satin stitches. This group of stitches are not pulled as tightly as other pulled-thread stitches and so the embroidery is more prominent than the holes.

Punch stitch

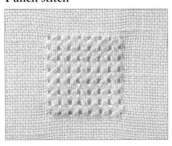

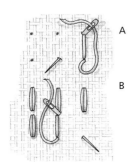

Punch stitch is one of the most common pulled-thread stitches and is often worked on its own. It is a square stitch worked in two steps.

Work rows of double straight stitches four threads apart following the illustration as a guide (A and B), then complete the square pattern with pairs of horizontal straight stitches. Punch stitch will form large holes if the stitches are pulled tight and if the fabric has a very loose weave.

Wave stitch

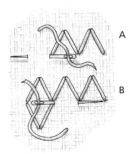

Wave stitch makes a trellis pattern similar to brick work. Pull the threads tightly to make large holes.

Work from right to left and back again across two threads and down four threads, always inserting the needle in a horizontal position (A). To begin another row, bring the needle down over eight threads and then turn the work upside down to stitch in the same way as before (B).

Coll filling stitch

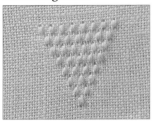

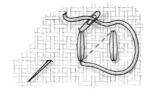

Coll filling is a surface stitch worked in rows from right to left. The threads are not pulled as tightly in this stitch making more of the embroidery stitch than the lacy or holey pattern.

Work three satin stitches vertically over four fabric threads. Space the groups of satin stitches in the second row between the previous stitches to form a brick-like arrangement.

Oblique filling

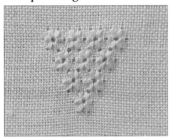

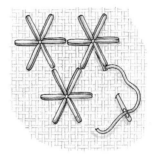

Oblique filling can create quite large holes in a loose-weave fabric if the threads are pulled tight. It can be worked as individual star-shaped eyelets or together as a filling stitch. Experiment with different threads.

Fill a block of eight fabric threads with six double stitches as shown. Make each stitch go through the same central hole and use the same outside holes for adjoining stars.

Three-sided stitch

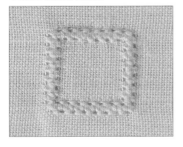

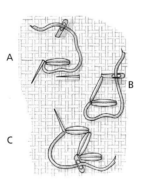

This stitch can be worked in rows as a filling but is often worked as a border. The stitches can be worked to form an attractive curved corner.

Work three-sided stitch from right to left, turning the fabric around to work in a different direction (A–C). The stitch is made up of three pairs of back stitches worked in a block of four threads. Work the stitch as a border, in rows or in a solid block with the next row sharing the same holes as the previous one.

Eyelets

Eyelets can be worked individually, in rows or as a grid pattern. The stitch can be made a different size provided all the stitches go into the same central square and are spaced evenly around the sides.

A small eyelet is worked over a block of four fabric threads. Use a strong thread (floss) that will not snap when it is pulled tight to form a large centre hole.

Drawn-thread work

Several types of embroidery are included under the heading drawn-thread work. It is often confused with pulled-fabric embroidery, but is a totally different technique. Fabric threads are withdrawn: the remaining weft or warp threads are then embroidered to create delicate lace patterns. Drawn-thread work is used today to decorate plain table linen

Withdrawing threads

1 Using a small, sharp pair of embroidery scissors, insert the tip of the scissors between two vertical fabric threads and cut across ten horizontal fabric threads. Use a tapestry needle to ease the horizontal threads out one at a time.

2 If the threads are not pulled out completely, the ends must be finished off neatly. Pull out all the horizontal threads up to the same vertical thread. Turn the fabric over and darn each thread in for about 1cm/½in.

3 You can also finish the ends off with buttonhole stitches. Work the buttonhole stitch over four or five threads along the edge of the channel. Trim the threads close to the stitching.

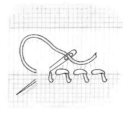

4 Hem stitch is the basic drawn thread stitch. It is used to group the threads into bundles and finish the edge. It can also be used to hold a hem in position on the wrong side.

5 Work along one side from right to left, grouping the threads into bundles of four.

6 Work hem stitch along the other edge. The threads can either form bars, or the bundles can be split in two to make a zigzag pattern

Right, from left to right: Double or Italian hem stitch, chevron stitch border, zigzag, twisted bars, straight bars, tied bars, double twists.

Working with wider drawn-thread bands

1 Pull out 20 threads and make a wide ladder border. Secure the thread (floss) at one end. Work a buttonhole stitch to hold it in the middle of the bars. Lift the second bar back over the first using the needle. Pull the needle through under the first bar.

2 Different patterns can be worked by twisting the bars in groups of two or in double rows as shown. You will need a wider band, between 25 and 30 drawn threads, to accommodate the extra row of twists.

3 Embroidery stitches can be used to tie the bars together. Twisted chain stitch or coral stitch are commonly used. Secure the embroidery thread at the end of the bar and work from the right side pulling the stitches tight.

4 Some stitches can also be used in place of hem stitch. Choose stitches that naturally pull the threads together in bundles. Both stem stitch and chevron stitch are suitable.

5 Strengthen wide borders by leaving a narrow band of unpulled threads between the rows. The outside edges are finished with hem stitch but the inner edges can be embroidered.

Above: This gown was made from fine cotton lawn and embroidered with silk. Drawn-thread work features on the bodice.

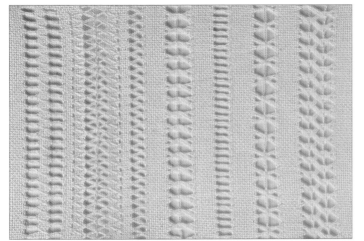

TIPS

• Use a fabric such as even-weave linen where threads are distinct.

• Always work in good light.

• When withdrawing threads, either pull them out singly straight across the fabric, or stop before the fabric edge.

Russian drawn-thread embroidery

As its name implies this technique originated in Russia. It is an exquisite fine embroidery that is very simple to work. Unlike other types of drawn-thread work, it is worked in blocks rather than rows and the open grid forms the background for simple motifs. The design is marked on the linen first and the border outlined in buttonhole stitch. The solid motifs are traditionally outlined with heavy chain stitches.

Getting started

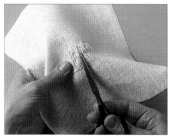

1 Mark the outer edge of the drawn-thread work with basting, ensuring that the square has an even number of threads in each direction. Cut the threads in pairs. Cut a pair of horizontal threads, then leave the next two threads uncut between two vertical threads. Turn and cut every second pair of vertical threads.

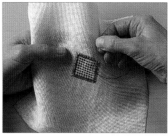

2 Trim the drawn threads close to the fabric and work buttonhole stitches neatly around the edges of the square. Stitch through every second thread to avoid bunching the stitches. Use a magnifying lamp to work buttonhole stitch and overcasting so that you can see exactly where to stitch.

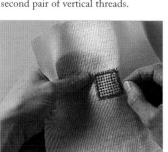

3 Beginning at the first pair of threads on the top edge, work two overcasting stitches over the thread bars. Work a stitch across the corner and then another two on the next bar.

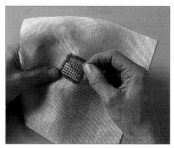

4 Feed the thread (floss) down to the next bar along the buttonhole stitches on the wrong side. Continue overcasting the bars in diagonal rows until the whole grid is covered.

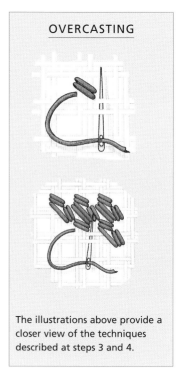

OVERCASTING

The illustrations above provide a closer view of the techniques described at steps 3 and 4.

Below: Russian drawn-thread work is often used to decorate table linen.

Needle weaving

This is a type of drawn-thread embroidery worked in narrow borders. Needle-woven borders are stronger than hem-stitched drawn-thread work because the fabric threads are densely covered with embroidery threads. Needle weaving is normally worked with coloured threads and can be used in conjunction with other embroidery techniques such as Hardanger.

STARTING AND FINISHING

Begin as for drawn-thread work by pulling out enough weft threads to form a wide band.

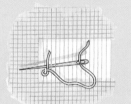

• Hold a long loop of thread down the thread bars and work wrapping or weaving stitches over the top to secure it in place.

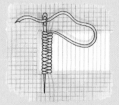

• Sew the end of the thread (floss) down inside the bar and snip off the end to finish.

• Finish off the ends of the band with buttonhole stitches or by sewing them in. Hem stitch the top and bottom edges as desired.

Ladder pattern

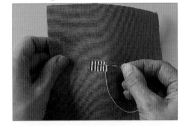

Overcast groups of threads to create a ladder pattern, or weave groups of threads together. These bars have been decorated with picots.

Woven bars

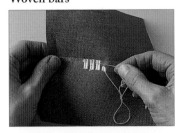

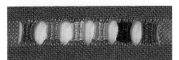

1   Begin in the centre between the groups of threads and weave from side to side until the bars are filled with stitches.

Zigzag pattern

Make a zigzag pattern by wrapping the completed bar with the next group of threads.

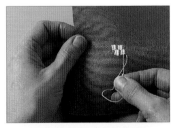

2   Woven bars can be split to create a number of brickwork patterns. Feed the needle up through the woven bars to reach the next starting point.

Broderie anglaise

This technique falls into the category of "whitework", a term that encompasses a number of techniques such as pulled-thread embroidery, drawn thread, Mountmellick and Casselguidi. All are traditionally worked using white thread (floss) on white fabric.

Broderie anglaise

Broderie anglaise is exquisite lacy embroidery combining fine surface stitches with eyelets of different sizes and shapes. The holes in the fabric are cut or punched with a round tool, such as a stiletto, and then overcast.

It was most popular at the end of the eighteenth century when caps, clothes and fine household linen were decorated with elaborate broderie anglaise patterns. Broderie anglaise is traditionally finished with a scalloped edge. The designs are usually formed from an arrangement of simple floral motifs. Mark the design on a closely woven fine cotton or linen.

Eyelets

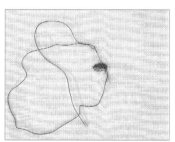

1 To make eyelets, work a row of tiny running stitches in a small circle, less than 5mm/¼in in diameter. Punch small eyelets with a stiletto or the point of fine embroidery scissors in the centre of the stitches. Work overcasting stitches around the edge and sew the thread end in.

2 Outline larger holes with running stitches as before, then cut across the centre of the hole both horizontally and vertically. Turn the fabric flap to the wrong side and overcast the edge. Trim any excess fabric from the wrong side. Larger oval eyelets are surrounded by padded satin stitches.

Scallops

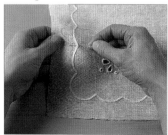

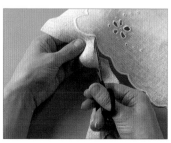

1 Outline the area with chain stitch for padding. Sew closely worked buttonhole stitch over the top.

2 Trim very close to the stitching with small, sharp scissors.

MOUNTMELLICK

Mountmellick work is a heavy type of peasant embroidery, worked with white crochet cotton on white cotton sateen.

• Traditional designs are inspired from the surrounding environs of Mountmellick in Ireland.

• The aim is to create a relief picture with a variety of raised or knotted embroidery stitches.

• Mountmellick embroidery is usually finished with a heavy knitted fringe.

Needlelace

This type of lace-making is most often associated with stumpwork, a style of embroidery that was popular in seventeenth century Britain. It is used to cover padded appliqué shapes and can be worked over wire to create three-dimensional petals and flowers. The delicacy and beauty of needlelace lies in the evenness and regularity of the stitches, so it must be worked on a firm foundation of threads (floss) or wire.

Needlelace is worked across a couched thread (floss) shape to give a firm foundation to the stitches. In stumpwork this is known as a cordonnet. The cordonnet and needlelace are worked over a piece of PVC or other firm fabric so that they can be made to the exact shape required. Once complete the cordonnet and needlelace are lifted off the temporary backing and stitched in place on the embroidery.

Right: Stumpwork birds with wired wings are clothed in needlelace. The needlelace shoreline sits on a space-dyed background of calico and scrim.

MAKING A CORDONNET

• Trace the required shape on to paper and cut out. Position the shape on top of a piece of calico. Cut a piece of PVC larger than your shape, place it on top of the calico and baste.

• Pin prick around the line to transfer the shape to the PVC. If the shape will be padded, pin prick slightly outside the line.

• Fold a length of strong thread (floss) in half and catch the loop end down on the marked line. Use thread in the colour that you will be working with. If the shape is to stand away from the fabric, for example, for a petal, add a piece of fine wire on top of the thread, leaving a wire stalk. This can be cut off later.

• Couch the double thread and wire down around the outline. Work the stitches closer together on tight curves and work two stitches in corners to make a sharp point. Slip the ends of the couched threads through the loop. Trim the ends to 1cm/½in and bend one end back on itself.

• Overcast the ends over the cordonnet only, to secure.

• Work the needlelace over the cordonnet without stitching through the PVC.

Getting started

Needlelace stitches are nearly all based on a simple loop or blanket stitch. Different patterns are created by stitching different numbers of stitches into loops and leaving some spaces in between others. This technique is intended to be finely worked: historically lacemakers would stitch hundreds of tiny stitches to the square 2.5cm/1in! There are many hundreds of needlelace stitches to choose from. Just a few of the more common ones are listed here.

Starting a new thread (floss)

You will probably need more than one length of thread (floss) to work a panel of needlelace. Don't use a piece longer than 45–50cm/18–20in in your tapestry needle otherwise it is likely to get tangled and become knotted as

you work, or if you are using fine silk thread it will unravel. As a rule, it is safe to continue working if your thread is about twice the length of the row you are about to start. If it is less you will need to start a new thread. Wrap the old thread around the cordonnet and leave a short end lying around the shape outline. Introduce the new thread by wrapping twice around the outline to secure it in place. The ends are held in place by buttonhole stitches at the end.

Increasing and decreasing

Increase or decrease the number of stitches at the end of a row. To increase, work extra stitches into the last loop. Then make sure you begin in the right loop to keep the pattern correct when you are working back

along the row. To decrease, miss the first loop and work along the row to the last loop. Then wrap the thread around the side of the cordonnet and continue as before.

Finishing

Once complete, twist any wire ends together and remove the excess. Work tightly packed buttonhole stitches around the edge of the needlelace, stitching under the cordonnet but not through the PVC.

From the wrong side (the calico side), clip the couching threads. Carefully lift the needlelace off the PVC. Use tweezers to remove any couching thread ends. Slipstitch the piece to the background as invisibly as possible. Mould the wire into shape at this point if required.

Bruxelles stitch

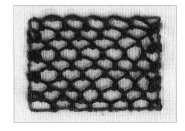

Bruxelles (Brussels) stitch is one of the most versatile needlelace stitches because it can be worked in pairs or trebles and can be whipped or corded.

Wrap the thread (floss) twice around one side of the cordonnet and work even blanket stitch along the top of the cordonnet. Wrap the thread around the cordonnet at the other end before continuing back along the last row of loops. Keep the same number of stitches in each row by missing the last loop.

Double Bruxelles stitch

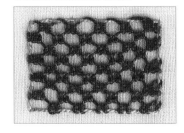

Work two blanket stitches along the top edge of the cordonnet then leave a space equal to two stitches before working another pair of blanket stitches. Continue across the row until you reach the other side. Wrap the thread around the side of the cordonnet and then work back across the row in the same way. Continue to fill the shape.

Whipped treble Bruxelles stitch

Work groups of three blanket stitches along the top of the cordonnet, leaving a space equal to two stitches between them. Work across the row. Wrap the thread (floss) around the side cordonnet. Whip the thread back over each loop (including the last one). Wrap around the cordonnet, then work blanket stitches into each loop and continue as before.

Point d'Anvers

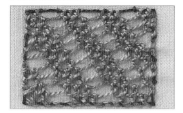

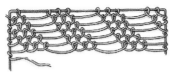

Work three blanket stitches along the top edge of the cordonnet and then leave a space equal to three stitches and work another three. Wrap the thread around the side of the cordonnet. Work back across the row making one stitch into the long loop and two more into the loops between the three stitches above.

Pea stitch variation

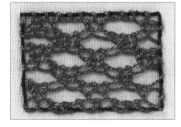

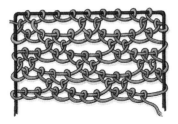

Work blanket stitches across the top of the cordonnet. Wrap the thread around the cordonnet side, then work two blanket stitches into the first two loops. Miss two loops and work blanket stitch into the next two until the row end. Wrap the thread around the cordonnet. Work one stitch into the small loop between two stitches and three into the long loop. At the end of the row wrap the thread twice around the cordonnet and complete the pattern.

Corded Bruxelles stitch

This is a more stable, denser variation of Bruxelles stitch. It can be adapted for double and treble Bruxelles stitch.

Work a row of blanket stitches as for Bruxelles stitch. Wrap the thread around the side cordonnet and take it straight back across to the other side without making any stitches. Wrap the thread around the side cordonnet twice and then work a row of blanket stitches into each loop catching the straight thread.

Goldwork

Today, goldwork is a generic term that covers all types of metallic thread embroidery. Traditional threads (floss) such as Japan gold, Russian braid and gold cord have a proportion of real gold in them which creates a wonderful effect when the light catches different facets of the thread.

Materials

There is a wonderful selection of exquisite metallic and silk threads (floss) to choose from.

1 Japan gold

Japan gold was traditionally made from fine ribbons of real gold coiled around silk floss. Today gold or silver lurex threads are wrapped around a thread core. Japan gold must be couched on to fabric because the metal layer will rip if stitched.

2 Braids and cords

There are many different heavy metallic threads (floss) that can be couched on to fabric. These provide a wide range of textures. They are available in many colours.

3 Metallic threads (floss)

Some metallic threads can be stitched by hand and some can even be used in a sewing machine. To test a thread's flexibility, run your nails down it. If this makes it unravel, it is only suitable for couching.

4 Purl

Purl is made from fine wire that is coiled to form a tiny spring. It is made in a continuous length that can be cut to size and stitched like a bead. Rough purl has a soft polished finish and smooth purl is highly polished and shiny. Check purl has a sparkly appearance because the wire spring is kinked. Pearl or wire purl is heavier in weight and is usually pulled out and couched on to fabric.

5 Gold kid

These are shiny metallic pieces of leather which can be cut up and applied to goldwork. Keep the pieces small and work stitches over the top to blend them into the design. Imitation kid has a synthetic backing.

6 Felt

Felt is used as a padding for gold kid and purl. Use yellow felt with gold threads and grey with silver. Make graded shapes to build up a thick pad with the largest shape on top.

7 Silk threads

Use silk thread for couching gold threads. It has a wonderful sheen and is strong and elastic. Use a yellow colour with gold threads and grey with silver.

THREADS (FLOSS)

• The first metallic threads (floss) were made in such a way that it was physically impossible to stitch them through fabric.

• New synthetic metallic threads have recently been developed that can be stitched in the same way as any other embroidery thread. They are easy to use and do not tarnish, but give a uniform sparkle that unfortunately has none of the softness or warmth of real gold.

• It is essential to buy good-quality gold thread because the cheaper imitations will quickly tarnish. The same applies to the fabric that the work is stitched on and all other embroidery threads used in the design.

• Natural threads and fabrics, such as cotton or linen can be used, but silk is without question the most suitable fibre. Its aptness lies not only in its wonderful sheen, but also in the strength and elasticity of the thread and the rich colours that offset the gold so well.

• Most metallic threads are simply laid over the fabric and couched down. The couched threads can be almost invisible or can play a big part in the design.

Couching

In the Middle Ages underside couching was devised as a method to secure rigid gold threads to a background fabric. This method of couching, where stitching is worked from the wrong side of the fabric and the laid threads (floss) pulled to the back, is now obsolete. However, couching (from the right side) remains the principal method of attaching thread to the background.

To begin, stretch the fabric in an embroidery hoop or frame and run a length of silk thread over a wax block. This helps to prevent the couching thread from twisting as you stitch. Cut a length of gold thread (to be couched) and tape the ends to prevent them from unravelling.

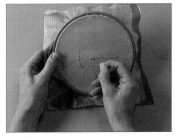

1 Pin the length of gold thread (floss) along the design line leaving a 2.5cm/1in tail. Bring the silk thread up next to the gold thread and make a straight stitch at right angles across the thread. Work further straight stitches 5mm/¼in apart. Thin gold threads are usually couched in pairs so that they lie closer together.

2 Leave about 2.5cm/1in at the end of the row. Use a large-eyed embroidery needle to take the embroidery thread through to the wrong side. It is better to make a large hole that will be covered by the gold thread than to snag or tear the fabric by forcing the thread through with too small a needle.

Using string

Use string to make raised areas of goldwork. The string can be of varying thickness and the spacing altered to create different effects. If possible, use a string to match the metallic thread. String can be dyed if a good match is difficult to find.

1 Cut lengths of string the same size and stitch down in parallel rows on the fabric. Leave a gap between each row. Work double oversewing stitches at each end and catch the string down on long lengths.

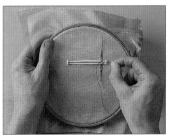

2 Couch the gold threads over the string, working double stitches at each side. Take the ends of the thread to the wrong side as before. A basket-weave pattern can be created by couching over alternate pairs of string.

Right: The skill in goldwork lies in the careful manipulation of the exquisite threads (floss). It takes time and effort to create a successful goldwork design. While it is good to be innovative, don't be tempted to distort and mangle the metallic threads in an attempt to be original.

Far right: Goldwork can be enhanced by other embroidery stitches such as bullion knots. These are the same shape as cut purl and look very effective.

COUCHING A PATTERN OR SHAPE

CREATING PATTERNS

Metal threads (floss) can be couched in different patterns by working stitches between the previous stitches or by stepping to one side. See below.

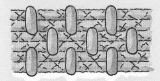

BRICKWORK

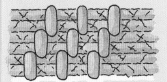

STEPPING

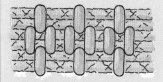

REPEAT PATTERN

Above and right: Use fine thread to create couched patterns.

CIRCLES

• To make circles, fold in half a long length of gold thread.

• Couch the folded end at the centre of the circle.

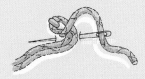

• Coil the double thread around, couching at right angles to the gold thread.

• When sewing in the thread ends, stagger them to make a smooth outline.

ANGLED SHAPES

Pointed shapes are outlined with a double length of gold thread. For a very sharp point, work one thread over each gold thread.

• Couch pairs of gold threads down each side of the shape, leaving a 2.5cm/1in tail of thread at the point. Continue couching pairs of threads down each side, alternately until the shape has been filled.

• Once complete, take the gold threads through to the wrong side and tie off.

Purl

Purl is a long metallic spring produced specially for goldwork. It can be cut up and stitched like beads or couched down like a gold thread. Purl is pliable and can be cut into lengths up to 1cm/¹⁄₂in when stitched over padding. There are several types of purl, such as check and smooth, which reflect the light to give different effects.

Purl looks very effective when stitched randomly on padded felt. If cut in short lengths, it can also be used as a powdering over the background of the design.

1 Use a small pair of craft scissors to cut purl because the wire will quickly blunt embroidery scissors. Cut the purl at right angles with a quick, clean cut. Let the purl fall into a small dish to keep it safe.

2 Using a strong thread or a double length of silk thread, pick up the purl with the needle point. Take the needle to the wrong side. The purl can be stitched to lie flat or worked over other pieces of purl or string.

Padding

One of the main characteristics of goldwork is the attractive play of light on the different threads (floss). To increase this effect, areas can be padded and covered with gold threads, kid or purl. You can use string or card (card stock) as a padding material but felt is the most common choice. Match the colour of the padding to the thread colour – yellow for gold and grey for silver.

1 Decide on the shape and size of the padded area. Cut a felt shape that size and then cut two or three smaller sizes to fit underneath.

Attaching kid

1 Cut the kid to the required shape. Hold it in place with your thumb. Bring the thread up next to the shape and stab stitch through the leather to the wrong side. Work around the shape, stab stitching every 5mm/¹⁄₄in.

2 Place the smallest piece in the middle of the shape and catch it down with stab stitches. Sew on the other layers in this way.

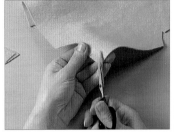

3 Sew the purl, kid or gold threads on top, stitching into the felt in the middle and through all the layers at the edge.

Right: This goldwork uses a variety of techniques. The delicate wadding is a soft contrast to the gold thread (floss) and kid leather.

Beadwork

Beads conjure up images of exquisite, heavily-encrusted evening wear and beautiful accessories such as bags or slippers. But beads can also be used to add detail and texture to other embroidery techniques such as cross stitch, canvas work, appliqué and freestyle embroidery.

Beads come in all shapes and sizes and can be stitched individually or couched in rows. Whatever their size, the technique for stitching them is basically the same. No special equipment is required although tiny seed beads and thin bugle beads have such tiny holes that a special beading needle may be needed.

Beading needles are exceptionally long and fine and are ideal for threading large numbers of beads for couching. It is usually possible to use a fine ordinary between needle for all but the tiniest beads. You will probably find the shorter length of this type of needle easy to handle. If a bead gets stuck on the needle part way down, do not force it over the eye. If you cannot get it back off the needle, crush the bead with small parallel pliers and choose another.

Getting started

Use a double thread (floss) for sewing beads if possible. Fold a long length in half and thread the cut ends into the needle. Bring the needle up through the fabric leaving a thread loop underneath. Take the needle back down through the fabric and the loop, then pull tight to secure. This is a very secure way to begin sewing. If a single strand is used, begin with a knot and stitch back through the knot for extra security. Tip a few beads into a small flat dish that has a rim ready to start. It is easier to pick the beads up with the point of the needle against the edge of the dish.

Couching

 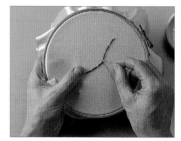

1 Couching is a quick and neat way to attach a long row of beads. You can also see at a glance what the line will look like before sewing the beads in place. Any beads that lie together well can be used. Thread two needles for couching. Secure the first double length at the beginning of the line to be covered. Thread on the beads in the required order.

2 Bring the second threaded needle up between the first two beads. Take the thread (floss) over the string of beads and back down on the other side. Sew a couching stitch between every bead. At the end of the line, remove any excess beads and take all the threads through to the wrong side and sew in the ends securely.

Above: Carefully selected beads add subtle interest to the design of this hand- and machine-embroidered fan.

Making a bead net

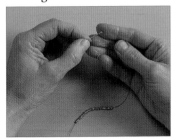

1 Thread a fine needle with a long length of waxed thread (floss). For row 1, thread on an odd number of beads: 25 is a good number. Let the beads lie on the tabletop so that they do not fall off the end of the thread.

2 To make the second row, add two beads and take the needle back through the fourth bead (the second bead on row 1). Carry on adding two beads and catching the fourth until you reach the end.

3 On the next row add two beads between the previous pairs.

4 Keep adding rows in this way until the netted fabric forms.

Above: This stunning smocked purse is decorated with a bead net and tassels.

Attaching single beads

Bring the thread up to the right side of the fabric and pick up a bead. Let the bead drop down to the end of the thread and sew back through the fabric at the end of the bead.

Attaching bugle beads

Bugle beads are sewn in the same way as small beads. Thread a bugle bead and stitch back down where the other end will lie. Hold the first bead in place with your thumb to get the length right. Take the thread across the back to the left-hand side and attach as before.

Sequins and beads

Sequins can be attached with a small bead. Bring the thread up through the fabric and thread on first a sequin then a small bead. Take the needle back through the hole in the sequin and the small bead will hide this.

Machine embroidery

Whether your sewing machine is a wonder of modern technology or an older swing needle model, it will be suitable for machine embroidery. Technical advances may have produced sewing machines that can stitch sophisticated, computer-generated patterns, but machine embroidery is mainly worked in the basic straight and zigzag stitches and therefore well within the scope of most machines.

Using the presser foot

There are two methods of working machine embroidery: with the presser foot in place on the machine; or using a darning foot instead of a presser foot, known as freestyle machine embroidery. Practise the different techniques on small pieces of fabric first and keep them in a notebook for future reference.

Movement is slightly restricted when working machine embroidery with the presser foot and with the feed teeth up, since the machine will allow you only to work backwards and forwards and not from side to side, but a variety of effects can be created using a basic straight stitch.

1 Thread the machine in the normal way with a synthetic sewing thread. Stitch in a straight line and stop with the needle in the fabric. Lift the presser foot and swing the fabric around ready to stitch the second row. Lower the presser foot and stitch again. Continue in this way until you have formed a block of straight lines.

2 With the needle still in the fabric, turn the embroidery around so that the next stitching lines you work will be horizontal. Stitch backwards and forwards across the previous stitching to create a cross-hatched pattern. Change the thread colour to build up layers of different coloured lines.

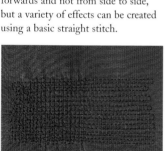

3 Straight stitches can be used to make parallel lines too. Sew across one or two stitches before beginning the next line. Stitch at right angles to form a regular grid pattern and fill in with diagonal lines to increase the texture and density of the stitches.

4 Altering the length of the stitches will produce different textures. Long stitches have a smooth appearance whereas small stitches tend to bring the bobbin thread up and make a slightly textured line. Use a different colour in the bobbin to emphasize this effect.

5 Heavier embroidery threads, which cannot be threaded through the needle, can be wound on to the bobbin. Work with the fabric upside down and stitch in the normal way. The embroidery thread will then look as if it has been couched down.

Zigzag setting

Machine zigzag, or satin stitch, is commonly associated with appliqué, particularly fusible web appliqué, where the raw edge of the applied fabric is visible. Densely packed zigzag, worked over the raw edge creates a neat outline.

1 Set the machine to a wide zigzag for machine embroidery. You may need to lengthen the stitch and loosen the tension slightly so that the stitches lie flat. Iron interfacing to the wrong side of the fabric before you start stitching if your fabric is delicate.

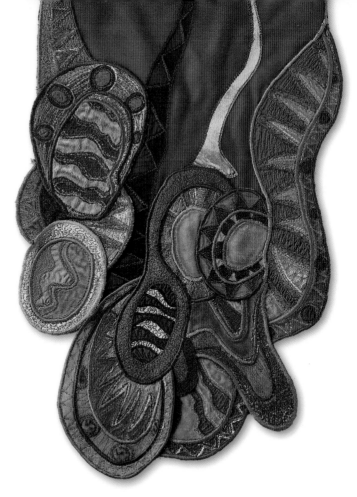

2 Work a row of zigzag stitches. Stop with the needle in the fabric. Turn the fabric around and stitch the next row.

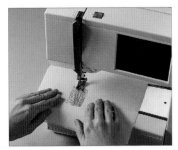

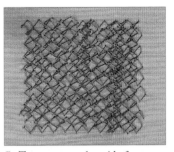

3 The rows can be worked slightly at an angle to produce a rough texture. Go back over some of the rows to increase the density of the stitches.

4 Work rows at right angles to the first set to make a denser cross-hatched pattern. Leave the needle in the fabric at the end of the row and swing the fabric

Top: Appliqué and satin stitch have been used to effect in this vibrantly coloured silk and satin scarf.

5 To create a regular grid of diamonds, work a row of zigzag stitches and stop with the needle in the fabric at the end of the left swing. Turn the fabric around and work the second row guiding the fabric carefully to allow the needle to stitch into the points of the previous stitches. You will find it works better if you sew the rows quite quickly.

Using different feet

Most sewing machines have a selection of different feet which can be used for machine embroidery. An ordinary general-purpose foot is fine for basic straight or zigzag stitches, but you should change to a clear-view foot if you want to stitch along a curved line or in a precise direction.

Use an embroidery foot that is cut away underneath for working satin stitch because this will be flattened by an ordinary foot. A cording foot has a groove underneath or a hole on top, to guide a cord or braid under the presser foot.

Using a cording foot

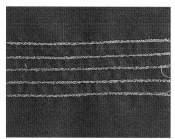

1 Place the braid on the fabric and put it under the cording foot. Make sure the braid is well under to ensure it does not bundle up under the foot. Work a couple of straight stitches in the end of the cord, then alter the stitch width to make a zigzag across the braid from one side to the other. Stitch slowly, letting the braid feed under the foot. Use the side of the foot as a guide when working multiple rows.

Machine-wrapped cords

Machine-wrapped cords are very attractive and quite easy to make. Use them as an added decoration on embroidery. You can make these using an ordinary foot and with the width set at its widest. Alternately, use a foot with a large groove or hole to let the cord go through easily, especially if the cord you are covering is thick. Any smooth, round cord is suitable, including lengths of wool (yarn).

1 Insert the cord through the hole in the foot and work one or two straight stitches to secure the threads.

2 Set the machine to its widest zigzag, and the stitch length at zero. Loosen the top tension slightly. Hold the cord on both sides of the cording foot and feed it through slowly as you stitch. Work over the cord again until it is completely covered.

Above: Machine-wrapped cords, appliqué, hand and freestyle machine embroidery on water-soluble fabric have been incorporated into this fan design.

Left: Examples of the basic wrapped cords.

Freestyle machine embroidery

This type of machine embroidery is worked with a darning foot, a special machine embroidery foot or a spring needle and with the feed teeth lowered. The fabric lies flat against the needleplate, so that the stitch forms correctly. The fabric is stretched taut in a hoop before beginning to stitch. With no restriction from the presser foot, movement becomes much more flexible and the stitching multi-directional.

Even if you are used to working with a sewing machine, this type of embroidery takes time to perfect. Think of it as drawing with pencil and paper, only here the paper (fabric) moves, rather than the pencil (needle).

NEEDLES

Ordinary machine needles can be used for machine embroidery, although needles with larger eyes, which accommodate heavier threads, are available. Try size 90/14 to begin with and move on to size 80/12.

Hoops

Two types of hoop are suitable for free machine embroidery. A traditional wooden hand embroidery hoop can be used, or one of the new flat metal and plastic spring hoops that are specially made for machine embroidery. These are designed to fit easily under the darning foot and hold the fabric taut.

To use a wooden hoop, place the fabric right side up on top of the outer ring. Press the inner ring firmly in position. If the fabric slips, tighten the outer ring and refit the fabric.

Alternately, place the fabric right side up on the plastic ring. Squeeze the handles of the ring together and press down into the plastic ring. Release the handles to secure the fabric.

Above: Freestyle machine embroidery is used to define the design suggested by the painted background.

Beginning freestyle machine embroidery

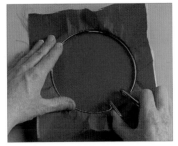

1 Insert a new needle size 90/14 in the machine. Loosen the tension slightly and fit the darning foot. Bring the thread up through the needle plate and lower the feed teeth.

2 Place the fabric and hoop under the foot. Hold the top thread and turn the hand wheel until the bobbin thread appears. Pull it through the fabric. Make the stitch length zero.

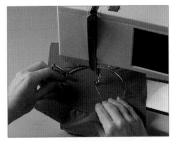

3 Lower the foot. This engages the stitch mechanism. Hold the thread ends and work a few stitches to secure the threads. Snip the thread ends if working an open pattern.

Vermicelli stitch

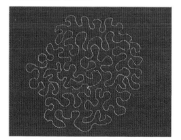

In vermicelli stitch the fabric is moved in all possible directions. This will help you learn to control the movement of the hoop and the speed of the machine. Work with the machine at a moderate speed and move the hoop to create a squiggly line as shown. Try not to jerk the hoop as this will make the thread or needle snap.

Loose spirals

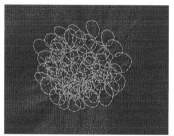

Spirals are formed by moving the hoop in a circular movement. Begin in the centre and work your way outwards. Stitch at moderate speed and move the hoop slowly and smoothly to make tight curves with lots of small stitches. The spirals can be formed outside or inside the line. It takes practise to make circles smooth with even stitches.

Jagged spirals

Jagged spirals are worked at a fast machine speed. Hold the hoop securely by the rim and secure the thread with a couple of straight stitches. Move the hoop in a circular movement as before. If you can get the speed of both the machine and the hoop right, jagged spirals will form. Try not to jerk suddenly or the needle will break.

Tight spirals

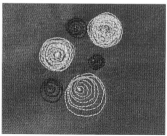

Tight spirals are slightly more difficult to work.

Bring the bobbin thread up to the surface and secure with a few stitches. Lift the darning foot and trim the thread neatly. Lower the darning foot and sew at a moderate speed moving the hoop in a circular motion. Work slowly out from the centre and try to form a near-perfect circle. Spirals can be quite open or densely filled. If necessary, you can stitch back over the previous stitches to fill in between lines.

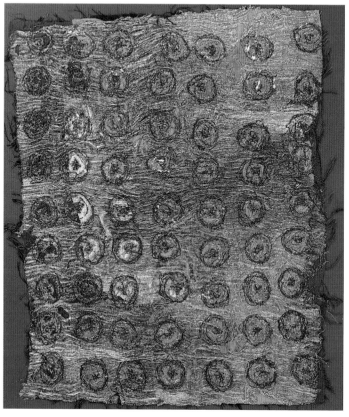

Left: This colourful design features machine-embroidered circles on multi-coloured metallic organza.

Creating different textures

Altering the tension of the machine changes the appearance of even a simple line of straight stitches. Tightening the top tension will bring the bobbin thread up to the surface and create a textured effect. You can emphasize this whipped effect by using a different colour in the reel and in the bobbin.

The top tension is always loosened slightly to begin freestyle machine stitching, so it makes quite a difference when the top tension is tightened completely. Take care that the top tension is not so tight that it causes the needle to bend and break.

If you want to create even more texture, loosen the lower tension by turning the screw on the bobbin case. If you are nervous about being able to get it back to the right setting again, try this tip. Before changing the lower tension, fit a bobbin in the case and let it dangle by the thread. You should be able to make the case drop bit by bit by jerking the thread lightly. This is the correct lower tension.

Whipping

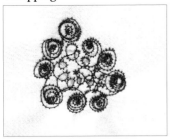

Tighten the top tension and work whipped loops and spirals. You can alter the tonal appearance by changing the speed of stitching. If you stitch slowly, the top thread will sometimes be couched by the bobbin thread. Increase the speed and the stitches get smaller and the bobbin thread covers more of the top thread.

Whipping with loops

Bring the top tension back slightly and loosen the lower tension. Move the hoop quickly to pull the bobbin thread out and make quite distinct loops. As the spiral size increases, the loops are pulled out further. Experiment to create different effects by changing the colour and texture of the bobbin thread.

Loop texture

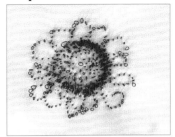

A different texture is created if the top thread is pulled out completely. Cut the top thread between the loops every so often and pull it out carefully. Use this technque for landscape backgrounds or filling large surface areas.

Whipped spots

If the lower tension is loosened considerably and the top tension tightened enough, much longer loops will form. Use this setting to make very textured whorls or little spots. Leave the thread ends until last, then sew them through to the wrong side.

Whipping on muslin

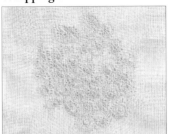

The fabric you use will affect the final appearance of the stitch, too. If you work whipping on a loosely woven muslin the fabric threads will be pulled and distorted, too.

Gathering on felt

Tighten the top tension and fit the felt under the darning foot (this will be the wrong side). Move the felt in a circular movement to stitch fairly big spirals and loops. The tight top thread will cause the fabric to gather. do not use an embroidery hoop.

Zigzag and satin stitch

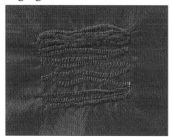  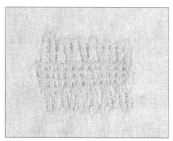

1 Set the machine for the widest stitch and loosen the top tension slightly so that only the top thread shows in the stitched sample. Work up and down, varying the speed of the machine in relation to the movement of the hoop to produce lines of zigzag and satin stitching.

2 Wider areas of satin stitching can be built up by overlapping adjacent rows. Or the width of the stitch can be changed as you work to produce thick and thin lines. Move the hoop with one hand and turn the stitch width dial with the other. Try to make the transition even.

3 When you work satin stitch on a loose-weave fabric such as muslin you can create machine embroidery that looks like traditional drawn-thread work. The swing of the needle pulls the fabric threads together to produce a lacy effect.

Effect of the background fabric

Machine stitching looks quite different on different types of fabrics. For example, a design stitched on a smooth fabric has a smooth finish compared to one stitched on velvet or a pile fabric, where the stitches seem to sink into the background.

The background does to some extent affect the type of embroidery you choose. On transparent fabrics, such as muslin, the threads can be seen from the wrong side of the fabric and the stitches tend to pull the fabric and create small holes. Satin stitching on loose-weave fabrics such as scrim pulls the threads together to produce an extremely lacy effect. Straight stitching works better on net where, there is considerable contrast between the stitching and the background.

Below: Machine embroidery on bubble wrap, a non-traditional fabric, creates a most unusual effect.

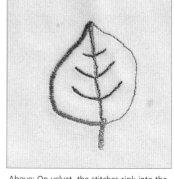

Above: On velvet, the stitches sink into the pile to give a very soft effect.

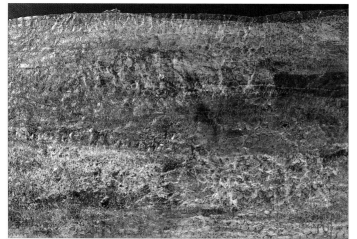

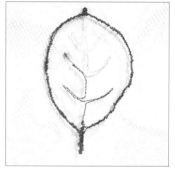

Above: The stitching on net is very prominent. Take care not to tear the fabric when machine stitching.

Using water-soluble fabric

Water-soluble fabric allows you to create three-dimensional pieces of embroidery that can be attached to another background or used to create sculptured pieces. The soluble material, which looks like clear film (plastic wrap), is fitted in a hoop and machine embroidered as if it were fabric. Even if you intend to work zigzag stitches, use straight stitch initially because the zigzag stitches will unravel if worked on their own.

The material is dissolved in water leaving the embroidery behind.

There are two types available: a thin clear plastic sheet that dissolves in cold water, and a pale green muslin that is soluble in hot water.

Open circles

Care must be taken when working open work on water-soluble fabric. Check that all parts of the embroidery outline are joined so that the stitched piece does not fall apart in the water. Hold the embroidery up to the light to check for gaps. If necessary, go back over some lines to close gaps.

1 Stretch the soluble material in the hoop. Slip the hoop under the darning foot and bring the bobbin thread up through the soluble material as you would for normal machine embroidery.

2 Set the machine for straight stitch with the stitch length almost at zero. Lower the darning foot and work a few stitches to secure the thread. Trim the ends. Begin to move the hoop in small circular movements.

3 Ensure that the circles touch one another, interlocking all over the material. Overstitch the circles several times and with different colours if appropriate. The denser the stitching the stronger the piece will be.

Filled shapes

Flowers and other solid shapes can be created with a solid filling stitch. The soluble plastic will tear quite easily so a piece of net can be fitted into the hoop at the same time for added strength. Pieces of fabric or thread can also be sandwiched between the two layers before stitching.

1 Mark the shape to be stitched with a water-soluble ink pen.

2 Outline the shape with rows of stitching, then fill in the shape.

Dissolving the soluble fabric

Fill a shallow dish with water and place the embroidered piece in it. Agitate the embroidery between your fingers until the material dissolves away. Rinse and leave to dry flat. You could try pinning very fine pieces to polystyrene, so that the shape does not distort when in the water.

Above: Shapes stitched on water-soluble fabric have been applied to the lid of this small beaded purse.

Templates

Enlarge the templates to the desired size, using a photocopier, or trace the design and draw a grid of evenly spaced squares over your tracing. Draw a larger grid on to another piece of paper and copy the outline square by square.

Cable pattern

Feathered heart

Feather/ring design
with lattice pattern

Lover's knot

Quilting templates,
p.154

Feathered wheel

Feathered triangle

Plaited border

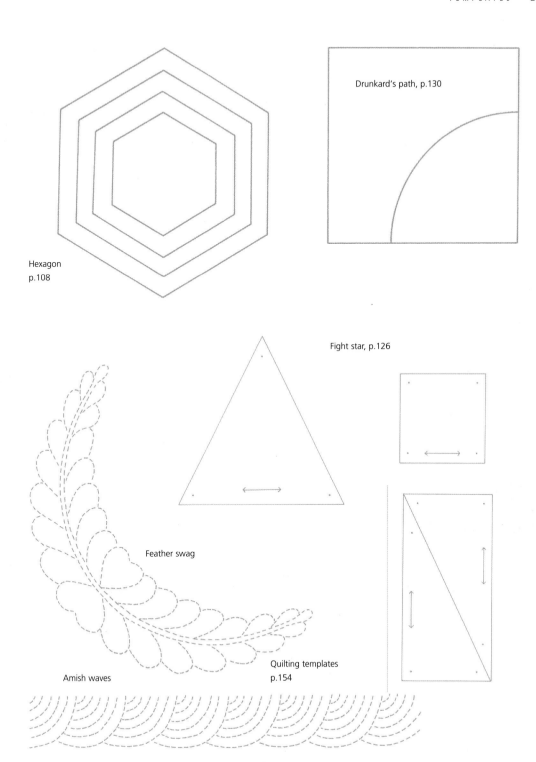

Drunkard's path, p.130

Hexagon
p.108

Fight star, p.126

Feather swag

Quilting templates
p.154

Amish waves

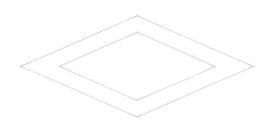

Le Moyne Star and Virginia Star p.128

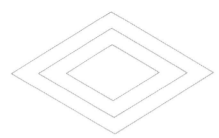

Tumbling blocks, p.107

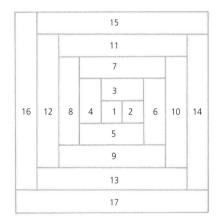

Log cabin, p.135

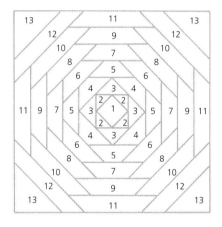

Pineapple log cabin, p.136

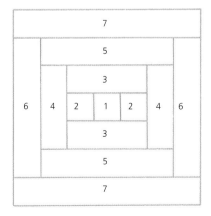

Courthouse steps, p.137

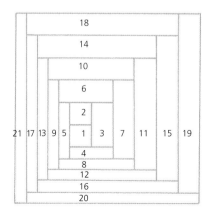

Off-centre log cabin, p.137

Stained glass appliqué,
p.148

Baltimore quilt, p.144

Blackwork, p.220

Reverse appliqué,
p.150

Mountmellick, p.230

Shadow appliqué,
p.146

Italian and trapunto quilting,
p.160–1

INDEX

accordion pleats 60
acetate 27, 32
Aida 208
alpaca 25
American block quilts 117–25
angora 25
Antwerp edging stitch 190
appliqué 101, 140–51, 158
    Baltimore quilt 144, 251
    Broderie perse 145
    Hawaiian 147
    joining blocks 152–3
    machine sewing 142–3
    raw-edge 140
    reverse 150–1, 251
    shadow 146, 251
    stained glass 148–9, 251
    traditional 140
Armenian edging stitch 190
Asanoha design 162
Assisi embroidery 218

back stitch 46, 180
basting 45
ballpoint needles 15
Baltimore quilt 144, 251
band stitches 184
basket filling stitch 196
basting 33, 45
batiste 19, 21, 24
batting 82, 100, 101, 153
battlement couching 203
beadwork 170, 238–9
beeswax 96
bias 37
bias binding 54, 167
binding 54
quilts 102
blackwork 219–21, 251
blanket stitch 47, 184
blanketing 22

blind tucks 59
blind-hemming (blindstitching)
    16, 49
block quilts 117–25
bobbins 14, 17
bodkins 10
Bokhara couching 201
bolster cushions 85
bonded fibre fabrics 30
border stitches 184
bound buttonholes 72
bound seams 50–1
box pleats 60
Bremsilk 32
brick stitch 196, 212
broad cross stitch 211
broderie anglaise 20, 21, 230
broderie perse 145
Bruxelles stitch 232, 233
bugle beads 239
bullion knots 192
bull's head 199
burlap 19, 20, 21
butter muslin 19
buttonhole bars 76
buttonhole foot 16
buttonhole stitch 184, 185
buttonhole wheel 194
buttonholes 70–3
buttons 74–5

cable stitch 67, 177, 179
calico 19, 21
camel 25
canvas 15, 19
embroidery 19, 208
captive rice stitch 215
carbon, dressmaker's 10, 44, 154,
    174
Carpenter's Square 157
Caselguidi 224
cashmere 25
Cathedral Windows 58
Catherine wheel 194
Cat's Cradle 125
cellulose 27
Ceylon stitch 202
chain stitch 178, 179
chalk, tailor's 10, 44
challis 22
chambray 19
checked fabrics 34, 40–1
cheesecloth 19
chequer stitch 216
Chequerboard 138–9
chequered chain stitch 178

chevron stem stitch 202
chevron stitch 67, 187, 188
chintz 19, 145
Churn Dash 121, 122
closed buttonhole stitch 185
closed Cretan stitch 182
closed feather stitch 176
cloud filling stitch 199
coll filling stitch 225
colour washing 173
colouring fabrics 172–3
colour wheel 98
compasses 96
composite stitches 176
computer-generated stitches 49
Contrary Wife 122
cool wool 22
coral stitch 177
cord
    machine-wrapped 242
corded Bruxelles stitch 233
corded quilting 161, 251
cording foot 16, 242
cordonnet 231–3
cordonnet stitch 181
corduroy 19, 39
corners
    flanges 83
    mitred 83, 101, 166
Cornucopia 144, 251
cotton, mercerized 33
cotton fabrics 18, 19–21
    pre-shrinking 35
couching 183, 236
    battlement 203
    beadwork 238
    Bokhara 201
    goldwork 234–6
    needlelace 231–3
    pendant 183
    Romanian 201

satin stitch 183
counted-thread embroidery
    208–17
Courthouse Steps 137, 250
craft knives 96
crazy patchwork 132–3
crêpe 22
crêpe-backed satin 23
Cretan open filling stitch 202
Cretan stitch 182
crewel wool 209
crocheting 30
Crockett Cabin 120
crocodile, mock 28
cross stitch 183, 210, 211, 218
crossed tucks 59
Crosses and Losses 120
crow's foot 195
crushed organza 28
Cupro 27, 32
curtains 86–91
    café curtain rods 86
    calculating fabric quantities 88
    curtain clips 86
    curtain hooks 87, 91
    heading tapes 89–90
    hold backs 86, 87
    linings 89–91
    self-headed 91
    sheer 87, 89
curves, stitching 16, 48, 52, 130–1
cushion stitch 215
cushions 82–5
cutting out 39–44
cutwork 222–3

damask 19, 21, 31
darning 16, 68
Darting Birds 123
darts 44, 62

decimal/imperial conversion chart 102
decorative fabrics 28–9
decorative seams 52–3
denim 15, 19
detached wheat-ear stitch 199
devoré velvet 28, 29
diagonal basting 45
diamond stitch 185
diamond straight stitch 213
diamond-filling quilting 159
directional fabrics 39–41
Dobby weave 31
dog's tooth check 22
double Bruxelles stitch 232
double buttonhole stitch 184
double chain stitch 178
double face knit 22
double feather stitch 176
double hems 57
double herringbone stitch 187
double knot stitch 177
Double Pinwheel 118
Double Wedding Ring 167
drawn-thread work 226–9
drill 19
Drunkard's Path 130–1, 249
duchesse satin 23
Duck's Foot in the Mud 117
dupion 23
Dutchman's Puzzle 114, 121

Eccentric Star 124
echo quilting 155, 159
edging stitches 190
elastic 15, 63
elastomeric yarns 26, 31
Electric Fan 114
embroidery 169–247
English crazy patchwork 132–3
envelope opening 83
equipment 10–17
embroidery 170
Eton taffeta 32
evenweave fabrics 24, 208, 227
eyelets 76, 217, 225, 230

fabric markers 10
fabric structures 30–1
fabrics 18–31
fan stitch 217
fancy herringbone stitch 186
fancy stitch 199
fasteners 74–9
fat quarters 96, 99
feather stitch 176
Feather Wreath 156
feathered chain stitch 179
felt 25, 26, 234
felting 30, 31
fibres, fabrics 18

Fight Star 126–7, 249
filling stitches 196
fir stitch 217
fishbone stitch 196, 198
flanged cord 85
flanges 83
flannel 22
flannelette 19
flap opening 84
flat fell seams 53
flaws in fabric, checking for 35
fleece 26
Flock of Geese 120
floss 170, 209
Flower Basket 119
flowers, embroidery designs 206–7
fly stitch 193
frames
    embroidery 170, 175
    quilting 96
fraying 50
    freestyle machine embroidery 243–4
freezer paper 96, 141
French knots 192
French seams 51
    mock 51
fur fabrics 28, 29, 43
fusible bonding web 10, 96
fusible interfacings 33
futi 23

gaberdine 22, 27, 31
gathering 63
    smocking 64–7
gauging 67
georgette 23
gingham 19, 20, 21
glue 96
gobelin stitch 212, 213
goldwork 234–7
graded seams 52
Grandmother's Flower Garden 106, 108–9
graph paper 96
griffin stitch 201

gutta 172

habotai 23
hair fibres 25
half back stitch 47
half cross stitch 211
half Rhodes stitch 214
hand-rolled hems 57
Hands All Around 117
Hardanger embroidery 208, 222–3
Hawaiian appliqué 147
heavy chain stitch 179
hem stitch 47, 226
hems 56–7
    blind 16, 49
    machine stitching 16, 57
    narrow 57
herringbone stitch 186, 187
herringbone weave 22
hessian 20, 21
Higaki design 162
Holbein stitch 218, 220
Honey Bee 121
honeycomb filling stitch 202, 203
honeycomb stitch 66, 67
hooks and eyes 76
hoops
    embroidery 170, 175, 243
    quilting 96
Hopscotch 114
hound's tooth weave 22
Hungarian stitch 213

in-the-ditch quilting 154, 158
Indian cotton 20, 21
insertion stitches 190
interfacings 33
interlaced herringbone stitch 187
interlaced insertion stitch 191
inverted pleats 60
ironing see pressing
Italian quilting 161, 251

Jacob's Ladder 123
jacquard weave 19, 24, 31
Japan gold 234

jean zippers 78
jean-point needles 15
Jenny's Star 121
jersey 15, 20, 21, 26, 27

khaki 19
kick pleats 60
kid, goldwork 234, 237
kloster blocks 222-3
knife pleats 60
knit fabrics 19, 20, 30, 31
    double face 22
    jersey 20, 26, 29, 33
    seams 50
knitting stitch 214
knotted buttonhole stitch 184
knotted cable stitch 177
knotted insertion stitch 191

lace 17, 20, 21, 28, 29, 31, 42
lace stitch 223
laced herringbone stitch 186
ladder stitch 185
lamé 28, 29
laminated fabrics 30, 31
lapped seams 52
lazy daisy stitch 193
long-tailed 193
Le Moyne Star 121, 126, 128–9, 250
leaf stitch 198
leather, imitation 28, 29, 31, 43
Leno weave 31
Light and Dark 134
linen 18
linen fabrics 24
linen stitch 211
linen thread 33
lingerie 51
linings 32
    curtains 89–91
Log Cabin 134–8, 152, 250
long quarters 96, 99
long and short stitch 197
long-armed cross stitch 210
looped edge insertion stitch 191

looped edging stitch 190
Lover's Knot 156, 248
Lurex 28, 29, 208
Lycra 26

machine sewing 48–9, 142–3
machine-wrapped cords 242
Magic Triangles 114
making up the quilt sandwich 153
man-made fibres 18, 27
Margaret's Choice 114
marking up fabric 44
    patchwork 96, 104
    pleats 60
Maru Bishamon design 162
masking techniques 174
Matsukawabishi design 162
measuring up 88
mercerised sewing cotton 33
metallic fabrics 28, 29, 208
metallic thread 209, 234
metric/imperial conversion chart
    102
microfibre 26
Milanese stitch 213
mirrors, shisha work 204
mitred corners 83, 101, 166
modal 27
mohair 22, 25
moiré 27
Molas 150
moleskin 19, 20
mosaic quilts 106–16
mosaic stitch 212
Mountmellick work 230, 251
muslin 19, 20, 21

nap, fabrics with 39, 50
natural fibres 18, 19–25, 32
needle weaving 229
needlelace 231–3
needlepoint 19, 209
needles 10
embroidery 170, 243
sewing machine 15, 243
net 26, 28, 31

bead 239
    embroidery on 246
    Lurex 29
net tracks and wires 87, 88
Nottingham lace 20
nylon 26
nylon jersey 32
nylon net 26, 28

oblique filling 225
Off-Centre Log Cabin 137, 250
Ohio Star 117, 126
ombré 39
open Cretan stitch 182
open fishbone stitch 198
organdie 19, 20, 21, 28, 29
organza 23, 28, 29
    crushed 28
ottoman 23
outline back stitch 67
outline quilting 154, 159
outline stitches 176
overlap opening 83
overlocking 49
oversewing 47

padded satin stitch 197
padding, goldwork 237
panné velvet 29
paper lamé 28, 29
paper patterns 38–44
parallel lines quilting 159
patching 69
patchwork 95–139
Patience Corner 121
pattern cutting 38–44
patterned fabrics 39–41
pea stitch 233
peachskin 26
peau-de-soie 26
Pekinese stitch 181
pencil pleats 89, 90
pendant couching 183
Persian yarn 209
picot 223
pin cushions 10

pin tucks 59
pinch pleats 89, 90
pine stitch 217
Pineapple Log Cabin 136, 250
pinked seams 52
pinning fabrics 45
pins 10
piping 55
    buttonholes 73
    cushions 85
piqué 20, 21, 27, 31
plaid fabrics 34, 40–1
plaited gobelin stitch 213
plastic fabrics 29, 43
pleats 60–1
point d'Anvers 233
pointed twill 24
polyester 26
polythene fabrics 29
poplin 31
poppers 77
Port and Starboard 114
pounce bags 175
preparation, fabric 34–5, 44, 99
press studs 77
presser foot 240
pressing
    curved seams 111
    darts 61
    patchwork 111
    pleats 60
    smocking 64
prick and pounce 154, 175
prick stitch 47
printed fabrics 19, 20
printing, block 173
protractors 96
pulled fabric embroidery 224–5
punch stitch 224
purl 234, 237
Puss in the Corner 117, 123
PVC (polyvinyl chloride) 29, 31,
    43

quilter's quarter 96
quilter's tape 10, 155
quilting 95–167
    diamond-filling 159
    echo quilting 155, 159
    equipment 96
    free-motion 158
    hand sewing 157
    in-the-ditch 154, 158
    Italian (corded) 161, 251
    machine sewing 16, 158
    medallion 156
    outline 154, 159
    parallel lines 159
    Sashiko 162
    selective 159
    shell-filling 159

    tied 163
    transferring design 96, 154-5
    trapunto 160, 251
    wholecloth 156
quilting hoops and frames 96
quilting pins 96
quilting thimble 96, 157

Railroad 165
raised chain band 188
raised chevron stitch 188
raised cup stitch 195
raised lattice band 189
raised stem stitch band 188
raised stitches 188
ray stitch 216
rayon 27
released tucks 59
repairs 68–9
resist techniques 172
reverse appliqué 150–1, 251
reverse cushion stitch 212
Rhodes stitch 214
ribbed wheel 194
ribbon embroidery 170, 205
ribbon stitch 206
rice stitch 215
rickrack braid 31
Road to Heaven 103, 119
Robbing Peter to Pay Paul 130
rolled hems 57
Roman filling burden stitch 200
Roman filling stitch 198
Roman Pavement 109
Romanian couching 201
rotary cutting sets 96, 105
rouleaux loops 72
rouleaux turners 10, 72
rulers 96
running stitch 46, 181
Russian braid 234
Russian drawn thread embroidery
    228

safety pins 10, 96
sampler quilts 121, 152

Sashiko quilting 162
sashing 101, 102, 152–3
satin 23, 31, 42
satin stitch 197
scallop stitch 217
scalloped tucks 59
scallops 230
scissors 10, 96, 105, 170
scrim 20, 21
scroll stitch 177
seam allowances 38
seam bound hems 57
seam rippers 10, 48, 96
seams
    binding 54
    clipping curves 52
    decorative 52–3
    plain 50
    taped 50
    trimming 52
    types 50-3
seeding 198
self-bound seams 51
selvage 37
Seminole 138–9
sequin fabrics 29
sewing machines 12–17
shadow appliqué 146, 251
shantung 23
sheaf stitch 189
sheer fabrics
    curtains 87, 89
    cutting out 42
    darts 62
    seams 51
shadow appliqué 146
shell-filling quilting 159
shepherd's check 22
shirring 63
shirting 19, 21
shisha work 204
Shoo Fly 124
shot twill 32
shrinkage, pre-shrinking fabric 35
silk fabrics 15, 18, 23
slip basting 45
slip stitch 47
slot seams 53
smocking 64–7
snap fastners 77
spaced tucks 59
spacing foot 16
spandex 26
spirals, machine embroidery 244
split stitch 181
Spoon and Bobbin 121
spring needles 15
square filling stitch 200–1
stained glass appliqué 148–9, 251
stamping techniques 174
Star of Hope 121

Star of India 126
star stitch 214
stem stitch 67, 180, 188, 202
stencilling 174
Steps to the Altar 124
stitch binding 30
stone-washed denim 19, 21
Straight Furrow 134
straightening fabric ends 34
straightening grain 35
stretch fabrics
    interfacings 33
    lining 32
    seams 50, 51
striped fabrics 34, 40–1
striped woven band 189
strong thread 33
stumpwork 231
sueded fabrics 26, 28, 29, 43
Sunshine and Shadow 106,
    112–13
surface honeycomb stitch 67
synthetic fibres 18, 26, 33

taffeta 26, 32
tailor's chalk 10, 44
tailor's tacks 44
tape measures 10, 96
taped seams 50
tapestry wool 209
tassels 80–1
    corded 81
tears, repairing 68, 69
templates
    appliqué 104, 251
    patchwork 96, 104, 249-50
    quilting 104, 248-51
Tencel gabardine 27
tension, machine-sewing 16
tent stitch 211
terrycloth 21
tête de boeuf 199
thimbles 10, 96, 157
thread 10, 33, 209
    appliqué 96
    embroidery 33, 170, 209

    quilting 96
thread eyes 76
threaded back stitch 180
threaded herringbone stitch 186
threading a sewing machine 14
three-sided stitch 225
ticking 19, 21
tie-dyeing 172
tied herringbone stitch 187
tied quilting 163
tissue paper 10
top-stitching 15, 33
towelling 21
tracing wheels 10, 44
tramming 208
transfer paper 96
transferring designs 154–5
trapunto quilting 160, 251
trellis couching 200
Trip Around the World 106,
    112–13
tucked seams 52
tucks 58–9
Tumbling Blocks 106, 107, 250
Tussah silk 23
tweed 22
twill 22, 23, 31
    pointed 24
    shot 32
twin needles 15
twisted chain stitch 178
two-patch quilts 106

understitched seams 50
unpicking 10, 48, 96
upright cross stitch 210

Vandyke stitch 185
vault stitch 216
Velcro 77
    curtain tape 89
velour 29
velvet 21, 26, 27, 29
    devoré 28, 29
    embroidery on 246
    machine-stitching 17

    nap 39
    panné 29
    printed 28
velvet stitch 216
Venetian picot 190
vermicelli stitch 244
vicuna 25
vinyl 29, 31, 43
Virginia Star 126, 128–9, 250
viscose
    acetate 27
    printed 27
voile 19, 21

wadding 82, 100, 101, 153
waffle stitch 215
washable fabrics
washcare symbols 36–7
water-soluble fabric, embroidery
    on 247
wave stitch 67, 224
wax resist 172
wedding quilts 156
Welsh quilts 156
welt seams 53
whipped back stitch 180
whipped chain stitch 179
whipped running stitch 181
whipped treble Bruxelles stitch
    233
whipping, machine embroidery
    245
whitework 224–30
wholecloth quilts 156
winceyette 19, 21
Windmill 117, 119
Windmill Blades 136
wing needles 15
wool, tapestry 209
wool fabrics 18, 22, 25, 26, 35
    pre-shrinking 35
worsted 22
woven fabrics 30, 31
woven wheel 194

zephyr 19, 21

SUPPLIERS

United Kingdom
Barnyarns Ltd
PO Box 28
Thirsk
North Yorkshire, YO7 3YN
for sewing and embroidery supplies

Bogod Machine Company
50–52 Great Sutton Street
London, EC1V ODJ
for sewing machines and overlockers

Coats Cafts
McMullen Road
Darlington
Co. Durham, DL1 1YQ
*for machine embroidery and
sewing threads*

Delicate Stitches
339 Kentish Town Road
Kentish Town
London
NW5 2TJ
for fine natural fabrics

DMC Creative World
Pullman Road
Wigston
Leicestershire, LE18 2DY
*for counted-thread fabrics, embroi-
dery thread and crewel wool*

Duttons for Buttons
3 Church Street
Ilkley, LS29 9DR
branches in Harrogate, Keighley,
York and Leeds
for buttons

Harrison Drape
Bradfor Street
Birmingham, B12 0PE
for curtain equipment

House of Smocking
1 Ryeworth Road
Charlton Kings
Cheltenham,
Gloucestershire, GL52 6LG
for all smocking supplies

La Maison du Patchwork
29 rue Jeanne d'Arc
87290 Châteauponsac
France
*for patchwork and quilting holiday
workshops*

Newey Goodman
Sedgley road West
Tipton
West Midlands
DY4 8AH
for sewing equipment

Quorn Country Crafts
18 Churchgate
Loughborough
Leicestershire
for patchwork fabrics

Ribbon Designs
PO Box 382
Edgware
Middlesex
HA8 7XQ
for silk ribbons

United States
Aardvark Adventures
PO box 2449
Livermore, CA94551
for fabrics, threads and trims

Herrschers
Hoover Road
Stevens Point, WI 54481
for general tools and equipment

Nancy's Notions
PO Box 683
Dept 32, Beave Dam
WI 53916
*for sewing, quilting, beadwork,
appliqué and embroidery*

Australia
Coats Patons Crafts Pty Ltd
89–91 Peters Avenue
Mulgrave
Vic 3170

DMC Needlecraft Pty Ltd
51–55 Carrington Road
Marrickville
NSW 2204

Simply Stitches
153 Victoria Avenue
Chatswood
NSW 2067

Canada
Dressew
337 W Hastings Street
Vancouver, BC

ACKNOWLEDGEMENTS

The publisher would like to thank the talented stitchers who generously loaned their treasured embroideries and patchwork quilts for inclusion in this publication: Daphne J Ashby, p. 219 and p. 236; Josephine Bardsley, p.131; Gilda Baron, p.172; Marilyn Becker, p.205 centre; Samantha Bourne, p.197; Corynna Bridgwood for the canvas work cushion on p.6; Rosalind Brook Ross, p.189 and p.195; Sarah Campbell for the felt hat, p.30; Constance Cole, p.145 (designs by Patricia Cox); Kay Dennis, p.231; Diana Dolman, p. 238; Greta Fitchett, p.141; Peggy Field, p.243; Joy Frey, p.241; Katharine Guerrier, p.127; Hilary Hollingworth, p.67; Jane Hopkins, p.242; Shelagh Jarvis, pp.58–9 (based on a workshop with Jenny Rayment); Heide Jenkins, p.223; Denise Jones, p.209; Helen Keenan, p.151; Barbara Laine, p.162 (left); Ann Mockford, p.239; Sheena Norquay, p.158; Jenny Parks, p.109 (top left); Doreen Plumridge, p.99; Kath Poxon, p.121; Rosemary Richards, p.148; Jane Rodgers, p. 247; Marie Roper, p.143; Samiah Faridi Saeed, p.244 and p.246; Chris Slade, p.66; Lola Sotorres, p.129; Jean Spencer, p.113; Isabel Sunderland, p.126; Jean Syson, p.156; Angela Thompson, p. 224; Gisela Thwaites p.125 and p.157; Caroline Wilkinson p.134 and 163 (bottom right); Judith Wilson, p.149; and Eiko Yamano p.133 (top).

Many thanks to the following people for stitching the many samples that appear in this publication: Sue Copeman, Barbara Lethbridge, Joyce Mallinson, Brenda Monk, Lynn Simms, Barbara Smith, Adele and Hayley Wainwright and Rita Whitehorn.

Thanks also to the following companies for assisting with photography for this book: Bogod Machine Company for the loan of the sewing machine; Bradshaw & Bradshaw, and Derby House for loaning fabric, Simplicity Ltd for the loan of the jacket on p.7 and p.31, the bridesmaid dress on p.29 and p.31, the evening gown on p.32, the velour top on p.63, the velvet jacket and trousers on p.70; and the child's outfit on p.79.

Thank you to the following for granting permission to reproduce images: p.137 left, reproduced by permission of the American Museum in Britain, Bath ©; p.102, Christies Images Ltd 1999; p.115; p.133b, p.165 and p.167 The Bridgeman Art Library; and p.106, p.182, p.203 V&A Picture Library.

Notes

Notes

NOTES

NOTES

NOTES

NOTES

NOTES

NOTES

RY WOLLSTONECRAFT
Vindication of the Rights of
Woman
VIRGINIA WOOLF
To the Lighthouse
Mrs Dalloway
LLIAM WORDSWORTH
Selected Poems (UK only)
RICHARD YATES
Revolutionary Road
The Easter Parade
Eleven Kinds of Loneliness
(in 1 vol.)

W. B. YEATS
The Poems (UK only)
ÉMILE ZOLA
Germinal

WILLIAM LANGLAND
Piers Plowman
with (anon.) Sir Gawain and the
Green Knight, Pearl, Sir Orfeo
(UK only)
D. H. LAWRENCE
Collected Stories
The Rainbow
Sons and Lovers
Women in Love
MIKHAIL LERMONTOV
A Hero of Our Time
DORIS LESSING
Stories
PRIMO LEVI
If This is a Man and The Truce
(UK only)
The Periodic Table
THE MABINOGION
NICCOLÒ MACHIAVELLI
The Prince
NAGUIB MAHFOUZ
The Cairo Trilogy
Three Novels of Ancient Egypt
THOMAS MANN
Buddenbrooks
Collected Stories (UK only)
Death in Venice and Other Stories
(US only)
Doctor Faustus
Joseph and His Brothers
The Magic Mountain
KATHERINE MANSFIELD
The Garden Party and Other
Stories
ALESSANDRO MANZONI
The Betrothed
MARCUS AURELIUS
Meditations
GABRIEL GARCÍA MÁRQUEZ
The General in His Labyrinth
Love in the Time of Cholera
One Hundred Years of Solitude
ANDREW MARVELL
The Complete Poems
W. SOMERSET MAUGHAM
Collected Stories
The Skeptical Romancer (US only)

CORMAC McCARTHY
The Border Trilogy
IAN McEWAN
Atonement
HERMAN MELVILLE
The Complete Shorter Fiction
Moby-Dick
JOHN STUART MILL
On Liberty and Utilitarianism
JOHN MILTON
The Complete English Poems
YUKIO MISHIMA
The Temple of the
Golden Pavilion
MARY WORTLEY MONTAGU
Letters
MICHEL DE MONTAIGNE
The Complete Works
THOMAS MORE
Utopia
TONI MORRISON
Beloved
Song of Solomon
ALICE MUNRO
Carried Away: A Selection of
Stories
MURASAKI SHIKIBU
The Tale of Genji
VLADIMIR NABOKOV
Lolita
Pale Fire
Pnin
Speak, Memory
V. S. NAIPAUL
Collected Short Fiction (US only)
A House for Mr Biswas
R. K. NARAYAN
Swami and Friends
The Bachelor of Arts
The Dark Room
The English Teacher
(in 1 vol.)
Mr Sampath – The Printer of
Malgudi
The Financial Expert
Waiting for the Mahatma
(in 1 vol.)

IRÈNE NÉMIROVSKY
David Golder
The Ball
Snow in Autumn
The Courilof Affair
(in 1 vol.)

FLANN O'BRIEN
The Complete Novels

FRANK O'CONNOR
The Best of Frank O'Connor

MICHAEL ONDAATJE
The English Patient

GEORGE ORWELL
Animal Farm
Nineteen Eighty-Four
Essays
Burmese Days, Keep the Aspidistra
Flying, Coming Up for Air
(in 1 vol.)

OVID
The Metamorphoses

THOMAS PAINE
Rights of Man
and Common Sense

ORHAN PAMUK
My Name is Red
Snow

BORIS PASTERNAK
Doctor Zhivago

SYLVIA PLATH
The Bell Jar (US only)

PLATO
The Republic
Symposium and Phaedrus

EDGAR ALLAN POE
The Complete Stories

MARCO POLO
The Travels of Marco Polo

MARCEL PROUST
In Search of Lost Time
(in 4 vols, UK only)

PHILIP PULLMAN
His Dark Materials

ALEXANDER PUSHKIN
The Collected Stories

FRANÇOIS RABELAIS
Gargantua and Pantagruel

JOSEPH ROTH
The Radetzky March

JEAN-JACQUES
ROUSSEAU
Confessions
The Social Contract and
the Discourses

SALMAN RUSHDIE
Midnight's Children

JOHN RUSKIN
Praeterita and Dilecta

PAUL SCOTT
The Raj Quartet (in 2 vols)

WALTER SCOTT
Rob Roy

WILLIAM SHAKESPEARE
Comedies Vols 1 and 2
Histories Vols 1 and 2
Romances
Sonnets and Narrative Poems
Tragedies Vols 1 and 2

MARY SHELLEY
Frankenstein

ADAM SMITH
The Wealth of Nations

ALEXANDER SOLZHENITSYN
One Day in the Life of
Ivan Denisovich

SOPHOCLES
The Theban Plays

MURIEL SPARK
The Prime of Miss Jean Brodie,
The Girls of Slender Means, The
Driver's Seat, The Only Problem
(in 1 vol.)

CHRISTINA STEAD
The Man Who Loved Children

JOHN STEINBECK
The Grapes of Wrath

STENDHAL
The Charterhouse of Parma
Scarlet and Black

LAURENCE STERNE
Tristram Shandy

ROBERT LOUIS STEVENSON
The Master of Ballantrae and
Weir of Hermiston
Dr Jekyll and Mr Hyde
and Other Stories

BRAM STOKER
Dracula

HARRIET BEECHER STOWE
Uncle Tom's Cabin

ITALO SVEVO
Zeno's Conscience

GRAHAM SWIFT
Waterland

JONATHAN SWIFT
Gulliver's Travels

TACITUS
Annals and Histories

JUNICHIRŌ TANIZAKI
The Makioka Sisters

W. M. THACKERAY
Vanity Fair

HENRY DAVID THOREAU
Walden

ALEXIS DE TOCQUEVILLE
Democracy in America

LEO TOLSTOY
Collected Shorter Fiction (in 2 vols)
Anna Karenina
Childhood, Boyhood and Youth
The Cossacks
War and Peace

ANTHONY TROLLOPE
Barchester Towers
Can You Forgive Her?
Doctor Thorne
The Eustace Diamonds
Framley Parsonage
The Last Chronicle of Barset
Phineas Finn
The Small House at Allington
The Warden

IVAN TURGENEV
Fathers and Children
First Love and Other Stories
A Sportsman's Notebook

MARK TWAIN
Tom Sawyer
and Huckleberry Finn

This book is set in CASLON, designed and engraved by William Caslon of WILLIAM CASLON & SON, Letter-Founders in London, around 1740. In England at the beginning of the eighteenth century, Dutch type was probably more widely used than English. The rise of William Caslon put a stop to the importation of Dutch types and so changed the history of English typecutting.